NOTES ABOUT THE AUTHOR

Born in Kroonstad in 1950 (in the then Orange Free State). Completed dentistry at Pretoria University in 1974 and MBL at UNISA in 1994.

First practice was in Wandsworth London, in the post-coalminers strike era in the 70's - Spent a total of five years overseas.

Sports achievements - played rugby for Northern Free State schools and earned SA University colours for boxing.

Business ventures: Property development in Brenton-on-Sea near Knysna and in Sunnyside Pretoria.

Current interests: Sport in general, the outdoors, philosophy, wildlife and classic European sports cars.

Married with three children and currently lives in Pretoria.

Articles on Olympic matters by the author appeared in The Sunday Times, The Saturday Star, Beeld, Mail and Guardian, Business Day, Insig Magazine, Project Pro magazine, and Finance Week.

The author has been on the Agenda and Spieël actuality television programmes, as well as on radio where he was interviewed by 'Radio Sonder Grense' and Classic FM.

Special thanks to

In the beginning - MBL study material:
My Spanish connection - Alfred Bosch, Pere Miro and Josep Rojas.
Staff at the IOC Museum - Michéle Veillard in particular.

Towards the end - Book research:
Iaan Bekker for inspiration, guidance and a splendid cover.
John Donaldson for advice and valuable information.
Ze Otto for creating the dollar wreath.
Ben Groenewald for information regarding security (or lack of it) at Atlanta.
The IOC's Patricia Eckert, Ruth Perrenoud, and Michelle Veillard - always friendly, helpful and efficient.

Throughout - Mariaan my wife and companion.
Also Louis, Lidia and Elmarie for constant help, support and information.

I would like to acknowledge the IOC's permission to use postcards of official posters.

THE
GAMES
CITIES
PLAY

PIETER DE LANGE

Published by

C.P. de Lange Inc.
P.O. Box 25412, Monument Park 0105, South Africa.
Tel: (012) 327-5544/3
Fax: (012) 327-5515/8

Reproduction:
Repro Touch
P.O. Box 73143, Lynnwood Ridge, Pretoria 0040.
Tel: (012) 344-4575

Printed by:
SIGMA Press
P.O. Box 23255, Gezina, Pretoria 0031.
Tel: (012) 333-6141

ISBN: 0-620-21998-X

First edition, first print 1998

CONTENTS

Introduction   9

Personal Recollections
NOCSA - October 1993   13
The Johannesburg Bid - September 1993   13
Lausanne, My First IOC Interview - July 1993   14
The Final Lap - June to September 1997   15

Chapter 1
The Relevant History of the Olympic Games,
and How it Translated into the Modern Games   17
  •   The Birth of the Modern Olympic Games   19

Chapter 2
The Role and Importance of Sport in Present Day Society   21
  •   Relevant Changes in Society - Technological Developments   21
  •   Post-business Society   22
  •   The Global Games   23

Chapter 3
All the Olympic Hosts and Bidding Cities of the Modern Games   27
The Pre-World War II Games - A Fragile Beginning   28
  •   Athens 1896 - The Beginning of it All   29
  •   Paris 1900 - A Great Exhibition, Pity about the Olympics   32
  •   St Louis 1904 - The Anthropological Flop   34
  •   London 1908 - Solid Support   37
  •   Stockholm 1912 - The Harmonious Games   41
  •   Antwerp 1920 - Reward for being Trampled in the Trenches   44
  •   Paris 1924 -"Chariots of Fire" Games   47
  •   Amsterdam 1928 - With a Little Help from our Friends in the East   49
  •   Los Angeles 1932 - "Buddy can you Spare me a Dime?"   53
  •   Berlin 1936 - The "Sieg Heil" Spectacle   57

Chapter 4
The Innocent Period   61
  •   London 1948 -The Austerity Games   61
  •   Helsinki 1952 - Pure Sport at a Price   64
  •   Melbourne 1956 - Away from it All   67
  •   Rome 1960 - The Classic Games   71
  •   Tokyo 1964 - The Awakening of a Giant   74

Chapter 5

The Tumultuous "M" Games   78
- Mexico City 1968 - Thin Air and Rich Tequila   79
- Munich 1972 - The Tragic Games   84
- Montreal 1976 - The Case of the Pregnant Male   90
- Moscow 1980 - The Grey Games   96

Chapter 6

Los Angeles 1984 - The Low-cost Commercial Games   105
- A Temporary Power Transfer   105
- Extensive Facilities   105
- Stunning Profits   107
- Just a 'Nice Games'   107
- Widespread Popular Support   108
- Quirky Personalities   108
- Incidental Strategic Success   109
- LA Sport   110
- Five Golden Rings   111

Chapter 7

Seoul 1988 - A Diplomatic Tour de Force   115
- The Seoul Dynamo   115
- Seoul's Selection   115
- Impending Embargoes   117
- Media Might   119
- Internal Battles   120
- The Tokyo Mould   121
- Steroid Sprints   122
- All is Well   123

Chapter 8

Barcelona 1992 - A Great but Costly Games   125
- The Divisive Origins   125
- A Bruising International Campaign   127
- Real Local Support   129
- Numerous Strategic Objectives   130
- Urban Renewal   133
- A Complex Socio-economic Legacy   136

Chapter 9

Atlanta 1996 - The Second Best Games?   138
- The Security Set-up   139
- The Transport Mess   140

- The Successful Partnership   141
- Atlanta and Los Angeles - Different Eras, Strategies and Results   142
- Conclusions   144

Chapter 10

Sydney 2000 - Can They "Hack" it?   148
- Inventions, Innovations, Interesting Facts and Unique Features   148
- Harsh Realities of the Costly Environment and the
  Precious Bottom Line   151
- Greener than Thou   152
- Costing the Bottom Line   152
- The Inevitable Power Struggles   154
- Areas of Agreement   155
- IOC Reaction   156
- Lessons from Atlanta and Pointers for 2004   156
- Finances   156
- Strategic Contrasts with Atlanta   157
- What will the Games be Like?   158

Chapter 11

Cape Town 2004 - The African Dilemma   160
- Africa - The Have-not Continent   160
- The First African Games   163
- Crime, Grime and Sleaze   164
- The Different Strategic Approaches   166

Chapter 12

Cape Town 2004 - The Bid   170
- The Philosophical Approach to Cape Town 2004   170
- To Support or not?   171
- The Debilitating Weaknesses   171
- A Population in Isolation   172
- Underdeveloped Infrastructure   174
- Accommodation   174
- Transport   177
- A Tale of Two Studies (and a Multiplicity of Figures)   180
- A List of Pronouncements on the Job Creation Aspects of a
  Cape Town Games   183
- The Jolly Jumper   184
- Telecommunication   184
- Security   185
- Sports Facilities   185
- Transport Infrastructure   185

- The Capital Cost Conundrum   186
- The Capital Budget   187
- Private Sector Load   188
- Odds and Ends   189
- Public Support for Cape Town 2004   191
- The Battle of the Bid   192
- A Chronology of Events   193
- Interesting Events and Controversial Comments Concerning the
  Management of Cape Town's Bid   201
- Cape Town 2004 - The Bottom Line   205
- If Not Cape Town, What Then?   205

Chapter 13

The Five Finalists for 2004   209
- Public Support   210
- Economic Strength   210
- Distribution of Competition Sites   212
- Transportation   212
- Accommodation   213
- The Flexible Budgets   215
- Sports Venues   216

Chapter 14

Athens 2004 - Classic Games or Greek Tragedy?   219
- Cape Town's Hangover   219
- Caustic Comments   221
- Lessons from Lausanne   222
- The Olympic Road to Ruin?   222
- Will Athens be Able to Cope?   224

INTRODUCTION

My Olympic saga, as it were, started with an interview with Gert Potgieter (ex world-record holder in the 400 million hurdles) in his offices at Pretoria University's vast LC de Villiers sports grounds on 4 February 1993.

In my notes the concluding statement was that Gert Potgieter felt there was "a definite need for a study of this kind and that the possibility exists to make valuable contributions". Well, I concluded my research project for UNISA's MBL degree, and "Johannesburg and the Olympic Games of 2004" now forms part of the IOC's official archives at the administrative head office at Chateau de Vidy in Lausanne, Switzerland.

Quite frankly I got carried away, and in financial and immolation terms, the research set me back quite a bit. But the result was a study that received higher marks than I would ever have expected. Ironically, Gert and I later found ourselves on opposite sides of the fence concerning Cape Town's bid.

The research took me on two overseas trips where I had interviews with representatives of the IOC: that is the representatives of the International Olympic Committee, COOB 1992; the Barcelona Olympic Committee for 1992, the Barcelona Tourism Bureau, the Manchester Bidding Committee; Manchester 2000 and the British Olympic Association.

On a personal level, the travels, the interviews (both here and abroad), and the resulting friendships, have been a mind broadening and enriching experience. It is probably because the Olympic Movement and all its processes are, on the one hand, so noble in aspiration and universal in application while, on the other hand, so down-to-earth in practical implementation, and fallible in terms of human relationships. For example, during my first interview with Pere Miro, the then Deputy Sports Director at the IOC, he explained that one of their most pressing problems with the Atlanta Games at that stage (July 1993) was just to determine the legal ownership of the competition sites. On the question of Atlanta's surprise election ahead of the sentimental favourite Athens, he said that there was so much infighting amongst the Athens bid proponents and there were so many technical weaknesses in the proposal, that it could not be taken seriously. (Apparently important lessons have been learned because the 2004 Athens effort was much more credible.)

It is important to distinguish between the IOC's very professional staff at the headquarters in Lausanne and the 110 IOC members spread across the globe. An IOC member is elected to represent that organisation in a specific country. Sam Ramsamy, for example, represents the IOC interests in South Africa, as the Royal Princess Anne does in Britain. It is against the IOC members that international authors like Andrew Jennings have directed their accusations of excess and corruption. The Olympic Family basically consists of IOC members, IOC staff, representatives of the International Sports Federations of various Olympic sports and National Olympic Committees of all the countries and regions recognised by the IOC, organising and bidding committees as well as the relevant sponsors for the duration of a specific Olympic Games.

The first international interview with John Limna of the British Olympic Association was at their offices in Wandsworth, London. I was surprised and delighted to find that their offices were just around the corner from where my first dental practice was in the seventies. I always walked my little Cockney girlfriend home past the church opposite the present BOA offices. The dental surgery had become a pizza parlour in the meantime, (much more palatable I suppose).

My next stop was Manchester and it was raining as usual. Actually, Manchester's inner city was much more attractive architecturally than I had expected, but after Barcelona, to find a restaurant open and willing and able ... It was always "sorry sir, we close at such and such a time", just when I was desperately in need of a decent meal. Of course, you just cannot beat the Latins when it comes to 'joie de vivre'.

The Turisme de Barcelona offices are situated in a magnificent period building. I was looking around so much that it was an effort to concentrate on the interview with the helpful and knowledgeable Josep Rojas.

The local interviews were just as interesting, but in a different, more intense way. My first interview for the book was with the forthright Wendy Ackerman, wife of Raymond Ackerman of Pick-'n-Pay Stores. She became so emotional when she narrated the details of the bitter power struggle between them and NOCSA's Sam Ramsamy, that the whole conversation had to be abandoned. I left feeling emotionally drained myself and only then did I begin to realise how harsh and ruthless on a personal as well as a financial level *(the idealistic Ackermans put in R8 million of their own money to finance the bid initially)* this seemingly fraternal movement can be. The Olympic Charter emphasises "a spirit of friendship, solidarity and fair play"[1] but the present-day bids, both on a national and international level, seem to signify the opposite. Has it always been like this? Christopher Hill wrote in his Olympic Politics that Madrid did not oppose Barcelona's bid but "played the politics of generosity, though with knives in their pockets".[2] Has it become more intense with the big sponsorship era?

Each country's National Olympic Committee usually holds an internal contest between the local cities, so that the national bid can be determined. It seems as if the National Olympic Committees of different countries do not always feature equally prominently in the Olympic Games. Of course "the IOC enters into a written agreement with the host city and the NOC of its country" (Olympic Charter).[3] But in some cases such as Barcelona, the NOC just seemed to play a background role, whilst in Sydney the NOC is in a very prominent position in the whole organising set-up. The Olympic Charter also states that the local NOC determines the formation of the Organising Committee for an Olympic Games (OCOG).[4]

The competing cities play their own little games. There usually is tremendous competition between them and enormous pressure from the public, so it is very tempting to play the numbers game and to present the relevant statistics in the most favourable manner possible. It is quite convenient to shift large sums around and to dress up the capital and operating sides of the budget to suit particular circumstances. The operating side is more or less matched to the income, which is large because of the huge TV revenues, and quite predictable because it is negotiated well in advance. So it is customary that bidding cities would show a relatively small profit: e.g. the 2004 finalists predicted a range of profits from $36,7 million for Athens to $2,1 million for Rome. The present attitude is that to show too large a profit in this section is slightly vulgar and besides, it has to be shared, usually with the National Olympic Committee involved (see chapter on Sydney). The operational expenses include those required for the actual hosting of the Games, such as feeding, housing and transporting members of the press corps, the athletes, officials as well as the rest of the Olympic family, organising the actual sports events and all its associated facets, such as the huge and technologically intensive media requirements. Of course, aspects such as administration and security feature prominently on the operating side.

The capital side has more to do with the building of the necessary infrastructure in terms of transport, accommodation, etc. And that is where the convenient grey areas start to open up because some of these expensive items appear on a city's public programme anyway, so they can be brought forward, and convenient terms such as accelerated spending can be brought into play to calm otherwise restive citizens. "It was bound to be done sometime anyway, so don't fret, we know what we're doing", is the typical patronising tone adopted by aspiring Chief Executives (CE's) of bidding or organising committees (OCOG's). In his book The Bid concerning Sydney's campaign to be appointed for 2000, Rod McGeoch mentioned that the Sydney Bid Committee felt that any item on the public programme in the "next 100 years" ought not to be seen as an Olympic expense if it is included in the capital programme.[5] Of course, if you need a large government safety net, you can load the capital side a bit with a extra few million in the hope that nobody notices. So the cities' favourite games are numbers and power games. The Berlin Bidding Committee for 2000 had to issue a formal apology after it had been disclosed in the press that they compiled a confidential list of personal sexual and bizarre habits of IOC members (they must have had intentions of using this information during the campaign). The IOC has tightened the rules applying to the dining and wining of

IOC members and especially the very expensive gifts previously presented by competing cities. However, the games that cities play remain the most fascinating aspect of Olympic competition because it is much more complex, more indicative of current socio-economic trends and less predictable than a mere 100 m event or a hockey competition. No wonder the well-known Frank Deford wrote in Newsweek in 1996: "Remember, the biggest Olympic Game of them all nowadays is getting the Olympics for your city".[6]

Footnotes
1. Olympic Charter 1995, p 11
2. Hill 1996, p 182
3. Olympic Charter 1995, p 59
4. Olympic Charter 1995, p 61
5. McGeoch 1994, p 187
6. Deford 1996, p 10

PERSONAL RECOLLECTIONS

NOCSA - October 1993

It was a hot Friday afternoon, the reception large and airy, and one could hear the occasional opening and closing of doors and shifting of chairs from the few offices nearby. Now and then the phone rang. Initially I had been more than ten minutes early, but it was already twenty minutes after the agreed time and I was kept waiting, waiting.

The receptionist was speaking to someone over the phone in intense, hushed tones which immediately attracted my attention; obviously she was talking about me because I was the only one around. "But you must see him," she insisted, "He took the whole afternoon off and came all the way from Pretoria". Oh hell, I thought, first Ramsamy gave me the run-around, never acknowledging a letter or responding to a message, now it's Dan Moyo who wants to duck out of our appointment. Luckily the receptionist's powers of persuasion prevailed and I was ushered through to Moyo's office where he and a more senior gentleman were waiting (probably reluctantly) to see me. When we were introduced, Dan and I immediately clicked and he broke into a broad smile. The elderly man was Bill Jardine from the NSC.

The ice was broken and we breezed through the questions. Dan was still on a learning curve, but so was I. Subsequently I did not gain a mass of information from the encounter, but managed to walk away feeling good about my first meeting with somebody from the ANC side. (Remember, this was a while before the 1994 election).

The Johannesburg Bid - September 1993

I was invited by Danie Malan to participate as an observer in Johannesburg's bid effort against Cape Town and Durban, and found all the proceedings fascinating. Because the first democratic elections were almost on us, the prevailing atmosphere was one of excited anticipation in terms of imminent international sports competition, mingled with lingering uncertainty as far as political changes and physical unrest were concerned.

The Johannesburg bid was led by the City Council, and at a meeting in one of their many impressive boardrooms, the video presentation came up for discussion. Now by that stage everyone sensed that the ANC was going to breeze to victory in the upcoming elections, so it was a rather ungraceful contest between Cape Town and Johannesburg to see who would field the more impressive collection of ANC figures in their presentation. Cape Town somehow seemed to have the edge, with Archbishop Tutu and Steve Tshwete already signed up. So Johannesburg looked at their likely support from the ranks of these "comrades" and Peter Mokaba of "kill a farmer, kill a boer" fame, was suggested. I was not sure whether as an observer I was entitled to voice an opinion. But I still objected to Mokaba's inclusion on the grounds that the Olympic Charter was all about love for your fellow human beings, peaceful co-existence and that kind of thing and that Mokaba's image was hardly in keeping with good neighbourliness or, in our case, sound race relations. But alas, no support. I received some understanding glances from certain City Council officials but nothing more. Cas Coovadia, who brought the civics on board, justified Mokaba's inclusion by saying that he was likely to be the next Minister of Tourism.

How sad, I thought, we have not yet entered the much promised democracy, but the new lot is just the same in one respect - might is right!

Lausanne, My First IOC Interview - July 1993

My first worry was Swiss francs. Would I be able to cash travellers cheques before 06:30 at Zurich Airport, before the early train, which I had to catch in time for my first IOC interview? I had been to Europe many times previously, but the standard of services for travellers was again a revelation. At that early hour, I had the choice of several banks or Change Agencies.

The airport and station were spotlessly clean and the shopping area both attractive and cosy.

At lunchtime I was dropped at the IOC Administrative Headquarters. I had enough time to walk along the picturesque lake and to study the signs indicating the present level of pollution, warning would-be swimmers that they had better stay out for a while. I could not resist a peep at the Chateau de Vidy, where the IOC president and the top IOC officials' offices are. A chauffeur was vigorously polishing a gleaming Mercedes-Benz 600 SEL. Apparently, this section is connected to the Administrative Headquarters via an underground corridor to ensure effective interaction throughout the year.

Make no mistake, Lausanne is lovely. The blue expanse of the lake with snow-capped mountains in the background, plenty of trees and greenery and a distinctive style of buildings all with their towering spires, are breathtakingly beautiful. Lausanne oozes a certain old-world style and charm and one senses a pace and tempo that is both businesslike and civilised at the same time.

The Administrative Headquarters are modern, light, airy and yet classical, with marble floors and walls and distinctive paintings in bright colours along the walls.

Apart from receiving prompt answers to my faxes, I had no idea what kind of reception to expect. It was warm and pleasant to say the least. Pere Miro, who was the Deputy Director of Sport, was extremely knowledgeable. He gave me a great deal of information in terms of how the IOC experienced problems with particular aspects of the Olympic hosts. I realised implicitly that once a city is appointed, the IOC is unlikely to change to another host halfway through the process. Inevitably there is a temporary transfer of power when a city is appointed as host and this is sometimes exploited.

It was valuable to be told about the challenges and problems from the IOC's managerial side. Pere also showed me the impressive Bid Books from the various candidate cities for the 2000 Games. The winner was due to be announced in September 1993. I found Sydney's (the eventual winner) Bid Books the most attractive and professional. I must admit Cape Town's Bid Books for 2004 were also superb and equalled Sydney's standard for 2000. I was also introduced to Jean-Michel Gunz, then Deputy Director, NOC relations. Pere Miro had recently been appointed as the Olympic Solidarity Director.

That was certainly one interview I will not forget.

The Final Lap - June to September 1997

The Cape Town 2004 hype was building up to a crescendo during this period, but unfortunately it consisted mostly of the same, often repeated but by now monotonous promises of zillions to be added to the gross domestic product and stacks of jobs to be created by the Olympic miracle machine. In the final weeks the groundswell of spontaneous enthusiasm became almost irresistible - South Africans are natural competitors and love nothing more than to strut their stuff in the international arena. But underlying one always senses a deep insecurity, which consists of a mix of guilt and recrimination about the past, a cynical view of the present and a prevailing uncertainty about the future. This unfortunately translates into an almost childlike eagerness to lap up prospects of quick fixes, whether they be from Olympic bid companies, politicians, lay preachers or weather prophets. The agonising dilemma of the beloved country was painfully demonstrated by the Pretoria News headlines of 19 August where one report proudly proclaimed how the bid has been instrumental in joyfully uniting city residents, whilst another headline grimly narrated details of " Three men torched to death in 'revenge attack' " in nearby Johannesburg.

The Olympic trivia consisted of Chris Ball feeling compelled to prove his Africanness by stating that his family has been in Africa for sixteen generations (which probably means they preceded Jan van Riebeeck) after being accused by Minister of Sport, Steve Tshwete, of running a bid company that was "too white" in complexion, and of political parties arguing about clauses inserted in the Olympic bill, which would have exempted the host city and organising bodies from legal provisions. The political Olympic squabble later almost turned into a real fracas when opposition parties accused the governing ANC of hijacking the first African bid. The Strategic Environmental Assessment of the CT 2004 Olympic bid was published in August and the executive summary compiled from this impressive collection of specialists studies again highlighted the enormous inherent potential for cost increases which in itself is an indication that the R21 billion expenditure predicted by Sam Ramsamy, NOCSA's President, in 1995 was much closer to reality than the overoptimistic budget presented by both bid companies.

Athens duly won, Cape Town did well to survive until the third round, mostly as a result of votes received from Buenos Aires supporters. In the first round CT and Buenos Aires were tied on sixteen votes, lowest of all. For a few days afterwards the newspapers were full of astonishingly naive excuses: "Africa deserted us" one CT official complained. I almost felt like shouting - Well, what do you expect when you propose to host the Games on the remote Southern tip of the continent? " We should have dealt with the crime issue in our presentation" wailed another dissapointed official, as if a murder rate 30 times higher than that of Greece can be made to disappear by the use of a few carefully selected slides. It reminded me of the time the Department of Bantu Education or whatever, had it's name changed for the umteenth time and a good friend of mine just sighed, "you can call a skunk by any name", he said. Well, violent crime is becoming our present skunk and if there is one lesson we should have learned by now it is that we should not try to con the outside world. For a change, we should admit serious shortcomings and rectify them first before we try to conquer the world. The tickets for wives of African IOC members was typical of the "see what we can get away with" syndrome. When our bid is credible, sincere and feasible enough, IOC members fom Africa and all over will support us.

UNISA - University of South Africa
MBL - Master of Business Leadership
NOCSA - National Olympic Commitee of South Africa
NSC - National Sports Council
ANC - African National Congress

CHAPTER 1

THE RELEVANT
HISTORY OF THE ANCIENT GAMES
and how it translated into the Modern Games

The history of the ancient Games is described by Nafziger in his excellent International Sports Law, as the history of the organised international sport competition.[1]

The first recorded Olympic Games were held in 776 BC, although earlier contests almost certainly took place. In other parts of the world, organised sport certainly did take place even earlier. Boxing contests were recorded in the Nile valley as early as 4 000 BC. Tomb paintings in Egypt from about 3 000 to 2 000 BC depicted running, swimming, rowing, archery and wrestling, and the oldest organised sports competition on record, the Tailteann Games, were held in Ireland at regular intervals from about 1 800 BC until 1 200 AD.[2] The very ancient Games involved only one athletic event, a 200 m stade or foot race which was won by Caroebus of Elis, a cook. Other events, such as the pentathlon, wrestling, boxing and chariot racing were added over the next ten Olympiads. (An Olympiad indicates the four-year period between the Games).

For the first 50 Olympiads (200 years), participants travelled to Olympia from twelve or more Greek cities. Eventually, some 100 city-states participated and by the last 100 years, under Roman domination, athletes came from as far as Antioch, Alexandria and Sidon.

Shared religious beliefs greatly contributed to the success of the early Games: "The ancient Olympic Games in particular were based on religious traditions and flourished in a relatively stable political environment despite periodic conflict".[3] In its very origins, the Olympic Movement was based on a moral premise that is much more encompassing than mere physical competition: "The Olympic festival was seen as a way to promote goodwill and unity amongst city-states. The Sacred Truce or ekecheiria provided that for three months surrounding the Games, there was to be a suspension of all hostilities among the city-states whose athletes were invited to compete in the Games".[4]

Furthermore, "athletes also had to take an oath before a statue of Zeus to compete honourably during the Games. The common religion made for strict enforcement and acceptance of rules and ethical codes. These factors ensured the necessary sanctity and respect for the Games and provided a strong basis for the enforcement of rules to govern the contests and agreements among city-states".[5]

Andronicos describes the **spirit of competition** as follows: "The Games gave birth to yet another Greek idea, the attitude of a free man competing with his peers, naked, unfettered by any element foreign to his body, conforming only to the rules of the Game, with the sole aim of winning for himself an olive crown - in other words, a purely moral victory - and the praise of his fellowmen".[6] The root word for gymnasium, according to Frank Deford (in a superb National Geographic article in July 1996), gymnos, has nothing to do with sport, but means nude. So the contestants were nude males, the audiences were also limited to males, although the priestess of Demeter was allowed to attend.[7]

But this does not mean that the concept of **sportsmanship** was one of the abiding values - far from it: "Athletes participated for respect from the gods and their fellowmen. The concept of sportsmanship was, at best, inchoate. Winning was everything, losers were often jeered".[8] In fact, Christopher Hill in his book Olympic Politics, goes so far as to insist "There was no suggestion that the point was to take part, rather than to win".[9] "The wreath or death!" was the contestants' cry according to Howard Chua-Eoan in a Special Edition of Time International in July 1992 . He goes on to explain that to these ancient athletes, the concept of places or good performances did not exist, only winning. But victory certainly had its rewards. "Athletes were feted upon their return home; they received places of honour at local assemblies; they became pampered wards of the state, besieged by the admiration of non-athletes".[10]

It was not long before the first signs of sportive nationalism and commercialism appeared. A victor received an olive wreath, but Nafziger states that there was considerable evidence of compensation for athletes and a degree of **professionalism** among them.[11] A winner became eligible for enhanced status in both his community and in the realm of Zeus. The reputation of the city-state was thus enhanced and subsequently politics and sports became teammates. There is even a persistent myth that one victorious boxer became the king of Armenia.

The management of the ancient Games was not for the faint-hearted: "Olympia's judges gained a reputation for conscientious and unbiased performance of their duties. Wearing purple robes, brandishing whips and followed by whip-carrying servants, they imposed fines and penalties in order to discourage or punish infractions of the truce and the rules of each contest, as well as behaviour such as bribing opponents".[12]

In 365 BC, Elis lost a war and Pisa gained control over Olympia. The cult of Zeus was gradually weakened and the sanctity of Olympia was tarnished. The Games became increasingly **secular affairs** and, because the enforcement of the rules was more difficult, squabbling increased. Victors were now often professionals who travelled between different festivals to compete for a living.[13]

The Roman conquest of Greece further changed the character of the Olympics, making them more truly cosmopolitan and somewhat more professional. The Romans viewed the Games more as public entertainment than as contests for more noble purposes in the Greek tradition. The last of the ancient Games was held in 261 AD, whereafter emperor Theodosius decreed their termination.[14] According to Georges Du Brie in Sports World, Japan "The original Olympiads in ancient Greece ran for over 1 000 years, before being banned by emperor Theodosius because they had become pagan, commercialised, too professional and rife with cheating and greed for money".[15]

The Birth of the Modern Olympic Games

The idealistic French nobleman Baron de Coubertin sought to adapt the concept of the ancient Olympic Games to modern conditions, providing an opportunity to revive and instil in the youth of the world the virtues of fair play and soundness of mind and body through physical exercise and competition. There can be little doubt that De Coubertin's idealised vision of the Olympics led him to believe that the Games represented the finest expression of sportsmanship and that his planned Olympic Movement would symbolise all that is honourable in mankind.

As we approach the third millennium, many would argue that De Coubertin's ideals are more apparent today in the application of sports like running, that attracts mass participation by enthusiasts, instead of the very intense top international events dominated by a relatively small number of professional performers.

De Coubertin got his Olympic show on the road at an international congress in 1884. The outcome of this congress proved invaluable to the culmination of his efforts, yet did not proceed without controversy. Some of the delegates complained that they had been misled into thinking that they were about to attend a conference on amateurs, at which the Games would be of relatively minor importance. De Coubertin had to display some neat political footwork which remains such a notable feature of the Olympic Movement even today.[16]

The commission on the Games agreed to the conditions on which De Coubertin had always insisted. These conditions were:
- The Games were to be held at four-year intervals.
- The Games had to be modern in outlook, not a direct imitation of their ancient counterparts. The **spirit of competing** was expected to be the dominant feature and not winning at all costs.
- The first modern Games were destined to be held in Athens in 1896.
- The general principle of **amateurism** was established, but this issue elicited a great deal of discussion because of different views. Finally, it was agreed that a distinction be made between reward and compensation (for loss of earnings) and

that, very exceptionally unions, federations and societies might allow encounters between amateurs and professionals, provided that the prizes offered were not in money.

• Gate money, it was agreed, should under no circumstances be paid directly to athletes but to their parent associations. The possibility of these associations passing on compensation to the athletes was not excluded.

• Another principle established at this congress was that the Olympic Games be a contest between **true champions**, which meant that in each country and sport there should be preliminary contests.

• The members of the IOC were to be representatives overseas of the Olympic Movement and not their individual countries' representatives on the committee. This principle is still part of the Olympic Charter.

• Each country was to establish a national Olympic committee.[17]

Footnotes
1.   Nafziger 1988, p 11
2.   Deford 1996, p 46
3.   Nafziger 1988, p 12
4.   Nafziger 1988, p 14
5.   Nafziger 1988, p 14
6.   Nafziger 1988, p 14
7.   Deford 1996, p 46
8.   Nafziger 1988, p 14
9.   Hill 1992, p 84
10. Chea-Eoan 1992, p 12
11. Nafziger 1988, p 14
12. Nafziger 1988, p 15
13. Nafziger 1988, p 16
14. Nafziger 1988, p 16
15. Du Brie April 1997, (In CIO N74) p 47
16. Hill 1992, p 17
17. Hill 1992, pp 20, 21

CHAPTER 2

THE ROLE AND IMPORTANCE OF SPORT IN MODERN SOCIETY

Ball games probably originated outside caves in ancient times as rock or skull games or later as games played with animal bladders. But play was also associated with more serious elements of life. The concept of teamwork was surely developed on the hunt, and later extended to tribal tussles. Sport has inherited archery, chariot racing and the javelin from these sporting and hunting associations. One can imagine that both in hunting and fighting in ancient times, winning was vital because coming second often meant simply not surviving.

This "conquer at all costs" attitude was reflected in the ancient Games, but De Coubertin very idealistically proclaimed the motto of the modern Olympic to be: – "The most important thing in the Olympic Games is not to win but to take part". In fact, in 'Let the Games Begin' Frank Deford finds this laid-back concept of amateurism preposterous, and he contends that the baron has terribly distorted the way we came to think about sport. "In fact, nowhere in human nature has victory in competition ever been accidental".[1]

Well, sport certainly is a microcosm of life in general, where you are also supposed to play the game according to rules and where some individuals habitually try to get away with cheating. In 'The Politics of the Olympic Games', Epsy described the meaning of the modern Olympic Games as follows: "The modern Olympic Games symbolise the struggle between man's ideals and the reality within which we must live".[2] This is also reflected in the bidding process and the different problems the various hosts have had to face through changing times in recent history. The Games in Antwerp, Belgium in 1920 and in London in 1948, were held just after devastating World Wars. Both Amsterdam in 1928 and Los Angeles in 1932 had to contend with the effects of a crippling worldwide depression. Melbourne (1956) felt the heat of the Suez crisis thousands of kilometres away. Seoul, the 1988 host, initially had to face up to the threat of a Soviet block boycott led by North Korea, which luckily never materialised. What has given rise to the enormous importance that organised sport in general and the Olympics specifically have managed to gain in modern society?

Relevant Changes in Society - Technological Developments

The mass media and television in particular have assumed a significant role in popularising international sport. In 1960, CBS paid $394 000 for the television rights to the Rome Olympics. In 1992, NBC paid $401 million for the Barcelona Games. The television rights for Europe also showed dramatic increases, from $19 million for Los Angeles in 1984 to $243 million in 1996 for Atlanta.[3]

In a speech to the Sydney Bidding Committee, Botella, the Deputy General COOB '92 SA quoted the official report by the Television Broadcast Research of the Games of the XXV Olympiad which shows that the 1992 Games were seen by an estimated global television audience exceeding 16,6 billion accumulative viewers in some 200 countries and territories worldwide.[4]

Indeed the technological developments that produced facsimile transmission of documents, video machines, affordable air transport, telephones and television, have contributed enormously to the creation of a global village with increasingly similar expectations, aspirations and interests worldwide. The overwhelming grief displayed by the world community recently in reaction to Princess Diana's tragic death, is stunning proof of the reality of a universal village.

Post-business Society

According to Drucker, societies have become more homogenous internally.[5] In the 1920's societies consisted of distinct groups with unique cultures. There were the blue-collar workers, farmers and businessmen. Each of these groups read different newspapers, largely went to different churches and usually lived in different parts of town. Each had distinct values and a particular lifestyle. In 1920, blue-collar workers in the manufacturing industry had become the largest single occupation group. In the 1950's they and their unions had become the dominant political force in every non-communist developed country.

Drucker goes on to say: "In the early 1970's industrial workers began to decline fast. By the year 2010 they will have shrunk in the developed non-communist countries to where farmers are now, that is between 5 % and 10 % of the workforce".[6]

"There seems to be general agreement that the US economy of the future will have a very large service component. The Hudson Institute (Johnson and Packer) estimates that manufacturing output by the year 2000 will be 17 % of GNP dropping from around 21 % of GNP in the late 1980's. During the same period, the output of service industries should increase from 69 % to 75 % of GNP".[7]

"Collectively services account for up to 70 % of the gross national product in the United States and other industrial nations".[8]

Drucker states: "The biggest shift, bigger than the changes in politics, government or economics, is the shift to the knowledge society in all non-communist countries. The social centre of gravity has shifted to the knowledge worker".[9]

The result of these socio-economic changes is that societies have become more homogeneous. "They see exactly the same television programmes as everybody else in American society. They take the same vacations. The new majority, the knowledge worker, does not fit any interest-group definition".[10]

Another by-product of the creation of large scale wealth is excess leisure time: "In this century, business has increased the capacity to produce wealth explosively. Half of the expansion in wealth-producing capacity was used to create leisure time through cutting the hours worked while steadily increasing pay. An American worker now puts in 1 800 hours a year compared to 3 300 hours in the early years of the century. Very little of the new leisure is used for intellectual pursuits. "The free hours are more likely to be spent in front of the television watching Dallas or sports".[11]

Yet the fact that we live in a knowledge society does not necessarily mean that people are less conscious of their separate identities. According to Drucker, "as people become 'westernised', more affluent, more mobile and more educated, they increasingly become more nationalist. They increasingly resent being 'colonials', even if the yoke is a light one. They demand the Japanese solution of being westernised but under their own control, management and government".[12]

Hoberman (in Allison) refers to three important sociological phenomena, one of which is sportive nationalism, which he defines as "the ambition to see a nation's athletes excel in the international arena that may be felt by many citizens without the prompting of national leaders".[13]

The Global Games

Based on the above discussion, we can assume that the widespread popularity of the Olympics is a product of ... a deep-rooted ancient urge in man to play and compete: "**Competitive impulse** is a basic human drive".[14]
- the **retention of nationalism** in modern societal attitudes - Hoberman predicts that sportive nationalism will remain a prominent feature of the political landscape in the foreseeable future.[15] "Any suggestion that national flags be abandoned and replaced with the Olympic flag would universally be rejected by the NOC's".[16]
- **technological marvels** that make it possible for the whole world to share events and ceremonies. Nissiotis states: "The Games have reached those millions who can enjoy themselves through television as if they were present themselves".[17]
- excess leisure time for modern workers: "Leisure activities have become more popular".[18]
- **the knowledge society** which has resulted in more shared interests and perceptions worldwide. In his Mega Trends, Naisbitt described ten major transformations that he sees taking place now in our society. First on his list is the shift from an industrial to an informational society.[19]

- the spectacular development of **sports performance** and the achievement of "almost superhuman records".[20]
- "the progressive participation of **more and more nations**, particularly those new nations which can compete as independent and free people".[21]

All of the above factors are also relevant for other major events. Why should the Olympic Games be more special than, for instance, other world championship events? "It is the **ethical content** of the Olympics which makes them a thing apart. Without that, and with the new **overt commercialism**, the Games could become just another fixture in the sporting calendar".[22] Indeed, the concern over ethics is prevalent in most societies today: "We have been searching for the solution to ethical matters in business for centuries. Today ethics continue to be hot".[23] "Everyday decisions of the government and business firms are judged in terms of right or wrong, regardless of the effects on efficiency and productivity".[24] To Samaranch, president of the IOC, sports activity is "the largest social force of our time".[25]

It is clear that the Games have taken on **social significance** far beyond mere sport. "The Olympic Games, when viewed both as **microcosm** of and as actor in international relations, provide an unique opportunity to examine at one time the numerous forces on the international scene".[26]

Maybe one can also see the Olympic Games as a sporting United Nations where all the problems and developments of the present society are mirrored for everyone to see. Wallechinsky reckons that the Olympics are no less **political** than the United Nations.[27]

Hill's opinion is: "The extraordinary public appeal of the Olympics rests partly upon the conviction that they are still the best, and in part on their claims to be unique, because rooted in a non-commercial idea, which still holds a **kind of magic**".[28]

Maybe it is because of its uniqueness that the pressures on and threats to the Olympic Movement developed.

Sport was gaining credence however, in economic, political and even academic circles, as something **exploitable** for certain desired results. "Business and economic circles saw potential monetary benefits. Politicians saw a means of reinforcing national identity. Academicians saw physical education as a valuable tool for the inculcation of normative values. All these forces that were operative in the revival of the Olympic Games, have played an increasing role in the Games as well as sport in general. As a result, participation in the Olympics is no longer just a pastime. It is a serious proposition for the athletes and for those involved, be they

nation-states, business organisations, the media or the spectators".[29]   Horst
Dassler, the great power manipulator and marketing operator, writing in the
Olympic Review, was far more forthright: "Elite sport has almost entirely lost the
ethical value which it owes to the Olympic ideal, and it is no use to lament what
is already gone, because any change in the situation would no longer be either
possible or one which could be controlled." Today the functions of elite sport have
a quite distinct aura:
- political propaganda
- economic propaganda
- spectacle and entertainment
- business interest
- to assist promotion of mass sport
- sociological influence on the masses.[30]

Allison also describes the changes that brought about the present challenges the
Olympic Movement faces: "Demise of the Soviet Union ends the Cold War and
removes the raison d'être of much investment in Olympic sport. As a result of
these changes, the Olympic Movement is cut off from much of its original spirit
and purpose, but dragged into **new territory** by its immense financial successes
and even greater potential in the age of commercial television. The old amateur
ethos declines to extinction; nobody believes in the separateness of sport from politics and commerce any more. Sport comes under the sway of the **immense pressures** of nationalism and corruption".[31]

From the above, it is apparent that one can identify **specific threats** to the Olympic
Movement:
- Gigantism - "We shall be discussing the size of the Olympic Games as there is a
number of participants which we cannot exceed without causing great harm to the
Games" (Samaranch).[32] Presently it is not so much the number of participants
which has increased to 10 200 for Sydney in 2 000 from 8 000 in Tokyo in 1964, but
the overall number of accreditations which is expected to swell to a crushing
150 000 in the next Olympics in Sydney in 2000.
- Doping - after the Johnson debacle at Seoul in 1988, there have been numerous
disclosures. Simson and Jennings in Lords of the Rings were very outspoken:
"There is something deeply worrying about the way the world's sports leaders
have misled us on dope-testing".[33] Since Atlanta, it has become apparent that even
with the latest technology, it is not possible to detect growth hormones without
resorting to blood tests.
- Commercialism - it is often asserted that the Olympic Movement is increasingly reflecting the characteristics of a multi-national corporation.[34] Samaranch was
quoted by Simson and Jennings as saying: "Olympic sport must not become
unequivocally the agent of world capitalism".[35] That is certainly the way it
appeared at Atlanta.

• Political threats - the dramatic increase in participating nations, which in London in 1948 numbered 59 and at Atlanta 1996 increased to 195, greatly enlarges the possible sources of terrorism.

Footnotes
1.   Deford 1996, p 48
2.   Epsy 1979, p vii
3.   Miller 1992, pp 50, 53
4.   Botella 1993, p 3
5.   Drucker 1989, pp 21, 22
6.   Drucker 1989, p 182
7.   Tosi, Rizzo and Carrol 1990, p 701
8.   Lovelock 1991, p 2
9.   Drucker 1989, p 167
10. Drucker 1989, p 22
11. Drucker 1989, pp 171, 172
12. Drucker 1989, p 32
13. Hoberman (In Allison) 1993, p 16
14. Hoberman (In Allison) 1993, p 17
15. Hoberman (In Allison) 1993, p 18
16. Hill 1992, p 241
17. Nissiotis (In Miller) 1992, p 172
18. Callahan, Fleenor and Knudson 1986, p 594
19. Naisbitt (In Callahan) 1986, p 468
20. Nissiotis (In Miller) 1992, p 172
21. Nissiotis (In Miller) 1992, p 172
22. Follows (In Miller) 1992, p 43
23. Freeman and Gilbert (In Tosi et al) 1990, p 716
24. Tosi 1990, p 716
25. Nafziger 1988, p 4
26. Epsy 1979, p ix
27. Wallechinsky 1992, p xiii
28. Hill (In Allison) 1993, p 102
29. Epsy 1979, p 5
30. Dassler (In Miller) 1992, p 192
31. Allison 1993, p 11
32. Hill 1992, p 242
33. Simson and Jennings 1992, p 236
34. Hill (In Allison) 1993, p 103
35. Simson and Jennings 1992, p 22

CHAPTER 3

ALL THE OLYMPIC HOSTS AND BIDDING CITIES OF THE MODERN GAMES

Olympic hosts.	Original bidding cities.
Athens 1896	
Paris 1900	
St Louis 1904	
London 1908	(Rome withdrew)
Stockholm 1912	
Cancelled 1916	World War I
Antwerp 1920	(Budapest first scheduled but loser in WWI)
Paris 1924	Barcelona
Amsterdam 1928	Lyons, Havana, Rome
Los Angeles 1932	
Berlin 1936	Barcelona, Buenos Aires
Cancelled 1940	WWII
Cancelled 1944	WWII
London 1948	
Helsinki 1952	Minneapolis, Amsterdam, Philadelphia, Detroit, Chicago
Melbourne 1956	Buenos Aires
Rome 1960	Tokyo
Tokyo 1964	Detroit, Vienna, Brussels
Mexico 1968	Buenos Aires, Lyon, Detroit
Munich 1972	Madrid or Barcelona (sources differ)
Montreal 1976	Los Angeles, Moscow
Moscow 1980	Los Angeles
Los Angeles 1984	Teheran (halfheartedly)
Seoul 1988	Nagoya (Melbourne and Athens withdrew)
Barcelona 1992	Brisbane, Birmingham, Belgrade, Paris, Amsterdam
Atlanta 1996	Athens, Manchester, Melbourne, Toronto, Belgrade
Sydney 2000	Beijing, Manchester, Istanbul, Berlin, Brasilia (Milan and Tashkent withdrew)
Athens 2004	Stockholm, Cape Town, Buenos Aires, Rome (Istanbul, St Petersburg, Lille, Seville and San Juan - eliminated in first round)

THE PRE-WORLD WAR II GAMES -
A FRAGILE BEGINNING

Chapter three is a sentimental reflection of the first few Olympic Games. Chapter four is a journey through the successful and idealistic post-war period (No references at the end of the more informal chapters three and four). In chapter five, the Games increasingly begin to reflect the complex and confrontational world we live in. From chapter six onwards, the immense pressures of increasing commercialisation and social expectations are examined. The information on the earlier Games was difficult to obtain: various sources which included the Official Reports by the Organising Committees (where available) and the ITV Book of the Olympics published in 1980, were used. All data regarding sports events were obtained from or verified in the Complete Book of the Olympics by David Wallechinsky.

ATHENS 1896 -
THE BEGINNING OF IT ALL

The rebirth of the Olympic Games took place in Greece where the whole Olympic concept originated. This decision was taken at the international Congress for the re-establishment of the Olympic Games in Paris in 1894. Ironically, the Greek government was not very enthusiastic and originally declined the honour, because it was not prepared to accept any financial responsibility.

De Coubertin had to rush to Greece to try and save the Games. Fortunately for him he found an ally in Prince Constantine, the heir to the throne and the grandfather of Crown Prince Constantine, a gold medallist in sailing in 1960. With the help of the Prince and the Hellenic Committee, a campaign was initiated to collect funds. The reaction was very positive and donations streamed in from Greece and abroad. A wealthy builder, Averoff, restored the 45 000-seat marble stadium below the Acropolis which dates back to the 4th Century. It cost Averoff one million drachmas, but his name is immortalised in Olympic history. De Coubertin managed to persuade 13 nations to attend: Australia, Austria, Britain, Bulgaria, Chile, Denmark, France, Germany, Hungary, Sweden, Switzerland, the United States and Greece. These countries sent 331 athletes to compete in 43 events, but most athletes had to pay their own way.

The opening of the Games was well attended with an eager crowd of over 50 000 people listening to the opening speech by Prince Constantine. The anthem, which was specifically composed for this occasion by Samarus, became the official hymn of the Olympic Movement. Greece had cast off the Turkish yoke of the Ottoman empire in the 1820's and these Games were part of the process of reviving the Greek culture.

On the sporting side, the first gold medal of the modern era went to American James Connolly, when he won the triple jump. Connolly later became a doctor and won a Pulitzer prize as a journalist. The discus-throwing event was also won by an American, much to the disappointment of the Greeks, who were quite serious about this ancient field event. The Greeks studied the classical sculptures of discus-throwers to help them perfect their technique, but when it came to the actual execution, the young American Robert Garret took the title with his last throw. Garret could only practise at home with a facsimile discus he made from a drawing, which proved much too heavy when he picked up the real thing in Athens for the first time. Garret also won the gold medal in the shot put.

The European crowd was fascinated by the "crouch" start adopted by the Americans in the 100 m heats. One of them, Thomas Burke, became the first 100 m winner of

the modern Olympic era. The USA ended up by taking 11 gold medals, compared with 10 for Greece and 7 for Germany. But in the overall medal count, Greece came out on top with 47, whilst the USA could only manage 19 and Germany 15. Some of the events did not take place: the sailing and rowing competitions were cancelled because of bad weather and the athletes complained of the very cold sea water near the Port of Piraeus where the swimming was held. Apparently one American competitor, Hoyt, jumped out immediately after diving in.

The marathon was unquestionably the most important event to the Greeks. The fact that this race was important to their national pride was reflected in the entries where 12 out of the 16 athletes were Greeks. The race was held on a very hot afternoon and the foreigners dropped out one by one. Most of them had never even attempted a race of this distance before, except for the Hungarian Gyula Kellner who had to qualify for the trip by winning a 40 km trial in Budapest. The Greeks took part in two preliminary races on the same course, from the marathon bridge to the Olympic Stadium, which of course gave them a considerable advantage.

There were some unusual incidents - the Australian competitor Edwin Flack who had won the 800 m event only a couple of hours before the marathon, was overextending himself at the 37 km mark and was beginning to stumble about. His companion, an Englishman, asked a Greek spectator to hold Flack upright while he rushed to get a wrap. The delirious Flack thought he was being attacked and punched the poor Greek so hard that he fell to the ground. Flack was eventually loaded on to a carriage and taken to the dressing room at the stadium where he was attended to by Prince Nicholas himself and revived with a drink consisting of an egg and brandy mixture.

As the race progressed, messengers were sent to the stadium on horseback and bicycles to reveal the identity of the leaders to the anxious 100 000 spectators in and around the stadium. There was a hush amongst spectators in the earlier stages when they were told that Flack was in the lead, but later on when a Greek major on horseback rushed to the royal box to inform the King and Queen that a Greek by the name of Spyros Louis was in the lead, the news spread around the stadium like wildfire. The small wiry winner was feted by royalty after his victory and admired by the Greek nation ever after. He was showered with gifts and offers which included watches, jewellery, wine, free haircuts, free clothing for life, free meals, free coffee for a year, a shotgun and a Singer sewing machine.

In Athens in 2004, the marathon will again take place along the same route ending in the original Olympic Panathenaic Stadium. The 1896 Games was a very successful event to such a degree that the Greeks felt it should remain permanently in Athens. De Coubertin had to defend his international concept of the modern Olympics against the King's determination that the Games should remain in Greece.

PARIS 1900 -
GREAT EXHIBITION, PITY ABOUT THE OLYMPICS

The second Olympic Games in Paris unfortunately turned out to be a poor side-show for the Great International Exhibition and as a result the events were spread out over 5 months. The Exhibition was professionally organised and drew millions of spectators. The Olympics with its amateur ethos drew small crowds and was treated with scorn.

Apparently some of the athletes did not even realise they were competing in the Olympic Games! The athletic events took place outside Paris and were the most successful. Irving Baxter, an American Indian, certainly drew attention with his high jump technique. He simply dived over the bar, landing on his hands and actually won the event with a height of 1,9 m.

The marathon took place on an extremely hot day and started and ended in the Bois de Boulogne. Only seven of the runners were able to finish. Michel Theato, a 23 year old delivery man for a bakery, took the lead shortly after the halfway mark and stayed in front until the end. Afterwards there was a lot of grumbling about him knowing all kinds of short cuts through the dark alleys in the older sections of the city, where his daily deliveries were done.

Interestingly enough, golf was part of the Olympic programme for the 1900 and 1904 Games. Ten women took part in the final nine-hole round of the ladies golf contest. Margaret Abbott, a 22 year old Chicago socialite became the first US woman to win an Olympic gold medal. She later told relatives that she won the tournament "because all the French girls apparently misunderstood the nature of the game and turned up to play in high heels and tight skirts". When Abbott died in 1955, she was unaware that the tournament she had won was part of the Olympics. Charlotte Cooper of Great Britain became the first female Olympic champion when she won the tennis tournament.

The French captured 28 gold medals, with the USA taking 20 and Great Britain going home with 17. The number of participants increased to 1 330 and 23 nations took part.

© IOC/OLYMPIC MUSEUM COLLECTIONS

ST LOUIS 1904 -
THE ANTHROPOLOGICAL FLOP

Again the Olympic Games played second fiddle to an international exhibition - this time to the World Fair. The 1904 Olympics were actually awarded to Chicago by the International Olympic Committee but after a serious controversy, President Theodore Rooseveldt intervened and the Games were moved to St Louis. This proved to be an unfortunate decision as the organisation was even less competent than that of Paris. Virtually all the competitors were American and in total there were only 687 sportsmen representing 12 nations. Rumours were that the St Louis establishments only served buffalo meat.

The British Isles were represented by one Irishman, and Olympic founder, De Coubertin, did not even bother to attend. The St Louis Games actually lasted over four months and apparently the promoters of the World Fair demanded all kinds of extra side-shows to keep the crowds entertained.

In Spalding's 'Official Athletic Almanac for 1905' which contains the Official Report of the Olympic Games, these side-shows are described as "the First Series of Athletic Contests ever held, in which Savage Tribes were the Exclusive Contestants".

These "Anthropology Days" as they were called, featured "Africans, Moros (Philippines), Patagonians, Ainu (Japanese), Cocopa (Mexican) and Sioux Indian Tribes". These unfortunate creatures were expected to take part in all kinds of athletic events, from pole-climbing to putting the 16 lb shot (7,27 kg). Obviously they did not fare particularly well at shot put, since it is an event that requires some specialised training to say the least. James Sullivan, the then Chief of the Capital Department of Physical Culture of the Louisiana Purchase Exposition and also Director of the 1904 Olympic Games, expected their way of life "should have enabled them to easily put this shot many feet further". The hypothesis which Sullivan wanted to test by featuring the so-called "Anthropology Days", was "that the average savage was fleet of foot, strong of limb, accurate with the bow and arrow and expert in throwing the stone".

In the numerous events and interesting contests, the Patagonians demonstrated "remarkable ability in tug of war but failed the other tests of strength, notably throwing the 56 lb stone" and the Pygmies showed enthusiasm only for the mud fighting and tree climbing. Solomon concluded that "the whole meeting proves conclusively that the savage has been a very much overrated man from an athletic point of view". A fellow academic, Dr McGee, held a less extreme opinion and reasoned that "the savages" would have become as proficient as many Americans if they had had the advantage of the use of a professional trainer for a short time.

Whether these ungracious events were included as a serious research effort or whether it was just a pretentious excuse to exploit the sensation value of the unusual participants, does not matter that much today, because crude as it might have been, this was the beginning of extending Olympic participation to all nations.

The first two black Africans to participate in the Olympics were Lentauw and Yamasoni from South Africa, who happened to be in St Louis as part of the Boer War Exhibit at the Louisiana Purchase Exposition. They entered the marathon and Lentauw managed to finish ninth, even though he was chased by two large dogs through a cornfield. The event was won by Thomas Hicks from the USA who was kept going by oral doses of strychnine sulphate mixed with raw egg white and some liberal brandy tots for the last 16 km. The event's organisation was terrible - the heat, dust and total lack of water facilities made conditions so difficult that only 14 of the 32 starters made it to the finish line. The winner's slow time of almost three and a half hours is an indication of the atrocious conditions and the lack of real depth amongst the entrants.

Comment

There is little doubt that the Olympic Games of 1900 and 1904 were the most unsuccessful ever. The fact that they were linked to international exhibitions has not escaped the International Olympic Committee's (IOC) attention. Even today, the Manual for Candidate Cities of the IOC, theme 8, states that the relevant authorities must provide a declaration that "no other important or international meeting or event will be taking place in the host city itself, in the vicinity or in the competition sites during the Olympic Games, or for one week immediately before or after".

LONDON 1908 - SOLID SUPPORT

The Olympic Movement as such was extremely frail and vulnerable after the Paris and St Louis disasters. The last thing it could afford was another failure.

Rome was actually scheduled to play host in 1908; but withdrew for financial reasons two years after being appointed. London was asked to step in at very short notice and by all accounts produced a well organised Games. The first comprehensive Official Report of an Olympic Games was also compiled. The Official Report hailed it as the greatest international athletic gathering ever held. Well, this greatest athletic gathering was attended by 2035 athletes from 23 nations and they competed in 21 different sports. The Official Report also emphasised that "in every civilised country Committees were formed beforehand, preliminary competitions were held, and every care was taken to select the best available national representatives".

There is no doubt that the British hosts realised that the Olympics were special, that these events and ceremonies constituted something more encompassing than just sports competition or a regular festival. On page 21 of the Official Report, it is said of the broader aspects of the modern Olympic Games "The **underlying idea** is that there is something in these periodical gatherings which give promises of results more important than those to be hoped for, from an ordinary athletic meeting, however representative and however extended in scope".

The hosts were not just sensitive to the Olympic ideals; they were extremely practical down-to-earth organisers as well. The reality concerning incessant cost increases is still with us to this day and was most aptly described in the 1908 Games report: "**If the question of finance has proved difficult in the past, that difficulty is not likely to diminish in the future, for Olympic balance sheets like other budgets are in the habit of proving their healthy existence by a vigorous growth**".

Of all the modern Olympic hosts, London in 1948 and Los Angeles in 1984 were probably the most capable as far as cost-containment was concerned. Virtually all other hosts had to contend with increased costs to a greater or lesser degree.

The Londoners had a clear idea and specific principles about the appropriate way to approach this huge event. "It is a well-known and generally accepted maxim of English life that undertakings such as these shall be carried out by private enterprise, and without help of any sort from the government, a distinction which other nations do not share". This meant that the British Olympic Association had to depend on its own efforts and "upon the support of the friends of the Olympic

THE GREAT
STADIUM
SHEPHERD'S·BUSH·LONDON

THE OLYMPIC GAMES 1908

PROGRAMME

6d

Movement". Fortunately, the Franco-British Exhibition was also due to be held in 1908 and the BOA was able to gain the help and co-operation of the executive of this exhibition. This gave them access to the sports arena that was constructed for the exhibition and which was then developed to serve as an Olympic Stadium. The agreement between the Olympic organisers, the BOA and the Executive Committee of the Franco-British Exhibition "provided that the Exhibition Committee should construct at their own cost all the racing tracks and buildings necessary for carrying out the Olympic Games, and should provide all necessary equipment, attendants, advertisements etc, and should advance to the British Olympic Association the sum of £2 000 for current working expenses". At last the Olympic Games benefited substantially from an Exhibition. Indeed one wonders how the organisers would have coped without these major facilities which were in place at the right time, for they had less than two years to prepare after the Italians withdrew.

Another interesting aspect of the 1908 Games was that the competitions in sculpture, music, literature, architecture and painting formed part of the Olympiad. The possibility of adopting a standard medal for the Olympic Games was also mooted for the first time. The idea was that one side should change with each Olympiad and that the other side should have a permanent face to be decided by the IOC.

On the sporting side, the Americans took most of the medals, but the intense competitive spirit spilled over in heated arguments and accusations of bias were levelled at British referees. This bickering between the two powerful English speaking countries became so vehement it almost put an end to the 1908 Games. The ill-feeling translated into frosty relations between the sporting bodies representing the two countries for some time after the Games. An example of the controversial decision was in the 400 m where three Americans, Carpenter, Robbins and Taylor, beat Halswelle of England. But the British judges ruled that Carpenter had impeded the Englishman and should be disqualified. They decided that the race should be run again without Carpenter. The two other Americans were furious when informed of this decision and withdrew, leaving Halswelle an open field to win a farcical one man race.

One of the most controversial endings to an Olympic marathon occurred when British officials almost carried the exhausted Italian Dorando Pietri across the finish line after he collapsed just a few yards short. Pietri was later disqualified and American Johnny Hayes got the gold, but Pietri remained the crowd's favourite and received a gold cup from the Queen. Both Dorando and Hayes were offered good money to turn professional, which they accepted. The most prominent two races were held in New York in 1908 and 1909, and both were won by Dorando. His opportunistic brother ran off with his fortune, while he remained a taxi driver in Italy.

When Reggie Walker, the 19 year old bank clerk from South Africa, won the 100 m sprint and beat the American and Canadian favourites "the crowd of 49 000 cheered wildly and threw their hats and programs into the air, while friends and officials competed for the right to carry him on their shoulders" according to Wallechinsky.

One US newspaper stated that "The Englishmen were gratified to see the monotonous succession of American victories broken by a Britisher, even if he was a colonist".

1908 was the only Summer Olympics where Great Britain beat the USA in the medal count, with Great Britain taking between 49 and 56 of the 97 possible gold medals (Wallechinsky states 56 and The ITV Book of the Olympics has the figure at 49) against the USA's 23 gold medals.

There were more overt political Games as well: the Russians tried to prevent the Finns from displaying their flag and the English applied the same pressure to the Irish.

But overall, the 1908 Games put the Olympic Movement back on the rails and the 90 000 people who paid to participate as spectators on the last day gave testimony to that fact.

STOCKHOLM 1912 - THE HARMONIOUS GAMES

As hosts, the Scandinavians have served the Olympic movement extremely well, with the 1912 Stockholm and 1952 Helsinki Games amongst the most harmonious and pure sporting events. Ironically, Stockholm followed after the 1908 London Games and Helsinki's predecessor was also London in 1948. Both Scandinavian Games helped to stabilise the Olympic Movement at crucial stages immediately after London had hosted the Games quite successfully at short notice (1908 and 1948). The Swedish hosts topped the medals table with 24 gold, the USA was just behind them with 23, leaving Great Britain with 10, and Finland with 9, far behind.

The 100 m was dominated by the Americans. They won all five of the heats in which they were entered. The final was marred by seven false starts, the first three by Ralph Craig who eventually won the race. Thirty six years later at the London Olympics, Craig, by then a successful industrial engineer, reappeared as an alternate on the US yachting team. There is no doubt that Jim Thorpe was the outstanding athlete of these Games. He won the decathlon by a huge margin and apart from his gold medal, received a jewel encrusted chalice by Czar Nicholas of Russia. Tragically, he lost his amateur status not long after his Olympic achievements, because he had earned $25 a week playing in a minor baseball league in 1909 and 1910. His name was erased from the records and his gold medals taken back. It was only on his deathbed 41 years later, that his amateur status was restored to him and his gold medals were handed to his children in 1983.

The Finns had to compete (unwillingly) as part of the Russian Empire. These political overtones spilled over in the Greco-Roman wrestling event between a Russian, Klein and a Finn, Asikainen who met in the middleweight semi-final and battled it out for 11 hours! This was the longest wrestling contest in Olympic history. The two stopped every half hour for a brief rest from the physical exhaustion and the hot sun. Finally, Klein gained the upper hand and pinned his man down. However the Estonian competing for Czarist Russia was so weary that he was unable to compete in the final and Johanson of Sweden won first place by default.

The 5 000 m proved to be a dramatic event: Hannes Kolehmainen had already won the 10 000 m two days earlier and he was taking part in his fourth long distance race in four days. Kohlemainen and Frenchman Bouin ran side by side down the final straight. Only 10 m from the line, the vegetarian bricklayer from Finland took the lead to win the race. Sadly silver medallist Bouin and bronze medal winner Hutson of Britain were both killed in World War I in 1914, within days of each other. Kolehmainen or "Hannes the Mighty" reappeared in Antwerp to win the 1920 marathon.

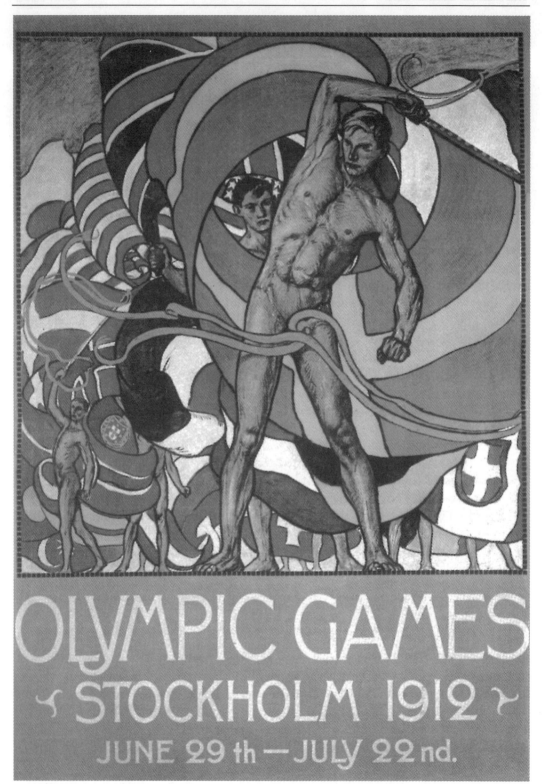

The marathon took place on a scorching day. After 30 km Tutu Kolehmainen, brother of Hannes, was forced to retire, and two South Africans, McArthur and Gitsham, took the lead. Three km from the finish, Christian Gitsham stopped at the refreshment stand for water. Kenneth McArthur promised he would wait for his teammate, but he kept pushing and opened an unassailable lead. It was only in 1996 that Josua Thugwane would again win the marathon for South Africa. There was a tragic side to the 1912 marathon: the 21 year old Portugese competitor, Francisco Lazaro collapsed from sunstroke and heart problems near the end of the race and was taken to hospital where he died the next day.

The first of a long line of swimming champions from the USA made his appearance at Stockholm, Duke Kohanamoku from Honolulu. He was called Duke because at the time of his birth the Duke of Edinburgh was visiting Hawaii. He won both his heats for the 100 m freestyle with ease, but because of a misunderstanding, the three US swimmers failed to show up for the semi-final on the Saturday night, so an extra heat was organised because a final without these three would have been absurd. But they had to better a time set by one of the finalists. Just to make sure, the Duke equalled the world record in the special heat. He won the gold with an effortless performance.

1912 was the second last Olympics where the supposedly friendly sport of tug-of-war formed part of the programme. At the 1908 London Olympics, the Liverpool Police pulled the US team over the line in a matter of seconds. The Americans vehemently protested that the British team was using special illegal boots whilst the Liverpudlians maintained that they were wearing run-of-the-mill police boots. The victors challenged the Americans to a pull in stockinged feet after the tournament, but unfortunately, the result of this impromptu match was not recorded. At Stockholm the tug-of-war proceeded without any controversies or serious incidents, but this time the Swedes came out on top and the British team in second place.

ANTWERP 1920 –
REWARD FOR BEING
TRAMPLED IN THE TRENCHES

The 1920 Games were officially opened by Albert, King of Belgium, and the IOC approved flag was flown for the first time at the Olympics. The 1916 Olympics due for Berlin had been cancelled because of the First World War (the opposite of the ancient Games in Greece, when wars were supposedly suspended for the duration of the Games).

The 1920 Games were awarded to Antwerp to compensate Belgium in some way for the terrible loss of human life suffered in the muddy trenches of World War 1. The losing nations Austria, Bulgaria, Germany, Hungary and Turkey were not allowed to participate. Actually, the 1920 Games were originally awarded to Budapest but switched to Antwerp at a later stage.

Apparently spectators were so few that the king of Belgium, Albert, remarked during the opening ceremony, "all this is quite nice, but it certainly lacks people". Obviously finances were a problem and by all account the facilities were unimpressive, to say the least. No official report exists and apparently even the list of results is incomplete. Even so, it is a fact that 1920 was the last time the manly sport of tug-of-war was included in the Olympic program with the British team taking gold ahead of the eight Dutchmen.

The standing high jump was still part of the Olympic programme and the rule was: "The feet of the competitor may be placed in any position, but shall leave the ground only once in making an attempt to jump. When the feet are lifted from the ground twice, or two springs are made in making the attempt, it shall count as a trial jump with result. A competitor may rock forward and backwards, lifting heels and toes alternately from the ground, but may not lift either foot clear from the ground or slide it along the ground in any direction". With this exception the rules are similar to the running high jump. The standing and running broad jump also formed part of the events.

Paavo Nurmi, the son of a Finnish carpenter, came second in the 5 000 m to the Frenchman Joseph Guillemot, but took revenge in the 10 000 m when he overtook Guillemot in the back stretch of the final lap to win by eight metres. But victory proved to be quite unpleasant as Guillemot vomited on Nurmi as soon as he crossed the finishing line. The cause of poor Guillemot's distress was a last minute change of schedule, which led to the starting time being brought forward by more than three hours at the request of the king of Belgium, leaving the Frenchman no time to digest a big meal.

The US team travelled to Belgium in a troopship and when they were shown their accommodation, which was in a school building, they threatened to go on strike. Somehow the matter was resolved and they did not carry out their threat to return to the ship's bunkers. Two and a half thousand athletes took part, representing 29 nations. The US resumed their domination of medals, won with 41 golds against 19 for Sweden and 15 for Great Britain.

PARIS 1924 -
"CHARIOTS OF FIRE" GAMES

For Paris, the second time around was much more successful with 44 nations represented by just under 3 000 athletes. Although the competition was of the usual high Olympic standard, the fanaticism of the French supporters, particularly in events where Americans were involved, was so intense it became a notable feature of these Games. The 1924 Games were the last to be attended by the founder of the modern Olympics, Baron de Coubertin, although six more Summer and Winter Olympics took place before he died of a stroke in 1937.

It was likely that criticism by the US Government levelled at the French occupation of the Rühr region fuelled the anti-American antagonism. It spilled over in violence when an American spectator, an art student called Gideon Nelson, was severely caned by an incensed French spectator at the rugby final between France and the US. Nelson was actually knocked unconscious by the blow in the face administered with a walking stick. This incidentally, was the last occasion that rugby was included in the Olympic programme and 30 000 French spectators were shocked to witness their team taken apart by the upstart Americans.

The 1924 Games were the "Chariots of Fire" Games, with Eric Liddle the favourite for the 100 m withdrawing from the race because it was scheduled on a Sunday. He nevertheless got his gold in the 400 m and set a new world record. Liddle's teammate, Harold Abrahams, took the 100 m gold for Britain. Johnny Weismuller - who later became synonymous with Tarzan in his movie career - took three gold medals in the swimming, a feat that was not equalled before 1964 when Dawn Fraser from Australia also managed the triple gold. Johnny definitely was the most popular American in Paris with a comedy diving act, performed between races where his partner was Stubby Kruger.

Paavo Nurmi firmly established himself as one of the legends of Olympic track-and-field, by winning the finals of the 1 500 and the 5 000 m, both in Olympic record time, with only 55 minutes rest in-between. When "The Phantom Finn" was first informed of the unfavourable athletics schedule, he decided to run a simulation three weeks before the two Olympic finals. He first ran the 1 500 m in world record time and then an hour later, incredibly, posted another world record in the 5 000 m.

The Americans, despite complaining about being accommodated in wooden huts, swept the medals table - 45 golds, followed by Finland with 14 and France with 13.

AMSTERDAM 1928 -
WITH A LITTLE HELP
FROM OUR FRIENDS IN THE EAST

Baron von Tuyll initiated the Dutch effort to host the Olympics in 1912 when he proposed Amsterdam with the support of Pierre de Coubertin. The Netherlands Olympic Committee did not yet exist and Von Tuyll had to launch the whole campaign on his own initiative. By 1990, the Baron had a Netherlands Olympic Committee behind him to lend more weight to his effort, but nevertheless Antwerp was chosen as the first post-war host. Amsterdam tried again for 1924 against cities like Lyons, Havanna and Rome, but De Coubertin's wishes prevailed and Paris won. Von Tuyll was still the mainstay of the Dutch effort and he started talks with Amsterdam bankers in 1920 but soon realised that he could not expect much support because of the prevailing depression. By 1923, representatives of the National Olympic Committee discussed the possibility of a lottery loan with prominent bankers, but the proposal was eventually turned down because attendance levels at events were considered risky. "Meanwhile, the Committee was receiving almost daily schemes which would yield enormous amounts if put into execution. At first sight each of these schemes looked really enticing, but after careful examination they were found to be inspired by commercial instincts and generally for interests outside the Committee, while there was a doubt as to what benefit would be derived". (Official Report)

The Dutch Government was approached through the Minister of Foreign Affairs to investigate the possibility of floating a State sponsored lottery, and the success of the lottery, organised by the Swedish Olympic Committee for Stockholm 1912, was used as a positive example.

The expected expenditure was in the region of 2 million guilders and it was hoped the lottery could contribute half of it. Significant progress was made when the Amsterdam Municipality contributed 400 000 guilders and the Province of North Holland granted a subsidy of 100 000 guilders.

At the beginning of 1925, a Bill was being prepared by the Ministry of Education, Arts and Science to obtain the green light for an annual grant of 250 000 guilders over four years to the Organising Committee. In the meantime, all the Provincial Councils were approached for grants on the basis of the potential of the Games to create **increased foreign tourism** to the Netherlands in general.

The matter of finances was becoming urgent as the whole financial planning of the 1928 Games was to be reviewed at the May 1925 Olympic Congress, scheduled at Prague. Foreign newspapers were already speculating over the possibility that

THE NINTH
OLYMPIAD

BEING THE

OFFICIAL REPORT OF THE OLYMPIC GAMES
OF 1928 CELEBRATED AT AMSTERDAM

ISSUED BY THE NETHERLANDS OLYMPIC COMMITTEE
(COMMITTEE 1928)

EDITED BY G. VAN ROSSEM
SECRETARY GENERAL

TRANSLATED BY SYDNEY W. FLEMING

AMSTERDAM J. H. DE BUSSY, LTD.
PRINTERS & PUBLISHERS
60-62 ROKIN

Postcard for Amsterdam not available.

another city might have to be asked to take over from Amsterdam if the necessary finance could not be obtained.

The text of the proposed Bill was made public and the Dutch press received a good deal of reaction from the public. The heated debate focussed attention on the tabling of the Bill and it actually became a controversial political decision. Despite intense canvassing by members of the Organising Committee and a brilliant speech by the Minister De Visser, the Bill was defeated on the 6th of May 1925. The requests of the Provincial Councils for subsidies were also declined.

Somehow the whole process touched a raw public nerve. Whilst there was considerable public opposition when the Bill was being debated, the tables were now turned and the public demonstrated vociferous support for the Amsterdam Games. At the critical juncture, a Committee from Dutch East India cabled a guarantee for 150 000 guilders which somehow triggered an avalanche of positive response. On the initiative of the Association "De Nederlandsche Dagbladpers", the whole Dutch press started collection lists on behalf of the Netherlands Olympic Committee. Telegrams were sent to 40 'Burgomasters' in Holland on 14 May 1925 to request them to form collection committees. By the beginning of May, the Committee already had one and half million guilders at its disposal. The amount contributed by private institutions and persons, including the committees from Dutch East India and Sumatra's East Coast, came to over 630 000 guilders.

There were now sufficient funds to build a brand-new stadium and the Committee proceeded immediately to investigate the accommodation capacity of the city and its environs. The register showed that 35 000 beds were available in Amsterdam and 15 000 just outside the city. But the Police and Municipal Housing Commission turned down about one third of these as unsuitable. A register of acceptable Olympic accommodation was compiled for the convenience of visitors and it included hotels, guest houses and selected private residences. The contestants and officials were sent questionnaires in 1926 to determine their requirements and preferences, and they were expected to take up most of the hotel and guest house accommodation. The accommodation nerve centre was situated in the colourfully named headquarters " 't Koggeschip". Indeed the reports contained information on many aspects of the Games besides accommodation and finance.

In the November 1928 edition of 'Woord en Daad', a periodical for members of the Central Union and Christian Philanthropic Institutions, the following was published: "It soon appeared - and was verified throughout the whole of the Games - that in view of the fact that the number of visitors remained far below expectations, there was no question at all of an influx of shady characters, nor of excesses and general confusion and festive debauchery seriously lowering the moral standard. Neither was there an influx of servant girls; this is probably partially due to the early decision to engage only male staff for the buffets etc, at the stadium ... in addition to the fact that there is but little in Holland to attract people of loose morals". (There were definitely no condom vending machines at those Games).

In total 10 500 foreign visitors from 43 countries were accommodated and the housing section could ascertain that not a single serious complaint was received about the nature of the accommodation, or of charges being too high.

The Germans were back in the Olympics after the First World War. The Americans wanted to practise in the brand-new stadium and when they found it closed they rammed the gates in a car. And women could compete for the first time in track and field events. Previously they were only allowed to take part in tennis, golf, archery, figure skating, yachting, swimming and fencing.

However the 800 m event for women ended in controversy when several athletes collapsed in exhaustion. There was a general outcry that women should not be allowed to compete in events of more than 200 m. The IAAF actually proceeded to ban races longer than 200 m and "no women's race longer than ½ lap was run at the Olympics for another 32 years" according to Wallechinsky. The 3 000 m and marathon took place at Los Angeles in 1984 for the first time, and the 10 000 m was not a reality for females until Seoul in 1988.

Johnny Weismuller took his last two swimming gold medals before embarking on a movie career. Paavo Nurmi, the first flying Fin, also won gold for the last time in the 10 000 m. In his fabulous career he broke 19 world records in 13 events and one of his national Finnish records stood until 1949.

Perhaps the greatest compliment bestowed on the Dutch came from the Official Report of the 1932 Los Angeles Games which stated; "As a consequence of the great fidelity of the Dutch Committee to Olympic principles and an appreciation of the seriousness of its task, an organisation record was established that could well be taken as a basis upon which to build for the Games of the Xth Olympiad".

LOS ANGELES 1932 -
"BUDDY CAN YOU SPARE ME A DIME?"

This was to be the first time the Games were held outside Europe apart from the St Louis flop. But the organisers faced two large obstacles: the terrible effects of the world-wide depression and the relative isolation of California. Milton Friedman described the depression that started in mid-1929 as a catastrophe of unprecedented dimensions for the USA. The dollar income of the American nation was cut in half even before the economy hit the bottom in 1933. This led to the lowest number of competitors since St Louis in 1904; in fact, only St Louis and Athens in 1896 had fewer participants. Even the chaotic 1900 Paris Games saw a larger number of contestants entering. (1 319 for Paris against 1 281 for LA).

As a result only three teams took part in the field hockey tournament, and soccer had to be dropped completely.

The introduction of the Official Report of the Games of the Xth Olympiad again stressed the sentimental value attached to an Olympic Games. The combination of festival and fierce competition based on values of fraternal universality, seemed to evoke deep-seated emotions. The Report refers to the precious memories in a special eloquent way. "The Games of the Xth Olympiad have come and gone ... to us who were participants in their activities, their memories are still real and vivid, memories of a splendid spectacle, splendidly staged, splendidly acted. But in a very short while these memories will lose their sharpness. They will be softened and as time passes they will gradually become merged into a recollection almost dreamlike, as of a ship that passes in the night".

Most of the Official Reports describe the unique sentiments that accompany this event, the feeling that somehow makes Olympic competition something above mere competition, however intense. And intense the competition at Los Angeles proved to be. The Olympic Movement was now well established and the crème de la crème of the world's athletes saw to it that records were regularly shattered. Olympic records were broken, amongst others, in the 100 m, 200 m (both by American sprinter Eddie Folan), 1 500 m (by Luigi Beccali of Italy), 5 000 m (by Laun Lehtinen of Finland), 10 000 m (by Janusy Kusocinski of Poland) and lastly, a new marathon record by Juan Zabala of the Argentine. Other new world-records were set in the 400 m by William Carr of the USA, in the 800 m by Thomas Hampson of Great Britain and in the 400 m hurdles where, strangely enough, because of prevailing regulations, the first place was awarded to Bob Tisdall of Ireland whilst the world-record went to Glenn Hardin of the USA who only managed second place. This was because Bob Tisdall knocked over the last hurdle. The regulations prevented any record being recognised if the contestant did not manage to clear all the barriers.

© IOC/OLYMPIC MUSEUM COLLECTIONS

Women's athletics, then in its infancy, produced world-records or new world-records in almost every item and proved to be popular with the crowds. Mildred Didriksen, or Babe as she was known, set three new world-records in the 80 m hurdles, javelin and high jump. The Americans expected Cleveland's Stella Walsh to win the 100 m for them and she did win, but in Poland's colours as Stavislawa Walasiewicz. Increasingly, organisers had to contend with the determination of nationality where an athlete was born in one country and brought up in another.

The USA dominated the medal count even more convincingly than in Amsterdam: with 41 golds against second placed Italy's 12 in comparison to 22 in Amsterdam where Germany came second with 10. Amazingly, Swedish wrestler Carl Westergren won the heavyweight title after taking the light-heavyweight gold in 1924 and the middleweight crown in 1920!

The 1932 Olympics witnessed the debut of the technological era in terms of automatic timing devices and photo-finish recordings by camera. This led to the beginning of today's emphasis on winning at all costs.

As always, events off the track were just as fascinating. The song of the day was; "Buddy can you spare me a dime" but it was wine the French team was after in spite of the prevailing Prohibition. And wine they got, because after all, it was reasoned, it is part of the French culture.

Comparisons with the 1984 LA Games were inevitable and it is immediately apparent that in 1932, commercialism was still taboo. It is emphasised in the Official Report that, "Not a single note of **commercialism** was allowed to permeate the consummation of the task". It is difficult to believe that this city was the one to present the first fully commercial Games in 1984.

The 1932 organisers certainly had no illusions about the investment potential of the Games; "It must be remembered that the total income from the Games does not have charged against it the cost of any stadium or other facilities used in the Games which existed prior to the organisation of the Games and for the cost of which the Games did not have to pay. In the organic provisions for the Olympic Games, it is not possible that they shall ever be a **business proposition** where the word 'profit' could properly be applied". And it is to an extent due to investments made in sports infrastructure in 1932 that the 1984 organisers could reap a handsome profit. Indeed profit was not a very welcome term in 1932, and the organisers were quick to squash any rumours regarding profits being made when the funds of the Organising Committee permitted it to retire the Olympic Bonds.

This leads to another significant contrast between the 1932 and 1984 events, because the voters in 1928 voted overwhelmingly to have an Olympic Bond Act approved to finance preparations and investments for 1932 (amazing when one considers the level of unemployment at the time which approached 25 %). The 1984 organisers were denied access to any public funds or guarantees as a result of a special proclamation supported by local voters. The economic climate in 1984 was much more favourable, thus a significant change in attitude must have taken place. The same tendency is discernable with the current campaign by Stockholm for the 2004 Games, where modern Stockholm is really struggling to obtain significant popular support for its bid in contrast to the harmonious 1912 event in the same city.

Another significant difference between the earlier and later LA Games was that the 1932 organisers constructed the first Olympic Village which was considered very innovative and daring at the time. (In 1984, university campus buildings were utilized.) The Official Report stated that, "It is difficult for the members to believe that the Organising Committee was prepared to build an entirely new, specially designed and completely equipped international 'city' for the sole use of athletes and officials participating in the Games". The magnificent 105 000 seat stadium was another amazing feature of these Depression, but definitely not depressing, Games.

BERLIN 1936 -
THE "SIEG HEIL" SPECTACLE

Originally, the Games of the sixth Olympiad were awarded to Berlin - this was supposed to take place in 1916, but the First World War intervened and Berlin had to compete against Barcelona for the 1936 Games. The decision was due to be made at an IOC meeting in Barcelona in 193I. Dr Lewald presented Berlin's case and pointed out that the German city was more accessible to millions of Europeans than Barcelona, and he also emphasised that Berlin's claim should receive more attention because of the fact that the 1916 Olympic Games had been cancelled. Because of the revolution that had broken out in Spain shortly before this meeting, attendance was poor and approval first had to be obtained to allow absentee votes by letter or telegraph.

The end-result was 43 votes for Berlin and 16 in favour of Barcelona. Hitler's National Socialists came into power in 1933 but this development could probably not have been foreseen by the IOC. In any event, it would seem unlikely that Spain, torn apart by a civil war, could have been seriously considered.

On the face of it, the new German rulers were extremely favourably disposed towards the Olympic organisers. The newly elected German Chancellor inspected the Grunewald Stadium and Sport Forum in October 1933 and instituted major changes to the delight of the organisers. Firstly, Hitler asked why the capacity of the stadium was to be enlarged by increasing the physical depth of the stadium rather than simply expanding it - it was then explained to him that the existing lease contract with the Berlin Racing Association ruled out any possibility that the Stadium might extend over the race course. Hitler enquired if alternative race courses existed in the area and Dr Lewald replied that two race courses were in operation in Hoppegarten and Karlshorst and that the Grunewald course had been operating at a loss for some time. The German Chancellor simply decided that the race course must disappear since he thought it desirable that the whole Grunewald premises should be given over to the construction of a new sports centre. The Chancellor also expressed the desire for a large open-air amphitheatre to be included in the construction programme. The proposal for another planned building, the Sport Forum which was actually rejected on grounds of cost, was approved by Hitler who was quoted in the Official Report ; "When a nation has 4 000 000 unemployed, it must seek ways and means of creating work for them". Hitler was, of course, eager to show the nation and the world that his brand of National Socialism would really make a difference.

The new Chancellor intuitively realised that a Berlin Olympic Games could provide the ideal vehicle to demonstrate to the world what a great nation the

GERMANY
BERLIN·1936
1ST–16TH AUGUST

OLYMPIC GAMES

© IOC / OLYMPIC MUSEUM COLLECTIONS

Germans could be under his version of National Socialism. Hitler as a politician, an actor and a strategic planner, was more than just a shrewd operator. Paul Johnson wrote in 'A History of the Modern World', "But in Hitler's case there was always an artistic dimension to these satanic schemes". Johnson reckoned that Hitler should have been an architect; indeed, he put an architect in charge of war production. Hitler was constantly busy with architectural plans to rebuild his hometown Lenz. Even towards the end in the bunker, he was still studying plans for this town's transformation. Johnson has no doubt that "Hitler's artistic approach was absolutely central to his success". After all, he had to conquer the minds of the best educated nation in the world.

That is why the whole Olympic concept was so appealing to him: the scope for impressive visual structures, the fascination of the opening and closing ceremonies, the powerful symbolism of the Olympic aura, the intense focus of worldwide interest, the drama of top class competition and of course, the possibility to demonstrate his racial theory of Aryan supremacy which was central to his political dream. Hitler loved visual themes and although he exploited class differences when it suited him, it was not as visual and obvious as racial disparities.

So while the official publication of the Reich Commission for Physical Training wrote enthusiastically, "There is no other competition between nations in which the laurels of victory are so coveted but in which, on the other hand, the **spirit of combat** is so honourable and friendly", the newly elected Chancellor had plans and intentions which were, to say the least, slightly devious and somewhat unfriendly.

But the Games by all account were a grand spectacle. The Olympic torch was lit on Mount Olympus and carried to Berlin by a series of runners - the first ever for a modern Olympics. Twenty-five large TV screens were set up in theatres throughout Berlin for free viewing - another first for the Berlin Olympics. Leni Riefenstahl produced and directed a film of the Games. To this day it is still considered one of the finest sports films ever made. The imposing stadium and arena could accommodate up to 130 000 people. The organisation was superb, military bands were playing on almost every corner, entertainment of VIP's was lavish, and impressive looking uniforms were abundant.

Before the Games the organisers calculated that Berlin was within one hour's travel distance by train for five and a half million people, and within four hour's striking distance for 17 million Europeans. Berlin and Potsdam at the time already had a population of four and a half million. So six and a half million tickets were printed and an estimated half a million visitors spent over two million bed-nights in the German Capital. On the sporting side, the black American Jessie Owens won four golds in the 100 m, 200 m, 4 x 100 m relay and long jump and consequently immortalised his name in Olympic history. Jack Lovelock became the first New Zealander to win Olympic gold when he broke the world record in the 1 500 m. The marathon was won in style by Sohn Kee-Chung of Korea who set a new Olympic record. Because Korea was occupied by Japan at the time, Sohn had to run in Japanese colours and was even forced to adopt a Japanese name. The winner of the bronze medal, Nam Seung-Yang, was also from Korea and when the Japanese anthem was played they both registered a silent protest by bowing their heads. Sohn later carried the South Korean flag at the opening ceremony of the 1948 Games in London, and 48 years later he brought the torch in the Olympics Stadium in Seoul in 1988. Berlin attracted three times more competitors than Los Angeles. In one respect Hitler could claim that Aryan supremacy was proven: in the medal count Germany took 33 gold versus 24 for the US. This was the first time since London in 1908, that the US did not walk away with the highest number of gold medals.

The 1936 Olympics celebration was undoubtedly the first time, but not the last, that this event was utilised as a propaganda tool for a totalitarian government. It is an open question to what extent this exercise in political opportunism backfired. It certainly opened a lot of eyes to the extent of the Nazi threat and, in a number of countries, Jewish communities specifically asked for a boycott of the Games, a proposal that was nearly carried through in the United States.

In the overall medal count Germany could show 89 gold, silver and bronze whilst the US took 56 medals home.

CHAPTER 4

THE INNOCENT PERIOD

LONDON 1948 - THE AUSTERITY GAMES

The first post-war Olympic Games of the XIV Olympiad were held in London in 1948. The immediate post-war era was one of rising costs of both wages and goods, accentuated by severe shortages of materials. These were not called the "Austerity Games" for nothing, but the whole approach was also that of a different era with much less commercialism and more emphasis on the "love for sports". As always, the IOC determined the conditions under which these Games were held to prevent overt commercialism - many means of raising money were not permissible, e.g. the inclusion of advertisements in brochures and programmes.

The Organising Committee did not have to build any stadia or arenas and many venues were made available for the Olympics free of any rent or charge. Therefore, the Official Report concluded, "it is not possible to view the Games as a coldly calculated business proposition of which the principal motive is to make a profit". The main source of income was ticket sales, and after the initial shock when it was discovered that a number of tickets ordered from abroad were not taken up, local demand during the Games compensated for any potential loss. The upshot was a neat profit of £29 000 after £761 688 of expenses were taken care of. The "gross revenue from the sports" came to an impressive £546 000 Sterling. No wonder the tickets sold so well, as the cream of the athletes from 59 nations were competing in 136 Olympic events - the ideal prescription to get rid of the post-war blues.

Not even the extraordinary heat of 1948's summer could suppress general enthusiasm and admiration for Emil Zatopek's splendid victory in the 10 000 m race. Fanny Blankers Koen reaped the rewards of her secret wartime training programme and dominated the women's events by winning 4 gold medals! This amazing Dutch athlete took top honours in the 100 m, the 200 m, the 80 m hurdles as well as the 4 x 100 m relay. The 100 m men's final was also memorable, if only for the fact that it was won by Harrison Dillard from the USA who actually specialised in hurdles. Four years later, Dillard did win his favourite event in Helsinki. Bob Mathias won the decathlon at the age of only 17.

Millions of people all over the world followed the Olympic events closely by listening to their radios. The British Broadcasting Corporation transmitted in 43 languages to listeners on five continents. An interesting new development at the time was that 80 000 television sets were already functioning, mostly in private homes, and that allowed up to half a million people for any given transmission to view these events.

The Olympic competitors were housed in Royal Air Force camps at Uxbridge, West Drayton and Richmond Park. The overall principle was to put four to six competitors in one room, which probably fitted in with the prevailing ration book atmosphere of severe shortages and hardship.

The 1948 Games were awarded less than three months after the Second World War ended, so London had less than two and a half years in which to prepare and promote the Games. This was at a time when many people doubted if there would ever be an Olympic Games again. No doubt, the 1948 Games are fondly remembered by all who had a part in it.

HELSINKI 1952 –
PURE SPORT AT A PRICE

The 5 876 Athletes who took part in 17 different sports made it a memorable sporting occasion. The Helsinki Games attracted more competitors than Melbourne or Rome, and as many as Tokyo in 1964.

Emil Zatopek, the Czech locomotive, was once again unbeatable in the 10 000 m, but after also winning the 5 000 m, the Galloping Major of the Czech army decided to enter the marathon as well. The favourite for this event was the British Jim Peters, who began well and was in the lead as they were approaching the halfway mark. He was surprised to be overtaken by the novice Zatopek who then had the audacity to ask if he, Peters thought they were going fast enough! Zatopek took Olympic gold in his first marathon and his wife Dora took top honours in the women's javelin event. Zatopek also broke the Olympic record in the marathon by six minutes. He attributed his amazing performance to a vigorous training schedule in the lovely wooded hills of his hometown, Prague.

In the boxing, history was in the making as the 17 year old Floyd Patterson from Brooklyn USA won the middleweight contest convincingly; he knocked out his final opponent in 74 seconds. In the heavyweight division the Swede, Ingemar Johansson, was disqualified for "not trying" against his hard-punching American opponent. Many years later these two would meet twice for the World Heavyweight Championship. In their first contest, Johansson knocked Patterson down seven times before scoring the knock-out. In the rematch, Patterson prevailed and reclaimed his title. And in the light-middleweight division, Lazlo Papp had to work hard to earn his second gold medal against South Africa's Theuns van Schalkwyk.

Helsinki had to compete against the likes of Detroit, Minneapolis, Philadelphia, Chicago and Amsterdam before being awarded the 1952 Games. Finnish athletes had amassed a total of 80 gold medals since their first appearance at Stockholm in 1912 and excelled in middle-distance running, wrestling and javelin. There was great enthusiasm among the population as a whole for the Olympics. Actually, Helsinki first tried to secure the 1940 Olympic Games, but was beaten to it by Tokyo in 1936. Two years later Japan voluntarily relinquished this honour and the Games were entrusted to Helsinki. The outbreak of World War II in the autumn of 1939 however, rendered this event a non-starter. Helsinki was appointed as the 1952 host at the 1947 IOC session in Stockholm.

There must have been some doubt whether Finland, with an enormous burden of war indemnity, would be financially capable of staging the Games. Nonetheless, Helsinki prevailed by 15 votes and Finns all over celebrated joyously.

But there was a financial price to pay. The city of Helsinki as well as the Finnish state invested $30 million and there was also a loss on the Organising Committee's operational balance sheet. No doubt some of the capital investments would have occurred anyway. In any event the Finns were proud to be host to competitors from 70 different countries. The chairman of the Organising Committee stated: "The economic loss, however, is slight compared with the palpable goodwill the country, the city, and the Finnish people reaped in reward. Taxpayers were not called upon to bear any extra burden". The guiding principle was that the Organising Committee would be responsible for projects of a more temporary nature, whilst the city and the state undertook capital projects which were deemed to be of a permanent nature and asset to the city. The Olympic stadium was erected for the 1940 Games and the capacity was increased to 70 000. Germany and Japan competed again after not being invited to the 1948 Games. The Southern hemisphere countries made their presence felt and in the 100 m Australia, South Africa and New Zealand took the first 4 places. In the 4 x 100 m relay, the Australians dropped the baton at the last change-over, leaving a gap for the Americans to sprint to victory.

In fact, the Americans dominated the 1952 medal table. They took home 40 gold medals and 76 in total, in contrast to the USSR's 22 gold and 69 overall medal count. Surprisingly, Hungary came third, with 16 gold and Sweden fourth with 12 gold medals. Countries like Britain, Japan and New Zealand could only manage one gold medal each.

The income from the sale of an impressive 1,37 million entrance tickets contributed the biggest amount to the receipt side of the operational balance sheet, but this still left the Organising Committee with a loss of 49 million marks.

MELBOURNE 1956 - AWAY FROM IT ALL

The first Olympic Games south of the equator was held in tumultuous times: the Suez crisis caused Egypt, the People's Republic of China, Spain, Holland and Iraq to withdraw, and the Hungarian uprising resulted in severe tension between the Russian and Hungarian competitors, in contrast to the generally very relaxed atmosphere.

Sixty-seven nations represented by 3 184 athletes took part in the opening ceremony in the traditional style of an organised march by national teams. But it was the closing ceremony which really stirred the crowds when the athletes broke ranks and mingled freely while chatting to each other and waving happily to all and sundry. Since the Melbourne Games, this cheerful, colourful, mixed throng of athletes at the closing ceremony has come to symbolise the universality of the Olympic Movement and the sheer goodwill created after weeks of intense competition.

Perhaps Australia's very remoteness which counted against it in the bidding campaign stages, now served as an ephemeral magic carpet to whisk everybody concerned away from the crises that dominated elsewhere. There were organisational problems as well, as the strict quarantine regulations of Australia forced the organisers to move the equestrian events to distant Stockholm. The Torch relay was started in Athens, then flown to Darwin in the Australian Capital Territories by way of Istanbul, Barra, Karachi, Calcutta, Bangkok, Singapore and Djakarta, a distance of 13 756 km (8 544 miles).

Then came the overland phase where the torch was passed from hand to hand, hailed with civic and public receptions all along the 2 831 miles. It was carried southwards towards Melbourne via Brisbane, Sydney and Canberra. These were the first Games to be officially televised and this of course played a huge part in getting televisions into Australian homes.

Because of Melbourne's remoteness from Europe, Asia and America, the number of tickets that could be sold overseas was limited. Yet a total of 110 000 were sold outside Australia, of which 56 000 went to New Zealand and the Pacific Islands, 22 000 to the USA and Canada, and 18 000 to the United Kingdom. All in all 1,34 million of the 2,58 million tickets were sold. A huge air-bridge had to be established to ferry people in for the opening ceremony. This involved 200 aircraft from 20 international airlines, which flew in 4 276 athletes and officials and 600 journalists, photographers and broadcasters apart from spectators.

Accommodation was provided by 167 suburban hotels, schools, public utilities and private homes. The placement of guests in private homes was managed in a very sensitive manner: first the 5 600 homes of volunteers were assessed and grad-

(Equestrian events took place in Stockholm)

ed, then "due regard was had to business, social and sporting interest and the general compatibility of visitors and host". The Australians were convinced of the success of this system of matching compatibilities and claimed that many Melbourne hosts entertained visitors beyond their original commitment by taking them on excursions, picnics and other outings.

The capital outlay on the Games amounted to about £8 million sterling. The deficit on the operational side amounted to some £300 000, with "housing, catering and canteen costs" taking the biggest slice (£840 000) on the debit side. Ticket sales remained the biggest source of income at a net of £1,17 million. In the end, the financial loss was accepted philosophically - at least in the official report: "the Olympic ideal however, does not reckon with profit and loss. They are less than nothing compared with the dividends in goodwill, not only in sport, not only for Melbourne or Australia, rich though this may be, but indestructibly in the hearts of men and women there and everywhere".

Several African nations: Kenya, Ethiopia, Liberia and Uganda, competed for the first time. There were some fine performances on the sporting side too, nowhere more so than in the 10 000 m duel between Pirie, the bank clerk from Surrey, and Kuts, the Russian sailor. The Russian kept on varying his pace, but by the 20th lap the Englishman surged ahead and then suddenly slowed down, leaving Kuts a convincing winner in a time almost 90 seconds faster than Zatopek's Olympic record. The 5 000 m was much the same story - although Pirie was the world record holder at the time, he seemed powerless against the Russian's combination of pace and stamina. It was another Olympic record for Kuts. As the Russian tanks were rumbling down the streets of Budapest, tension boiled over in the swimming pool where the Hungarian and Russian teams were contesting in water polo. The Hungarians were leading comfortably when a Russian fist split open an Hungarian eyebrow and this led to general mayhem. The pool was alive with flailing arms and fists, and fighting broke out amongst spectators as well. Eventually, Hungary took gold, Yugoslavia silver and Russia bronze.

The Australians were delighted when Betty Cuthbert won three gold medals in the 100 m, the 200 m, and the 4 x 100 m relay. Interestingly enough, the first three women took the first three places in both the 100 m and 200 m. But the local successes were not limited to the track: in fact, the Australians took eight of the 13 swimming titles in Melbourne. Dawn Fraser, then 16 years of age, took two golds and a silver. For training she swam five hours a day in Sydney harbour and reckoned that the waves and currents really tested her.

In the boxing, the legendary Hungarian Lazlo Papp took his third gold medal in consecutive Games. He became the only East-European to turn professional and became the European middleweight champion in 1962, but had to pack it in and return home in 1964 when the Communist authorities revoked his passport.

Perhaps the most memorable moment is still the closing ceremony when, at the suggestion of a 17 year old Chinese boy, the march was of one multicultural nation and all wars, politics and national chauvinism were forgotten.

ROME 1960 - THE CLASSIC GAMES

After studying the number of sports events in the Games of Berlin, London, Helsinki and Melbourne, **"the Committee considered it useful to suggest a reduction in the number of the events included in the programme of the two preceding Olympic Games"**. Already the sheer size of the whole event was a source of concern. The Organising Committee was trying to keep the total number of athletes under 7 000 (in 1960 it meant only 1 000 entries for women). The acceptable proportion of officials to athletes was calculated at 25% which meant 1 800 of them. In the end, 6 441 athletes from 84 countries took part.

The other perennial problem the organisers had to contend with was to convince the local taxpayers that the capital expenditure was for projects which were not constructed solely to meet the requirements of the IOC. The Committee used the usual subtle phrases to convince everybody concerned of their noble intentions: the venues "were to be constructed in occasion of the Olympic Games but not because of these". The Olympic Stadium certainly seemed to be a worthwhile legacy, for it might serve out another Games in 2004 and in-between there were numerous great events such as the 1990 Soccer World Cup. The number of tickets sold amounted to 1,43 million, with Italians buying the bulk at 823 000. The most popular sport was athletics for which 448 000 tickets were sold. Not surprisingly, football was second with over 252 000 tickets and third, the swimming and water polo events, for which 181 000 tickets were demanded. All these tickets were bought by real people, so the demand for accommodation was huge, but the Province of Rome could offer an ample 22 255 rooms in hotels, pensions and inns. In the brief period from 1 January to 1 August 1960, 105 new hotels opened their doors for the first time.

It was at Rome that the USSR really first challenged the USA. Some African countries like Ethiopia and Kenya were also making their presence felt. Abebe Bikila from Ethiopia won the moonlight marathon running barefoot, beating fellow African Rhadi from Morocco by just 100 m. The athletes from Down Under certainly made their mark with the great Australian, Herb Elliot, taking the 1 500 m race in convincing style and smashing the world record at the same time. The New Zealand team had to be satisfied with only one gold at Helsinki, but in Rome the inexperienced Peter Snell's final dash in the 800 m left the other athletes standing as it were, to take the first gold for the All Blacks. One of those other athletes was Belgian policeman, Roger Moens, who happened to be the world record holder at the time. New Zealand's second gold was to follow soon after in the 5 000 m where their hopes rested on Halberg, an athlete with a withered arm from a rugby injury, whose confidence was dented after successive failures at Melbourne and other international events. Snell and Halberg were both trained by Lydiard who

inspired Halberg to believe in himself once more. It certainly worked on the day as he took the gold in convincing style.

For the Americans, Wilna Rudolph was the queen of the track. She sprinted to victory in the 100 and 200 m and was part of the victorious 4 x 100 m relay team — not bad for a woman who was born seventh in a poor family of 19 children, and who contracted polio from which she had miraculously recovered.

In the men's 100 m and 200 m, the victors were from non-English speaking countries for the first time in the history of the Games. Amin Hary from Germany took the 100 m after three false starts (two of which were caused by Hary himself), and the 200 m, where the Italian in the sunglasses, Livio Berrutti, drove the crowd wild by winning all the preliminary races as well as the final.

In the pole vault Don Bragg from California soared to 4,7 m and went on to play Tarzan in the movies. Cassius Clay took the light-heavyweight title in boxing by squeezing past Madigan of Australia. He was later known as Mohammed Ali and became one of the all-time great heavyweight champions years later. In wrestling, the Turks certainly impressed by taking seven gold medals. At the time, these were great modern Games held in an ancient city.

TOKYO 1964 -
THE AWAKENING OF A GIANT

On 26 May 1959, at the 55th General Session of the IOC, Tokyo was appointed as host for the 1964 Olympic Games. This decision came some 23 years after Tokyo was awarded the Games of the XII Olympiad which it relinquished in 1938 just before the Second World War.

Where Rome strove to contain the ever expanding Games, Tokyo certainly had no financial inhibitions in expanding its infrastructure. The Organising Committee decided early on that just meeting the required standards for sporting facilities and accommodation arrangements would not be sufficient without equally acceptable roads, transport facilities and environmental conditions.

Tokyo, as a populous city with huge industrial complexes, presented the planners with complex problems. But the requirements for the Games were fitted in with the existing ten year plan as far as possible. The 22 highways and roads plus expressways which consisted of either over-head or tunnel sections, cost $500 million. The underground railways were extended by 177 km over eight lines. At the port of Tokyo, landing and pier facilities were improved. The water supply and sewerage facilities were improved for the growing population. An unusually severe drought before the Games caused considerable anxiety, and water had to be pumped in from surrounding areas.

A lot of trouble was taken to prepare accommodation and eating facilities in a way that would be more amenable to overseas visitors. The Tokyo Metropolitan Government and The Shoko Chukin Bank made $1,66 million available as special loans to owners of approved Japanese type inns (ryokan) in order to make them more acceptable to foreigners. A huge campaign was launched at hotels, inns, sports centres and private homes to conduct special classes on food hygiene and to effect widespread bacteriological tests. The National Stadium, completed for the Asian Games a year before Tokyo was awarded the Olympic Games, was to serve as Olympic Stadium and the seating capacity was extended by 25 000 to accommodate 72 000 spectators in all.

The total costs led to a great deal of confusion and indeed controversy. The expenditures can be classified under different headings, mainly direct and indirect with regard to the Olympic Games.

The operational expenditure undertaken by the Organising Committee included items such as transportation of the Olympic family, managing Olympic Villages, and running the actual events, which included sporting and ceremonial affairs as well as general administrative and personnel expenses. This came to just over $26 million. The expenditure on the construction and expansion of sports facilities, of which $13 million was spent on the Komazawa Sports Park (football, hockey, baseball, volleyball and wrestling), was the largest item and came to over $46 million. These costs were carried by National Government, the Tokyo Metropolitan Government, and various local governments such as the nearby Yokohama City Authority. So the direct costs amounted to $72,222 million.

The indirect expenditures totalled an astounding $2,6 billion - which compares with Barcelona's $8 billion 28 years later, if one takes an average inflation of 5% per year. Even at 8% the Tokyo costs would soar to over $24 billion in comparison to Barcelona's. But the citizens of Tokyo and Japan had an impressive list of improvements to vital infrastructural areas, which no doubt boosted the international competitiveness further and helped to underpin future industrial growth. Indeed, The Economist's Atlas of 1989 points out that "The world first became aware of Japan's economic miracle in 1964 when Tokyo hosted the Olympic Games". It was after 1965 that the Japanese growth in GDP really soared above those rates of West Germany and the USA.

Let's not forget the 8 138 athletes who represented 93 countries and territories for just over two weeks and helped to sell two million entrance tickets. The most popular sport was football (616 000 entrance tickets), then athletics with 519 000, swimming and diving did amazingly well (154 000), also volleyball with 83 000 entrance tickets, and boxing, surprisingly, with over 72 000 sales.

The Olympic flame was lit by Yoshinon Sakai who was born in Hiroshima one hour before the atomic bomb was dropped in 1945.

Peter Snell, who surprised everybody by taking the 800 m gold in Rome, completely dominated the middle-distance events at Tokyo by easily winning both the 800 and 1 500 m races. This was only the third time in Olympic history where an athlete successfully defended the 800 m title and the first time that somebody added a 1 500 m to two golds at 800 m. Behind him in the 800 m Wilson Kiprugut came in third to gain the bronze medal, the first Olympic medal ever won by a Kenyan.

But there were many superstars on show. Al Oerter of the USA won the discus event for the third time in a row with his fifth throw: his distance of over 61 m earned him the gold medal, as well as a new Olympic record. This amazing performance took place a week after tearing the cartilage in his lower ribs. Doctors advised him to rest for six weeks after this injury, but on the day of the preliminary round, Oerter was there, wrapped with ice packs and fortified by painkillers. Amazingly, he won again at Mexico City and once more extended his Olympic record, this time to 64,78 m. His first Olympic record at Melbourne was with a throw of 56,36 m. So, from 1956 to 1968, he extended the Olympic record by more than nine metres! All the more amazing when one takes into account that he was involved in a near fatal car crash in 1957.

In the swimming pool, Dawn Fraser proved unbeatable in the 100 m for the third Olympics in a row. To celebrate, she pinched the Japanese flag at the Emperor's Palace, dived into the moat and swam away when police chased her. The Emperor made her a gift of the flag after she was finally caught. Don Schollander from Yale University took four gold medals in the 100 and 400 m freestyle as well as two for relays in the 4 x 100 m and the 4 x 200 m events. Abebe Bikila dominated the marathon throughout. This time he wore shoes!

© IOC/OLYMPIC MUSEUM COLLECTIONS

CHAPTER 5

THE TUMULTUOUS "M" GAMES

MEXICO CITY 1968 - THIN AIR AND RICH TEQUILA

The age of innocence was finally over. While most people remember Mexico City for the controversy over its height above sea level, it was the beginning of political and commercial turmoil that is still a threat to the Olympic Movement 30 years later.

Firstly, Mexico City was the first of the four M hosts: Munich, Montreal and Moscow followed. All of them required extensive government subsidies. In the case of Mexico City, 74 % of the expenditures of the Organising Committee was subsidised by the tax payer. Television revenue reached almost $7,5 million and increasingly became a dominant factor in determining which sports are acceptable in terms of good television viewing. Traditionally the Olympic power brokers had been the IOC, the National Olympic Committees and the Sports Federations but from now on the television moguls would increasingly influence Olympic fortunes.

Although the Official Report states $7,5 million as the total income for television rights, the specialist publication "Television in the Olympics" provides $9,75 as the total.[1] Overt commercialism only reared its head at Los Angeles in 1984 but in 1968 the athletes were already part of the intense rivalry between commercial interests. Horst Dassler, who played such an important role in creating the structure of the current business-orientated international sports world, had been paying athletes for a long time to wear his products, Adidas shoes. According to Andrew Jennings, in 'Lords of the Rings', Horst's father already recognised the importance of branding and it was extremely important for Horst to show the world that "Winners wear Adidas".[2] The problem was that these top athletes were still at the time supposed to be amateurs but with the increasing importance of television, things almost got out of hand at Mexico City. "The Shoe Wars" between Horst Dassler of Adidas and his uncle Rudolph Dassler of Puma almost spilled over into the change rooms and on to the tracks at Mexico City and was the subject of an article in Sports Illustrated in 1969 which revealed the extent to which the IOC, then under Avery Brundage, was turning a blind eye.[3]

Horst Dassler certainly proved to be one of the most adept operators in commercial terms the sports world has ever seen. When these events forced the athletics federation to rule that after the 1968 Games only running shoes without identifying marks would be allowed, Horst shifted "his attention from the athletes to influence federations with cash or by underwriting their programs and helping his friends to rise within them".[4]

But Adidas were on the scene long before 1968: Jessie Owens won his four golds in Berlin in 1936 wearing Adidas, and the three stripe image was constantly seen on winners' shoes. Apparently the young Horst was sent to Melbourne in 1956 by his father to counter his uncle's efforts to supply the athletes with Puma shoes. The inventive Horst bribed key personnel at the docks in Australia to prevent the Puma equipment from being unloaded.[5] This gave him plenty of opportunity to peddle his wares to the eager athletes. At Mexico City Horst Dassler supplied 83 % of winners with shoes and other equipment.[6]

There was also an element of political expediency connected to the Mexico Games although this is not widely recognised. According to Paul Johnson, the then Mexican President, Louis Echeverna "harboured ambitions to establish Mexico as the leader of the Third World as a model Big Government small state ... he increased the state's share of the economy by 50 % and the number of state-owned corporations from 86 to 740. The predictable result was hyper-inflation and a balance of payments crises". It is due to this free spending mood and also a result of the President's "Third World leader" ambitions that the huge subsidies ($57 million) could be obtained. But these same irresponsible policies led to wide-spread strikes and protests and tragically, less than a fortnight before the opening ceremony, the troops opened fire on thousands of unarmed students who were holding a rally in the Plaza de las Tres Culturas.[7] Hundreds of people were killed although the government maintained that the death toll was less than 50.

These events cast a dark shadow over the celebrations of the Olympic festival and competitors were not keen to travel to town at all.[8] Towards the end of 1976 Mexico's economy was chaotic and Lopez Portillo took over the reins and steered the economy back to reality. He was helped by major oil discoveries in 1977.

The IOC was widely criticised for not condemning the killings outright. According to Wallechinsky the IOC refused to take a stand and regarded the tragic incident as "an internal affair".[9] Yet the Olympic presence focussed the world's attention on Mexico and there is little doubt that the authorities felt the pressure of international criticism - without the Olympics there might have been more such incidents.

Compared to the tragedy at Plaza de las Tres Culturas, the fuss and furore over the height above sea level seems silly, almost comical. Some of the predictions were so outrageous they remind one of the dire consequences that were forecast for female athletes if they dared tackle long distances. One example is Manfred Kinder who wrote in Berliner Ausgabe on December 11, 1964 that "if athletes have to adapt themselves to an altitude of more than 2 000 m for six to eight days, my outlook is very pessimistic: they will fall like flies!". The editorial of Copenhagen's Extra Bladet on 20 October 1965 read: "Athletes from many European countries were invited to that city to take part in a sort of 'dry run' of the Games. All have returned saying: 'It's scandalous that Mexico City has been chosen to host the Games! At least half a year is needed to adapt to the oxygen-poor air. One's life would be endangered trying to break records' ...".[10] To try and dispel international fears, three international sports competitions were held in Mexico City prior to the Games and thorough research carried out at the same time. The third international sports competition took place a year before the Games and 2 564 athletes from 56 countries took part. As a result not one nation withdrew because of the altitude factor and it is generally accepted today that competition at altitude is a situation that can be prepared for to a much greater extent than high humidity. In fact altitude training these days is included as part of a normal training programme.

The Organising Committee certainly felt vindicated by the number of world records that were broken at the Mexico Games: 82 in comparison with 42 at the previous Games in Tokyo.

Of the total expenditure of $176 million, $53,6 million was for sports installations, $16,6 million for infra-structural improvements and $16 million for the Olympic village - the Organising Committee felt that at least these were permanent assets for the city. But considering the precarious economic situation at the time, the morality of the relative huge expenditure on sports infrastructure can be challenged and it would be interesting to know how well these facilities have been utilised ever since and whether the Mexican people consider it a worthwhile endeavour.

But Mexico City had to be ready and able to host a very large event with the highest number of athletes ever: 5 531, only a few hundred more than at Tokyo, representing 112 nations. Interestingly enough, according to Wallechinsky Rome played host to only 83 nations and Tokyo to 93.[11]

The traditional Mexican disposition for creating a festive atmosphere contributed to a pleasant and friendly Games overall, apart from some isolated incidences. Tommy Smith won the 200 m for the US and broke the world record previously held by John Carlos, who took bronze. Both these black Americans mounted the rostrum barefoot wearing civil rights buttons. When the Star-spangled Banner was played they bowed their heads and gave the clenched fist black-power salute. They later explained that they protested against the fact that the word "freedom" in the National Anthem only applied to white Americans. They were summarily suspended by the IOC and ordered by the United States Olympic Committee to leave the Olympic village. The IOC has always been very sensitive to the using of the Olympic platform to further any causes whether they be worthwhile or not, because it would detract from the dignity and the purity of the events and ceremonies. In 1992 the South African sports authorities wanted this country's sports representatives to wear "Peace and Democracy" stickers to Barcelona in the wake of the Boipatong massacre, but for the same reason this was not allowed by the organisers.[12]

Another minor, more comical occurrence at Mexico City took place when a fist fight broke out in the Olympic village between Polish competitors and competitors from French speaking West Africa. The Poles complained that they had been kept up throughout the previous night by loud "jungle music" and they retaliated by throwing water bombs.

The altitude made matters easier for athletes from high lying African countries. Kenyan athletes took gold in the 1 500 m (Kipchoge Keino), the 10 000 m (Naftali Temu) and the 3 000 m steeplechase (Amos Biwott). A Tunisian won the 5 000 m (Mohamed Gammoudi) and an Ethiopian (Mamo Wolde) took top honours in the marathon.

Bob Beamon from the US gave one of the most astonishing performances ever when he set up a new long jump world record of 8,9 m. The previous record was 8,35 m. The record was improved by over half a metre! "In the 33 years since Jessie Owens' world record in 1935, the world record had progressed by eight and a half inches. In a matter of seconds, Beamon had added another 21 3/4 inches (approximately 54 cm). Ironically - since Beamon completely bypassed the 28 foot barrier - the first 28 foot jump didn't take place until the 1980 Olympics".[13]

The tall Dick Fosbury launched a novel high jump technique which fascinated the crowds and won him gold. It became known as the Fosbury Flop. The huge Al Oerter who has never flopped in his life won gold in the discus event for the fourth time in a row. Al now had as many gold medals as he had children. David Hemery set a new world record in the 400 m hurdles for Great Britain.

In the gymnastics Vera Caslavska, the Czech gymnast, fascinated the crowds, especially when she chose "Mexican Hat Dance" as her music for the floor exercises. In boxing the popular Chris Finnegan from Great Britain won the gold medal in the middleweight division and then faced his most daunting challenge: he could not manage to produce urine for the drug test. He drank several glasses of water but nothing happened, then three or four pints of beer and still nothing. Eventually Chris was taken to a restaurant with the two Olympic officials tagging along carrying their testing equipment. This tough boxer had one apparent hang-up - "Now if there's one thing I've never been able to do, it's have a piss while someone's watching me. I can never stand at those long urinals you get in gents' bogs with all the other blokes having a quick squirt". Finally, at 13:40 Finnegan could provide the precious liquid and all was negative and well.[14]

Sex tests for women were first introduced at Mexico City. According to Simson and Jennings, Tamara Press from the Soviet Union who won gold in the shot put at Rome and Tokyo, as well as gold in the discus event in Tokyo, disappeared as soon as the sex tests were introduced.

Mexico City was certainly a tumultuous Games. But so was the whole world at the time: "China was in the throes of the Cultural Revolution; Czechoslovakia's burst of freedom was crushed by Soviet troops, the government of France was almost overthrown by student-led demonstrations, and civil rights and antiwar demonstrations were spreading across the United States".[15] Again the Olympics reflected the harsh realities of the world we live in.

Münchën ⚬⚬⚬ 1972   26.8 – 10.9

MUNICH 1972 -
THE TRAGIC GAMES

The Germans had the best of intentions with the 1972 Games in Munich. They wanted to show the world the friendly hospitable face of the newly industrialised West Germany. Understandably the Germans were keen to erase the memories of the militaristic Sieg Heil Games of 1936.

But the Games were too amiable: security was relatively lax. They had no inkling of the terror planned by the Palestinians. Apparently the Israeli secret service Mossad had two agencies involved in Munich and one did not know what the other was doing.[1] Another version is that the lack of co-ordination between the police of the city, the region and the state contributed to the inadequate response.[2] The IOC has been careful ever since to establish that a specific authority is ultimately responsible, especially where many different agencies and security groups are involved, which is usually the case with American cities. The IOC was very concerned at the time about security in LA in 1984 and this proliferation of security agencies certainly contributed to security problems at Atlanta.

On 5 September, eight Palestinian terrorists managed to get into the Olympic village and immediately headed for the Israeli quarters where they killed two Israelis and took nine others hostage. They laid down terms which included the release of 200 prisoners from Israeli jails and safe passage for themselves. A helicopter and the West German Police were waiting at a nearby airfield and a shootout ensued, causing a further 15 lives to be lost. All told 11 Israelis were killed that day - one athlete, two weight lifters, two wrestlers, four coaches and two judges. The last six volunteered as hostages in order to prevent competitors from being endangered.

This tragedy left a permanent scar on the Olympic Movement and to this day dominates the memory of the Munich Olympic Games. The IOC in the person of the then President Avery Brundage determined that the Games should go on so as not to give in to the Black September terrorist group or any others with similar ambitions. If the terrorist attack had not occurred, the 1972 Games would have been hailed as one of the most successful ever. Indeed the Takac report gave it the highest marks. It was only at Barcelona in 1992 where higher marks were awarded. Interestingly Munich got the Games ahead of Barcelona. This report takes into account all the organisational aspects: housing, feeding and transport of athletes and officials, the actual events in terms of preparations, information and management as well as the matters affecting the media.

Amazingly enough the terrorist drama brought unexpected benefits to the Olympic Movement: TV viewing in the US increased dramatically, and ABC which only paid $7,5 million for the Munich Games, as well as the associated advertisers, suddenly realised that they had actually acquired a bargain. Hill describes this aspect in Olympic Politics[3] "In those days 'The telecast still garnered relatively small audiences, and the advertising community could barely stifle a yawn'. The Munich kidnappings turned the Germans into major news and 'Even commercial advertisers realized a grisly profit : they had paid low rates in anticipation of the usual low Olympic ratings and were the unintended beneficiaries of the skyrocketing audiences as the crisis wore on' ".

If one looks at the figures in David Miller's 'Olympic Revolution', the jumps from Munich's $7,5 million to Montreal's $25 million (+230 %) is enormous and would support Hill's observation that the Munich massacre effected much higher viewer interest in the USA[4] but other publications put the value for Munich's TV rights much higher - $17 million.[5,6] If this figure is correct, the assumption is simply not valid because the increase to Montreal's $35 million would be just over 100% which was almost the norm for this era.

In terms of sporting achievements the Munich Olympics were a magnificent occasion. Mark Spitz proved himself to be amongst the all time great Olympians by taking a superlative seven gold medals in swimming. His dominance of the men's swimming events included the 100 m freestyle, 200 m freestyle, 100 m butterfly, 200 m butterfly, 4 x 100 m freestyle relay, 4 x 200 m freestyle relay and his share in the 4 x 100 m medley relay. On the women's side Shane Gould of Australia reigned supreme with five glorious gold medals. These included the 100 m freestyle, 200 m freestyle, 400 m freestyle, 800 m freestyle and 200 m individual medley.

In the pole-vault where the Americans had held a total monopoly on gold medals since Athens in 1896, the East German, Wolfgang Nordwig, ended the USA's incredible run of 16 wins in succession by clearing a height of 5,5 m. The American favourite Robert Seagren came second, but when he failed to clear 5,45 m for the third time Seagren went over to Adriaan Paulen, the IAAF official responsible for the event and thrust his pole into Paulen's lap. Seargen certainly had every reason to be furious because the Olympic pole-vault event was preceded by a series of disruptive and unsettling events.

East Germany lodged an appeal against a new model of Cata-Poles which was being used by Seagren and other prominent vaulters from the USA and Sweden. The East Germans complained that these poles contained carbon fibre. The manufacturers denied this, while the pole vaulters pointed out that the IAAF rules did not preclude any specific material. Nevertheless the IAAF banned the Cata-Poles on 25 July and the Games were due to start on 26 August. On 27 August, four days before the pole-vault event, the IAAF reversed the decision and lifted the ban. The affected pole-vaulters could heave a sigh of relief and get some practice. Then astonishingly the ban was reimposed on 30 August and all the poles confiscated by the IAAF officials for inspection. The vaulters found in possession of the Cata-Poles were handed new old poles. Nordwig who did not like the Cata-Poles jumped with his usual pole, and fortunately for him he had a habit of stuffing his ears with material to help him concentrate and to cut out all possible distractions to keep his mind from straying.[7]

In the meantime the giant Russian (154 kg) Vassily Alexeyev extended his formidable reputation by winning the gold medal for weightlifting. He was to remain unbeaten from 1970 until 1978 and set 80 world records in total. He was quite a voracious eater as well: he was spotted in Munich enjoying a breakfast of 26 fried eggs and a steak. He was married to a woman called Olympiada.[8]

In complete contrast to the huge weight lifters, the nimble and attractive Olga Korbett charmed TV viewers the world over and collected three gold medals in gymnastics.

The Munich Games attracted 7 147 competitors of whom 22 % were female. This number was only exceeded in 1988 when Seoul had to cope with 9 412 competitors by which time 35 % were women.

It was at Munich that the Soviet Union began its domination in medals. The USA still ruled in Mexico City with 45 golds against the Soviet's 29 but four years later the tables were turned and the Soviet Empire took 50 gold medals against the 33 for the Americans.

This trend was to continue with the Soviet Union establishing a virtual monopoly over the first place in the medal count from 1972 until Seoul in 1988 after which the Soviet Empire started to disintegrate, the sole exception being LA 1984 when the Soviet bloc boycotted the Games.

Munich certainly afforded the thousands of athletes the opportunity to compete in style by designing and creating sports stadiums and infrastructure that were attractive to look at, because everything evolved around a central visual theme, as well as being practical to actually use. South African architect Anthony Lange's description is quite entertaining - "in response the city developed a stunning athletic complex conceived as a landscape into which the various stadiums were gently moulded with their roofs of fabric and flex-glass lightly suspended above sculptured mounds, like Bedouin tents. Regrettably the nearby Olympic village was a mini-city of ugly exposed concrete apartment blocks".[9] The quality of these apartment blocks was unfortunately also poor and lots of problems with leaking roofs and damp walls were later experienced.

As always there was the slight matter of finance to contend with and the consortium formed by five government bodies, namely The German Federal Republic, The Bavarian Free State, The State City of Munich, The State of Schleswig-Holstein and the City of Kiel had to carry the can for the Olympic financial short-falls.

In 1970 the OBG (the Olympic Construction Company) was in the red to the tune of DM831 million but as the income from the sale of Olympic coins, from the Olympic Lottery and other sources such as a contribution of the Central University Sports Facility came on stream, the state sponsored share of costs diminished slightly to end at DM686 million in 1972.[10] The OC (Organising Committee) was unable to repay this loan and it had to be converted into a subsidy. The total costs of the 1972 Olympic Games according to the Official Report came to just under DM2 billion. At 8 % year escalation and an exchange rate of DM1,5 for a US dollar this would have translated into approximately $6,5 billion in 1992 which is about 30 % less than Barcelona's capital expenditures. Obviously Munich did not attempt a complete suburban facelift on the Barcelona scale, but the capital side included expenditure on improvements of public transport and road networks and other long term utilities such as student dwellings, children's day care centres and cultural facilities.

Apart from the tragedy brought on by the terrorist hostage drama, the Germans had every right to be proud of the strategy of the Munich Games and the consequent legacy for the city.

The load on the tax payer was hardly noticed for the Federal Republic was in a strong industrial growth phase, the solid foundations of which were laid by the astute Konrad Adenauer. After the Second World War the Russians chose to impose an "all-powerful paternalistic state, a Leninist centralized direction of nationalized industry, a huge Prussian-style bureaucracy and stress on equality, uniformity and collectivity" on East Germany and this formula eventually produced a radicalised version of the Nazi state which would had done Goebbels proud, according to Paul Johnson.[11] The first Chancellor of the Federal Republic of Germany realised that the "real antithesis to National Socialism was individualism, a society where private arrangements took priority over public, where the family was the favoured social unit and where voluntary principle was paramount".[12] Adenauer formed an alliance with Professor Ludwig Erhard, head of the Bizonal Economic Council, "whose free market economic philosophy based on low tariffs, free trade, cheap imports and high exports, was exactly suited to his own political philosophy". In 1949 the Chairman of the DGB (Deutschergewerkschaftsbund), the federation of 16 powerful industrial unions, Herr Boeckler, joined the Chancellor and the Professor as co-architects of the 'Mitbestimmung' (co-partnership of labour and capital) policy. "By the mid fifties, German labour had settled for what was essentially a non-political policy based on high profits, high wages and bonuses, high productivity, excellent social security and seats on policy forming boards"... "Adenauer was one of the most gifted statesmen of modern times; certainly the most wholly successful in recent German history. During his chancellorship, real incomes in Germany tripled".[13]

A recurring theme is that the successful development efforts tied to Olympic Games (Tokyo in 1964, Munich in 1972, Seoul in 1988 and Barcelona in 1992) took place after periods of relative poverty and stagnation as well as the replacement of dictators by democratic systems and relatively progressive free market policies.

The whole Olympic process in each of these cities served as a showcase for the industrial muscle of the particular host nation and also contributed to the internationalisation of the specific regions in terms of attitudes. For example the Olympics did not do anything for Moscow's dour image; LA on the other hand already had a strong identity which was enhanced by its Olympic associations. But without doubt Tokyo, Seoul and Barcelona were transformed in the eyes of the international public after their staging of the Olympics. Munich's memories unfortunately are tainted by the tragedy associated with the 1972 event. The innocent period after the Second World War during which London in 1948, Helsinki in 1952, Melbourne in 1956 and Rome in 1960 hosted the pure events, before commercialisation and political protests became the norm, bestowed permanent Olympic halos on the hosts, but according to my perception at least, not quite to the same extent as the successful developmental efforts did.

Montréal 1976

MONTREAL 1976 -
THE CASE OF THE PREGNANT MALE

Universally regarded as the epitome of Olympic financial mismanagement, the Canadians nevertheless by way of the Malouf Report expressed their pride in the staging of the first Canadian Games. When Montreal was awarded the 1976 Games the joyous celebrations carried on through the night. Yet six years later this was to turn into a financial nightmare with the local tax payers having to pay off the $1 billion deficit. This process was completed in 1996 just before the Atlanta Games commenced. Apparently the man with the illusions of grandeur, Mayor Jean Drapeau bragged that "the Games could no more produce a deficit than a man could have a baby".[1] The voluminous report on this financial fiasco by Quebec's leading judge Albert Malouf stated that "Drapeau had appointed himself foreman and project manager for Montreal's new Olympic facilities without the aptitude or knowledge for the job". The report asserted further on that, "The Mayor had commissioned unnecessarily luxurious and impressive installations dictated by 'considerations of aesthetics and grandeur' without serious study of the costs", yet even Judge Malouf's critical investigation accepted that for most Canadians the Games were "a source of joy and national pride".[2] The Montreal Star reported that 33 cranes were hired by the constructors of the Olympic Stadium for $1 million - an amount that is higher than the total purchase cost would have been and some of the cranes were not even used at all. No wonder the final bill was an eye watering $2,31 billion.[3]

For purposes of comparison the Montreal costs were 60 % higher than those of Munich and the consequent shortfall almost 300 % more. The Montreal shortfall was split between the Province of Quebec and the City of Montreal. Apart from the obvious overspending, the Montreal revenue programme was seriously hampered by delays in obtaining the necessary legislation to approve the Olympic Coin programme. The agreement of each province was required to run an Olympic lottery and this was also a tedious process. The coin and stamp programme plus the lottery income represented 80 % of the total operational income.[4] To add insult to injury it seems as though the Montreal Olympic Park was destined to run permanently at a loss. In 1979 it was still operating at a yearly deficit of $8 million and there was serious doubt if it could ever be run on a self financing basis. An inherent design fault meant that vast circulation spaces had to be heated and maintained.[5]

Montreal's proximity to the US border had the interesting effect that it is the only Olympic Games where foreigners bought most of the entrance tickets, namely 60 %.[6]

The Chinese issue had been simmering under the surface for quite some time. At Rome in 1960 the communist bloc IOC members wanted to have Taiwan expelled and the People's Republic of China (PRC) reinstated. Subsequently the Taiwanese were allowed to take part but under the name Formosa, which they did under protest. "In 1971 the IOC resolved that the PRC would be welcomed back if it respected Olympic rules although it also laid down that Formosa would not be excluded".[7] By April 1975 the PRC had joined the required number of international sports federations to apply for IOC membership but the PRC was only willing to join the IOC if Taiwan were expelled. This issue even had repercussions at the United Nations at this stage. The crucial decision was whether the PRC should be allowed to take part at Montreal? The situation was complicated by the Canadian Government's "one China policy" which was adopted in 1970 and which led to Canada's recognition of the PRC as the sole Chinese representative.[8] The Canadians would not accede to pressure from the PRC to refuse entry to the Taiwanese but stated that they, the Taiwanese, were not to use the word China or their flag or anthem. The problem was that the Canadians were in breach of an undertaking given in 1970 that no recognised member country would be denied entrance. The Canadian National Olympic Committee was furious at this political backtracking and there was even talk amongst IOC members of taking the Games elsewhere to the US or Mexico or an alternative suggestion was to stop the marching under national flags and to invite all NOC'S to use the Olympic flag instead.[9] The Taiwanese refused the IOC's offer to allow it to march in the opening parade as Taiwan and the team eventually packed its bags and left the day before the Games. The IOC President, at the time Lord Killanin, accused the Chinese of using their extensive purchase of Canadian wheat as a bargaining tool but this was denied all round. The counter argument was that if the IOC had done its homework it would have been cognisant of the existing policies of the Canadian Government.[10]

South Africa was not allowed to take part in the Olympic Games after 1960 but in 1976 "numerous African states boycotted the Games in protest against a rugby tour of South Africa undertaken by a New Zealand side. The protesters demanded that the IOC should bar New Zealand from the Games, which it of course had no reason to do, since rugby was not even an Olympic Sport".[11] The Adidas team were still at it: Patrick Nally who had close ties with Horst Dassler explained that 1976 was to be stage three of Horst's power strategies. Stage one involved the paying of competitors to wear Adidas kit. Stage two meant the takeover of sports federations. At Montreal a structured plan was intended to launch the Dassler and Nally era. They selected a mansion as headquarters, brought along their own chef and entertained lavishly and constantly. Simson and Jennings quote Nally on their aims, "We'd got commercial companies to bring money into the international federations, we could also show how we could help aspiring federation presidents with their campaign objectives". Nally had by this time secured a multi-million dollar deal with Coca-Cola for Havelange of FIFA. This meant that FIFA was building a new international headquarters in Zürich and appointing full-time professional personnel.[12]

Apparently Horst was very adept at building up valuable contacts within the Olympic organisations themselves. "Many of the key people who organised the Montreal Games were either employed by Adidas or acted as unpaid Adidas consultants. Consequently they kept Horst supplied with relevant information, crucial contacts or things like accreditation passes to get into restricted zones where the athletes could be contacted".[13] Nally remembered the little gifts Horst used to have on him; "Some expensive Omega watches always went with us" and after a cosy chat intermingled with some comments on how Adidas is looking for a new commercial openings in sport, Horst would say; "Oh, by the way, here is a little token of Adidas esteem" and one of the precious time pieces would casually be handed over.[14] Nally obviously enjoyed watching a smooth operator like Horst in action: "Travelling round Montreal with Horst was an education because he had a way of treating every individual as his friend".[15] It took Nally 14 months to tie up the deal with Coca-Cola and he had to fly almost constantly between Rio de Janeiro, Atlanta, Los Angeles, New York and Zürich before the complex four year involvement worth $5 million could be finalised.[16] Nally admitted that the deal was frequently on the verge of collapse because of legal complications. But somehow they put together the **first multi-national sponsorship of sport.**[17]

It is worth noting how this deal came about: Joao Havelange was elected as the new FIFA President in 1974 and he secured Third World votes by promising a soccer development programme as well as a world youth tournament. He approached Dassler for finances when the time came for him to deliver on his promises. Dassler was dependent on Adidas to sell his equipment but he could not afford to fund these tournaments from his own company's budget so he got Nally to put together a marketing package and present it to international companies.[18]

Oh yes, there were some splendid performances at Montreal outside the marketing sphere as well.

Alberto Juantorena from Cuba managed an Olympic first when he took gold in both the 400 m and 800 m and set a new world record. The tall Cuban also became the first man from a non-English speaking country to win the 400 m but he had to do a lot of running and actually lost 5 kg during the nine Olympic races. Maybe Juantorena had a bit of luck on his side as well because Mike Boit of Kenya had to watch from the stands because of his Government's decision to boycott the Games. Another fine athlete Filbert Bayi, the world record holder in the 1 500 m was prevented from taking part and New Zealand's John Walter made good use of the opportunity to take gold in the slowest 1 500 m time in 20 years. Lasse Viren from Finland repeated his incredible double win in the 5 000 and 10 000 m, to become the first man ever to achieve this feat in successive Games. But his victory did not escape serious controversy. Apparently the Scandinavians first perfected the technique of injecting oxygen-saturated blood into an athlete's veins just before an event and Viren was accused of using this method. Although it was not illegal, "Viren vigorously denied that he engaged in blood boosting and claimed that his training schedule was organised to peak at the Olympics".[19]

Guy Drut of France managed to keep a public promise he had made a year earlier, namely that he would win the 110 m hurdles in a time of 13,28 sec. Guy had a French father and an English mother and was an excellent all round athlete with impressive records in the pole-vault, long-jump and high-jump. Edwin Moses took the 400 m hurdles and set a new world record in the process. Incredibly it was his first international competition in this event. "The African boycott prevented a potentially historic show down. No matter how sympathetic one is to the movement to bring self-determination for blacks in South Africa, it is difficult not to be cynical when you realise that John Akii-Bua was not allowed to compete in Montreal because the leader of his nation's government, Idi Amin, was offended by human rights violations in another country".[20]

The Montreal marathon produced another unusual winner. Defending champion Frank Shorter was the favourite and when he took the lead after 25 km he seemed to be taking control of the race. Within a few minutes another athlete whom Shorter mistook for Lopes of Portugal appeared alongside him. It was actually Waldemar Cierpinski from East Germany who hassled Shorter by running as close to him as possible and stayed with him every time he tried to break away.

The converted steeplechaser won the marathon and in his confusion did an extra unnecessary lap. His team mates could not believe it. The East German soccer team was watching the race on television before their final match against Poland. "Goalie Jürgen Croy later recalled, 'We just sat there staring at each other, thinking that if this living example of mediocrity can lift himself up and win this marathon, and we don't beat Poland we are never going to hear the end of it' ". Poland was beaten in the final.[21]

In the gymnastics Nadia Comaneci charmed the world and scored ten out of ten seven times. Teofilo Stevenson won the heavyweight boxing as he had four years earlier in Munich and did again four years later at Moscow. It was only at Moscow that Stevenson was extended to go the full three rounds against Pyotr Levai from Hungary.[22]

Olympic history of another kind was made by Wilnor Joseph of Haiti who finished the second heat of the first round in such a slow time it would not have earned him a qualification for the 800 m final in 1900, let alone 1976.[23] His teammate, Olmeus Charles, made his mark in the 10 000 m by posting the slowest time ever in the Olympics. He came in 14 minutes after Carlos Lopes who won this heat, and the whole schedule was held up while the poor Charles plodded the last six laps on his own. The problem was that Haitian dictator Baby Doc Duvalier rewarded friends or trusted soldiers with free trips to the Olympics whether they were athletes or not.

The colourful Hasely Crawford took the coveted 100 m gold and in doing so became Trinidad's first Olympic champion. Wallechinsky writes that Crawford received more than his share of honours. "He was awarded the Trinity Cross Gold, his picture appeared on two poster stamps, an airplane was named after him, and six different Calypso songs were written in his honour".[24]

OLYMPIAD 80
MOSCOU MOSCOW MOCKBA

MOSCOW 1980 - THE GREY GAMES

The fact that a little bear Misha was picked as mascot certainly did not signify a bearish mood in commercial terms. In spite of the American-led boycott 200 sponsors took part in comparison with 168 in Montreal.[1]   Horst Dassler, as was to be expected, had the inside lane, commercially speaking. Horst managed a deal which gave him numerous marketing rights, including the clothing for all the athletes. At the time firms like Coca-Cola and Levi's were keen to establish manufacturing plants in Eastern Europe and Levi's actually supplied 64 000 pairs of jeans for Horst to sell and as samples. By then Horst had introduced the top executives to Russian leaders and they were impressed with his political contacts.[2] "This rapid proliferation of commercial brands linking themselves with the Olympics both alarmed and provoked Games organisers to consider a new strategy : exclusivity in terms of number of sponsors and their commercial sector". The table was set for Los Angeles to establish the model of exclusivity which became the central part of future Olympic sponsorship programmes.[3]

But it was the Soviet Union's invasion of Afghanistan a mere seven months before the Games that focussed the world's attention on the relative morality and effectiveness of boycotts as well as the question of awarding the Olympic Games to totalitarian regimes.

When Moscow was elected in 1974 its only opposition came from Los Angeles "After Moscow had won, Killarin made the unprecedented ruling that the votes should not be made known but that the choice should be announced as having been unanimous, because he feared that if Los Angeles had realised how few votes it had got it would not have tried again".[4]

The Soviets first took part in the Helsinki Games of 1952. Before that it was Tsarist Russia in 1908 and 1912. The Soviets soon managed to bring the Cold War into the Games. They went against tradition when they insisted that they should nominate the Soviet member of the IOC and not, as usual, leave it to the IOC to appoint representatives to a specific country. Obviously these Soviet IOC members "politicised the Games, in the sense that there were now disagreements along established political lines".[5] For the athletes their Iron Curtain opponents soon became the enemy because they quickly realised that these Soviets could not be described as amateurs in any sense and the press made a big thing of the US versus Soviet Union medal count.

It is still an open question whether the Soviet Union should have been awarded the 1980 Games. There is no budget available of expenditure incurred, no sign of feasibility or impact studies done beforehand and obviously no surveys of public opinion concerning the perceived benefits or drawbacks of the 1980 event.

Wallechinsky refers to the poor behaviour by spectators which he reckons was the worst since 1924 in Paris. The Americans, West Germans and Japanese were missing but nevertheless these aggressive fans took to booing and heckling the Poles and East Germans.[6] In the usual style of all repressive governments the security arrangements bordered on the paranoid with Moscow being totally sealed off from the rest of the country and athletes not even allowed to do a victory lap. Beforehand the capital was quite predictably purged of anyone who might compromise the display of Soviet harmony. According to Jennings the KGB were operating under instructions that the Moscow Games should be dope free. These KGB operatives subsequently infiltrated the anti-doping operation by posing as interpreters and assistants and either helped the athletes (doped ones, that is) to contribute somebody else's clean urine or if tested positive, simply to suppress the news of the results or erase it from the records.[7] The KGB Colonel described some of the techniques used by guilty athletes. "The Colonel also alleges that some athletes used the technique, relatively easy for woman, horrifyingly painful for men, of pumping clean urine into their bladders via a catheter".[8] Germany's professor Manfred Donike had to do the re-analysis of all the urine samples and apparently found evidence of a large number of athletes using testosterone.

If the Soviets were comfortable with and confident of arranging the excessive security and the suppression of bad news concerning drugs they were out of their depth as far as some organisational aspects were concerned. Jennings noted that "Staging a complex international event, like the Games, with the never-ending demands of the IOC and the sports barons was beyond most Moscow bureaucrats".[9]

Lord Killanin was about to stand down after eight years and a new IOC president was to be elected in Moscow. Horst Dassler was crucial for Juan Samaranch's campaign to get elected. By now Dassler was so influential he could virtually guarantee votes from all sections of the movement especially the Soviet bloc, the Latin grouping as well as from much of South Asia.[10]

But Moscow needed both Samaranch and Dassler to help them to comply with the stringent IOC demands as well as to obtain sponsorship. Obviously the Soviets were not too comfortable in dealing with complex marketing issues. Moscow served to consolidate the power of these two important figures in world sport. Samaranch was duly elected as the new President of the IOC and Horst Dassler was his kingpin. Jennings quotes Christian Janette who worked for Dassler and initially arranged for Samaranch to meet him at Samaranch's request. "I think that after being elected President Samaranch never did anything without advice from Horst Dassler, because he probably wanted to run the IOC as Horst Dassler ran Adidas".[11]

The boycott had a profound effect on many aspects of the Moscow Olympics. The organisers had to lower their expected number of foreign visitors from over

300 000 to more or less 70 000, 66 Olympic Committees stayed away, 81 nations were represented, against 141 in LA four years later and 92 four years earlier. For the first time since Mexico City the total number of athletes was below 6 000.[12] Amongst those staying away were both Chinas who were still locked in the battle for recognition.[13] But the tide was turning against the Taiwanese ever since the United States dropped its recognition of Taiwan in 1978 and switched Chinese recognition to the PRC.

The television rights were bought by NBC for $85 million. The boycott put them in a precarious position because there was a great deal of uncertainty at one stage if the 1980 Games were going to take place at all. NBC were covered by Lloyds of London for about 90 % of their expenditure, but when they eventually pulled out and announced that they would not cover the Games anymore, it was estimated that they nevertheless lost between $20 million and $40 million in lost advertising and expenses already incurred.[14] As a result the IOC also lost a great deal of income because they were entitled at the time to a third of the television revenues. According to an agreement reached in Munich, the organising committee was entitled to two thirds of the television rights and the IOC to one third of which one third would go to the various National Olympic Committees and another third to the international federations.[15]

The impact of television revenues on the IOC's finances is quite staggering when one considers that in 1972 when Killanin took over from Brundage the IOC was just over $2 million strong. Before the 1972 Games the hard-up IOC had to borrow against the promised television rights. When Samaranch took over in 1980 there was $40 million in the IOC kitty.[16]

This unexpected loss in revenue made the newly elected Samaranch realise that the IOC was becoming too dependent on the quadrennial boost from television and the need to diversify its sources of income became apparent.[17]

The four "M" Games: Mexico City, Munich, Montreal and Moscow, all turned out to be a burden on the taxpayers involved. Apart from the Germans who breezed through it, the other three economies were seriously affected: the Mexican Government was on a disastrous spending spree which precipitated hyperinflation and general economic mayhem, Montreal had to pay off debts for 20 years and the Soviet economy was in dire straits in the late eighties and precipitated the demise of the Soviet Empire. Because there was no accountability in the Soviet Union it is extremely difficult to ascertain how big a financial disaster the Games were.

Paul Johnson remarks that by 1981 Soviet Russia was struggling to meet interest payments on its $80 billion international debts. "By the beginning of 1982, the entire Soviet bloc was in as deep a recession as the West had been in the immediate aftermath of the mid-1970's crisis".[18] Of course the Olympic Games was a relatively small undertaking for the massive Soviet economy, but the lack of control over spending and the Afghanistan invasion at the same time meant a serious drain on resources. Unlike the Munich Games, which served as a showpiece for the vibrancy of the expanding German industrial base, the Moscow Games was just another tiresome burden on the back of the proverbial camel. There was obviously no sign of a co-ordinated development plan into which the Olympics could be made to fit. The 1980 Moscow Games can be best described as a last desperate effort by a weary and isolated bureaucracy to display the non-existent grandeur of the Soviet empire to an increasingly disbelieving world. Since the seventies "the 137 million Great Russians, a markedly ageing population compared to the non-Slavs, felt demographically on the defensive. It was significant, too, that among Muslims knowledge of Russian was declining".[19] On top of these unfavourable demographic tends, of which the religious Muslim counter culture was the most serious threat, there were problems with poor industrial production, especially when the West started to close down on the exports of new technology, the enormous burden of the East European allies, Poland's debt alone at a staggering $27,5 million and the consistently poor agricultural performance.

Johnson relates how Khrushchev, Premier of the Soviet Union from 1958 to 1964, toured the country after retirement and spoke to ordinary country people about their problems. Khrushchev wrote in his memoirs how he was struck by the direct question of a particular peasant who lived in a traditional food producing area; "Why, he added, should eggs and meat be unobtainable after fifty years of Soviet power? I look forward to the day when a camel would be able to walk from Moscow to Vladivostok without being eaten by hungry peasants on the way".[20]

If the Moscow Games had been held in a country with a semblance of a free press it would no doubt have gone down as a much bigger economic disaster than Montreal, where the press was able to focus on all the corruption and mismanagement. Today even diplomats tell stories about how homeless people seek shelter in the grand stadiums and how the Muscovites walk their dogs on neglected and cracked cycling tracks.

But in 1980 these stadiums were vibrant with excitement and the various racing tracks hot from use for serious competition. Waldemar Cierpinski described by his team mates as "this living example of mediocrity" in 1972, again won the marathon. As he crossed the line there were five other runners on the track doing their last lap, an Olympic record.[21]

In the absence of the Americans, Allan Wells from Great Britain won gold in the 100 m sprint. At 28 the Scot was the oldest winner of the 100 m in Olympic history. His father worked as a blacksmith and his mother was a cleaner at a hospital who also sewed nets for fishermen. Wells was trained by his wife.[22] The 200 m title also went to an European. Pietro Mennea representing Italy overtook Allan Wells with less than 10 m to go. At the 1997 World Student Games Mennea broke Tommie Smith's 11 year old world record. But later that year Allan Wells beat him in Torino in a European cup tournament. "For this insult, the otherwise blameless Wells had become known as 'The Beast' in Mennea's household". Mennea was a candidate for local office for the Social Democratic Party at the time, but he did now allow the official boycott policy of his party to thwart his long held Olympic ideals.[23]

The 800 m final was surely one of the most eagerly awaited showdowns in Olympic history. The spotlight was on the two English world record holders, Sebastian Coe and Steve Ovett. These two had set the athletic world alight with their performances in the years leading up to 1990. In 1979 Coe broke three world records in 41 days. He first bettered Jauntorena's world record by a full second, then 12 days later he set a new world record for the mile, becoming the first person since Peter Snell to hold world records for both the 800 m and the mile. Then on 15 August Coe broke Filbert Bayi's five year old record in the 1 500 m. In 1980 Steve Ovett entered the record books in a convincing manner. On the first day of July, Coe set a new 1 000 m world mark and less than an hour later Ovett snatched the mile world record away from his arch rival.

The experts were unanimous that Coe was the favourite for the 800 m, but felt on the whole that the 1 500 m could belong to either of the men. Ovett however issued a public statement in which he stated that he was certain of the 1 500 m but that he felt either of them could take the 800 m. The final 800 m turned out to be a slow race won by Ovett and Coe had to put in a desperate effort to manage silver. Ovett as usual declined the post race press conferences, but Coe poured his heart out, "I chose this day of all days to run the worst race of my life. I cannot explain why. I suppose I must have compounded more cardinal sins of middle-distance running in 1½ minutes than I've done in a lifetime. What a race to choose". Coe realised the 1 500 m was his last chance. "The 1 500 was going to be a hard event anyway, but now it's going to be the big race of my life. I must win it".[24]

The favourite for the 1 500 m, Steve Ovett must have been extremely confident when they lined up, because he had won 42 consecutive races at 1 500 m and one mile before the Olympic final. In the actual race the German, Jurgen Straub, was still leading with only 200 m to go and as they were coming into the final curve Ovett and Coe picked the same moment to deliver their final sprints. But it was Coe who took the lead and the ecstatic look of relief and delight on his face when he crossed the line has been seen on photos and posters all over the world. Straub came second and Ovett had to be satisfied with bronze.[25] The 5 000 m gold medal went to Miruts Yifter from Ethiopia who had the knack of making crucial mistakes. In 1971 he comfortably led a 5 000 m race but stopped running one lap too soon. At the Munich Olympics in 1972 he missed the start of his heat in the 5 000 m, but nevertheless took bronze in the 10 000 m. There were three different explanations offered for Yifter's mysterious failure to appear at the starting line; first that he was given erroneous directions to the check-in gate at the stadium; second that he simply spent too much time in the toilet before the race, and third that he got lost between the bathroom and the track. In 1976 he could not compete because Ethiopia boycotted the event. However at Moscow he made up for it by taking the 5 000 m gold with ease. When asked for a definite answer on the question of his age, which was reported as anything from 33 to 42 he replied, "I don't count the years. Men may steal my chickens, men may steal my sheep, But no man can steal my age".[26]

In the high-jump event Gerd Wessig of East Germany, a 21 year old cook, turned out to be one of the big surprises. He improved his personal best by over two inches to become the first man to set a world record in the high-jump in the Olympics. Wessig set this record after he had already earned the gold medal, which was the first time since 1896 that a jumper made another successful jump after winning gold.[27]

The pole vault was eagerly anticipated, since three different men had set world records in the same season. But "unfortunately the competition was marred by the incredibly boorish behaviour of many of the Soviet fans who whistled and jeered at foreign vaulters, particularly the Poles". But Poland's Wladyslaw Kozakiewicz won the gold medal without missing one jump and still had enough fighting spirit to make an obscene gesture to the crowd. He also set a new world record, the first at the Olympics since 1920, and he subsequently defected to West Germany.[28] Bruce Kennedy, originally a Rhodesian and an excellent javelin thrower must have set some kind of record in the bad luck stakes. In 1972 he went to Munich as part of the Rhodesian team but they were not allowed to take part as a result of political pressure. Kennedy was again selected for 1976 but Rhodesia was excluded. He married a US Citizen in the meantime and qualified for the US team for Moscow but again political manoeuvring prevented his Olympic debut. At least he could see the 1984 Olympics when he volunteered as an usher.[29] By this time Zimbabwe the former Rhodesia was in the Olympics again.

Footnotes

Mexico
1. De Moregas Spa et al 1995, p 19
2. Simson and Jennings 1992, p 33
3. Hill 1992, p 85

4.   Hill 1992, p 85
5.   Simson and Jennings 1992, p 34
6.   Hill 1992, p 85
7.   Wallechinsky 1992, p XXI
8.   ITV Book 1980, p 98
9.   Wallechinsky 1992, p XXI
10. Official Report, p 50
11. Wallechinsky 1992, p XI
12. Johnson 2 July1992, p 1
13. Wallechinsky 1992, p 101
14. Wallechinsky 1992, p 224
15. Wallechinsky 1992, p XXI

Munich
1.   Hill 1992, p 168
2.   Miller 1992, p 128
3.   Hill 1992, p 72
4.   Miller 1992, p 53
5.   De Moregas Spa et al, p 19
6.   Simson and Jennings 1992, p 69
7.   Wallechinsky 1992, p 95
8.   Wallechinsky 1992, p 608
9.   Lange 9 May 1995, p 21
10. Pro Sport 1973, p 55
11. Johnson 1983, p 581
12. Johnson 1983, p 581
13. Johnson 1983, p 584

Montreal
1.   Simson and Jennings 1992, p 63
2.   Simson and Jennings 1992, p 64
3.   Wilson 1988, p 22
4.   Feasibility Study for a London Bid 1978, pp 99, 100, 101.
5.   Feasibility Study for a London Bid 1978, p 111
6.   Feasibility Study for a London Bid 1978, p 72
7.   Hill 1996, p 46
8.   Hill 1996, p 48
9.   Hill 1996, p 49
10. Hill 1996, p 50
11. Hill 1996, p 36
12. Simson and Jennings 1992, p 65
13. Simson and Jennings 1992, p 66
14. Simson and Jennings 1992, p 66

15. Simson and Jennings 1992, p 67
16. Wilson 1988, p 180
17. Wilson 1988, p 181
18. Wilson 1988, p 180
19. Wallechinsky 1992, p 44
20. Wallechinsky 1992, p 69
21. Wallechinsky 1992, p 61
22. ITV Book 1980, p 137
23. Wallechinsky 1992, p 31
24. Wallechinsky 1992, p 11

Moscow
1. De Moregas Spa et al 1995, p 27
2. Simson and Jennings 1992, p 144
3. De Moregas Spa et al 1995, p 27
4. Hill 1996, p 121
5. Hill 1996, p 120
6. Wallechinsky 1992, p XXI
7. Jennings 1996, p 235
8. Jennings 1996, p 236
9. Jennings 1996, p 45
10. Jennings 1996, p 45
11. Jennings 1996, p 46
12. Wallechinsky 1992, p xi
13. Hill 1992, p 52
14. Hill 1996, p 122
15. Hill 1996, p 77
16. Wilson 1988, p 18
17. Wilson 1988, p 14
18. Johnson 1983, p 714
19. Johnson 1983, p 712
20. Johnson 1983, p 714
21. Wallechinsky 1992, p 61
22. Wallechinsky 1992, p 12
23. Wallechinsky 1992, p 19
24. Wallechinsky 1992, p 31
25. Wallechinsky 1992, p 39
26. Wallechinsky 1992, pp 44, 45
27. Wallechinsky 1992, p 90
28. Wallechinsky 1992, p 96
29. Wallechinsky 1992, p 129

CHAPTER 6

LOS ANGELES 1984 -
THE LOW COST COMMERCIAL GAMES

The 1984 Olympic Games were actually unique in several unrelated aspects. The Los Angeles Games will be remembered as a prominent chapter in superpower politics - Jimmy Carter organised a boycott of the 1980 Moscow Games in reaction to the Soviet occupation of Afghanistan and the Soviet bloc subsequently returned the compliment when 1984 came round.

A Temporary Power Transfer

There was also no competition from other cities to host the 1984 Games, so Los Angeles had a clear track ahead of them, and they were subsequently able to dictate terms to the IOC to an extent that was unheard of in Olympic terms because the IOC had no replacement to fall back on (although at some stage a dozen or so IOC members wanted to reject the Los Angeles bid, hoping that Mexico, Munich or even Montreal would have been able to take over the bid at short notice).[1] Los Angeles could insist that their own lawyers draw up the contract instead of those of the IOC. This meant built-in cast-iron guarantees against losses that could have involved taxpayers. The Los Angeles Olympic Organising Committee (LAOOC) also refused to sign the usual contract to which the United States Olympic Committee would have been party - this was entirely contrary to the Olympic Charter. The Games were handed over to an independent organising committee which accepted final responsibility jointly with the US Olympic Committee. This body would seek financial guarantees from private industry to cover losses and by doing so absolved the city of Los Angeles of all financial responsibility in clear violation of the IOC rules.[2] This shift in power was merely temporary because the IOC amended the host city contract after 1984.

Extensive Facilities

It was also physically possible for Ueberroth and his team to adopt a low cost approach because Los Angeles was already a highly developed city with the added bonus of a legacy of sports facilities from the 1932 Los Angeles Games. For example the magnificent 105 000 seat stadium had been built during the terrible depression years leading up to 1932. In order to utilise as many existing facilities as possible, the Games had to be spread out over a very large geographical area, roughly 400 km long by 80 km wide.[3] University campus buildings could be used as Olympic Villages so there was no need to construct new buildings. The 1932 Olympic Village was the first in the history of the Olympic Games and initiated a tradition which is still adhered to today.

Los Angeles 1984 Olympic Games

Stunning Profits

Peter Ueberroth certainly knew what he wanted to achieve: "We made a conscious decision to underestimate projected revenues as this was our only protection against unknown cost factors and an unstable international political environment" [4] He managed to get the IOC's approval for all profits of the 1984 Games to stay in the USA. Of course nobody had any idea of how large the profits would turn out to be. According to Hill, the IOC briefly considered abrogating the original agreement when Ueberroth began to reveal the real figures after the Games. [5]

The Games were intensely political because of the Soviet boycott and because the taxpayers of California refused to fund them. The Organising Committee was forced to create the first private enterprise Games and in doing so set a trend for the whole future development of the Olympic Movement. Miller expresses much the same sentiment: "Los Angeles was such a phenomenal commercial success, it changed the nature of the Olympic movement". [6] Simson and Jennings put it more bluntly: "The mountain of dollars from Los Angeles' 'Enterprise Olympia' soared past any expectations. When all the bills had been paid, there was a staggering $215 billion in the bank". [7] Writing in Olympic Preview, Ueberroth (President of LAOOC) stated that it might be difficult for some to believe that an event traditionally as costly as the Olympic Games, could be staged without direct cost to the citizens of the host city. Furthermore, Ueberroth asserted that the Los Angeles Games would benefit from commerce but predicted that it would not be a commercial Games. [8]

It is interesting to go back to the 1932 Los Angeles Games and compare the overriding commercial emphasis of 1984 with the prevailing attitude of 1932 which is reflected in the Games Report: "The record of our city's conception of its responsibility, and of its preparations from beginning to end, discloses one fundamental and guiding principle, which was to adhere strictly to the Olympic ideals and to make such contributions in its organisation of the Games as would strengthen and perpetuate those ideals. Not a single note of commercialism was allowed to permeate the consummation of the task". [9]

Just a Nice Games

The political developments were shaped by the international effects of the Soviet boycott as well as the international predicament of the IOC (no alternative hosts) and also by local citizens exercising their political clout. However, Hill states that in the case of Los Angeles "It was not the established political authority that asserted the peculiar value of capitalism, but the businessmen who ran the Games as a commercial exercise. Nor was it the government that revelled in chauvinism, but the people. Had there been no boycott, the Games would have been nothing like as popular as they turned out to be under the stimulus of anti-Soviet senti-| ment".[10] Another fact in the internal political scene was the restriction placed by the local taxpayers on public expenditure because they were concerned about the following:

• potential damage to the environment
• the financial costs and
• the possible daily disruption to their lives.[11]

Although there was no overt political message from the hosts, Ueberroth (in Miller) insisted: "There is no message from the Committee. Munich wanted to show that it represented the new industrialised, free and friendly nation. Montreal spent two billion dollars to prove it was not a stepchild to the United States. Moscow wanted to demonstrate that it was the most noble socialist state, that its ideology had worldwide acceptance. We haven't any message, except, let's have a nice Games".[12]

Widespread Popular Support

As stated previously, whatever support existed was probably enhanced by the Soviet boycott. Miller said that Ueberroth succeeded in enlisting thousands of volunteers to help make the Games possible. For example the Botswana participants lived as guests in private homes because they could not afford more than a few days in the village. Anyone that needed emergency medical treatment was attended to, free, by volunteer surgeons in the expensively equipped medical complex of the University College of Los Angeles.[13] In terms of local popular support, one can safely say that the Los Angeles event was a definite success because the OC could count on the free services of volunteers right across the socio-economic spectrum.

Quirky Personalities

Ueberroth, in the first place, had to deal with Madame Berlioux, at the time the IOC's Executive Director and "normally a tigress in support of the IOC's rights".[14] The President of the IOC in 1984 was the amiable Lord Killanin, who lived in a fairly modest house in Dublin and left the control of the IOC's day-to-day business to Monique Berlioux. Ueberroth stated that Berlioux's demands were encyclopaedic. "We had to make sure that a swimming pool was available, that Evian water was supplied, that there were exquisite flower arrangements, that the room service met her French tastes, that restaurant arrangements were made for the finest eateries, that appointments were not scheduled either early in the morning or late at night, and that her travelling staff received equally impeccable treatment".[15] Likewise Peter Ueberroth complained that the IF presidents are "accustomed to pomp and circumstance and are extremely status conscious". Apparently Primo Nebiolo, now President of the IAAF, pressurised Samaranch and Ueberroth constantly for special treatment and extra accreditations. Euberroth himself was however not "unequivocally admired" and Reich in Hill's 'Olympic Politics' suggested that his management style was authoritarian, erratic and unpredictable. He described Ueberroth's organising committee as a kind of "totalitarian Utopia".[16]

Incidental Strategic Success

Without its being planned as such the Los Angeles Games was a trendsetter for future bidders and the greatest beneficiary was the Olympic Movement as a whole. After 1988, there was a viable number of strong bidders to choose from. The IOC was thus able to confirm its grip on the whole hosting process by gradually introducing changes to the Olympic Charter (OC).

"Within less than a decade of Los Angeles being the only candidate for 1984, the pendulum had swung to the opposite extreme, with rival cities fighting tooth and nail to stage the billion dollar Olympic festival. It was Los Angeles, ironically, that began this commercial roller-coaster".[17]

This is how the Olympic scene developed after 1984:
1988 - two candidate cities: Seoul and Nagoya.
1992 - six candidate cities: Amsterdam, Barcelona, Belgrade, Brisbane, Birmingham and Paris.
1996 - six candidate cities: Atlanta, Athens, Belgrade, Manchester, Melbourne and Toronto.
2000 - six candidate cities: Beijing, Berlin, Brasilia, Istanbul, Manchester and Sydney (Milan and Tashkent withdrew).[18]
2004 - 11 candidate cities: Athens, Buenos Aires, Cape Town, Rome, Stockholm (St Petersburg, Lille, Istanbul, San Juan, Seville and Rio de Janeiro were eliminated before the final round).

In strategic terms the 1984 Games were noteworthy even though Los Angeles had no domestic objective to link the Games to any development as such.

The Koreans were very keen to emulate LA's success and were trying to discern formulas: "In the case of the United States (being such a powerful developed economy), there are no data available to suggest that any research has been done to determine the effect the Olympics had on the economy: Trying to assess how much effort was made to induce dollar income and collect overseas dollars, the Los Angeles Organising Committee does not have such data available, and such a concept was not present from the planning stage of the Olympics".[19]

Miller also noted that despite boycotts, "shameless nationalism, security against terrorism, traffic problems and unbearable smog, those people who believed that there would never be another Games after Los Angeles, had definitely been proven wrong".[20]

LA Sport

In the decathlon the gregarious Daley Thomson (UK) took his second successive gold. After his last item, the 1 500 m, he paraded a sweat shirt on his victory lap which read on the front, "Thanks America for a good Games and a great time". On the back, "But what about the TV coverage?": an obvious reference to ABC's biased coverage where virtually only American winners were portrayed.

The biggest surprise in the men's track and field was the victory in the discus event by Rolf Dameberg, a bearded 31 year old unemployed school teacher from Germany whose fourth round throw put him ahead of the US favourite Mac Wilkens. Sebastian Coe took the 1 500 m title ahead of Steve Cram, a British team mate, to become the first male repeat winner of the Olympic 1 500 m. The year before the LA Olympics, Coe was in hospital with a serious taxoplasmosis infection, and it was generally assumed that his international career was over. "His comeback was treated with scorn by much of the British Press".[21] The runup to the 1 500 m final turned into a survival battle. Said Aouita who later held the world record withdrew to concentrate on the less competitive 5 000 m, which he won in record time. Apparently Morocco's King Hassan gave Aouita a villa in Casablanca and renamed the Rabat-to-Casablanca express train in his honour after his 5 000 m victory. Former world record holder Sydney Maree had to withdraw because of a hamstring injury. World championship finalist Dragon Zdravković was sent home by Yugoslav officials for refusing to wear Adidas shoes. World record holder Steve Ovett had collapsed after his eighth place in the 800 m final and spent two nights in hospital suffering from bronco-spasms, which was attributed to the notorious LA smog. Despite advice to the contrary, Ovett took part in the 1 500 preliminaries and won his heat, where world championship finalist Pierre Delézé tripped on Ovett's heel and fell heavily. The fourth 1 500 m heat was won by Joaquim Cruz, the US based Brazilian who beat Coe convincingly to win the 800 m gold. Cruz had to pull out of the semifinals because of a head cold.

The legendary F Carlton Lewis took four gold medals, in the 100 and 200 m, the long jump and the 4 x 100 m relay where the victorious US team set the only track and field world record of the Los Angeles Games. In the 200 m final Pietro Mennea, who finished in seventh place, became the first track athlete to qualify for the final of the same event in four straight Olympics.[22] In the 400 m Gabriel Tiacoh won silver and became the Ivory Coast's first Olympic medallist.[23] Edwin Moses took gold in the 400 m hurdles, a victory which surprised no one since Moses had a victory streak in the winning of finals which lasted 9 years, 9 months and 9 days and which was only ended in Madrid in 1987 when he was beaten by young Danny Harris.

On the female side of track and field Valerie Brisco-Hooks became the first person to manage a gold in both the 200 and 400 m events. She actually retired in 1982 being 18 kg overweight following the birth of her baby boy. Brisco-Hooks was fortunate that the East Germans were absent and she had to overcome a mediocre start to take the 200 m gold. Only 28 women took part in the 400 m competition of whom the slowest was Zeina Mina from Beirut in Lebanon. Because of the civil war in her country at the time she could not train on a track for the whole year preceding the Olympics. She trained on beaches, in subways and did not mind her slowest status at the Games. She said she was just thrilled to be away from the bombs.[24]

The first Olympic women's 3 000 m race was held in 1984 and it was sensational for the wrong reasons. Mary Decker the US national hero was the favourite. Since beating the three times Olympic champion Tatyana Kazankina as well as world record holder Svetlana Ulmasova at the inaugural world championships in Helsinki, Mary Decker became a symbol of beauty and success to millions of young Americans. But there was a dark side to her personality as well. At the 1983 Millrose Games she shoved a Puerto Rican runner Angelita Lind to ground when the slower Angelita failed to move to the outside as Decker was lapping her. The press revelled in a huge pre-Olympic hype about the expected Mary Decker - Zola Budd confrontation but actually the shy barefoot runner from Bloemfontein in South Africa was not yet ready for this level of competition. Because SA was banned by the IAAF in 1976 and not allowed in the Olympics since 1960, Zola was forced to move to Surrey in England and to adopt British citizenship. Because of the vigorous anti-apartheid campaign in the UK her participation there became very controversial and the immature Budd struggled to cope with the enormous pressures. But she was immensely talented and broke Decker's world record by over six seconds early in 1984. In the 1984 final Budd was leading at about 1 700 m when Decker bumped against her leg. Just five strides later it happened again and Decker tripped on Budd's right leg as Zola tried to balance herself. Decker fell heavily, pulled a hip muscle and was sadly out of the race. The partisan crowd of 85 000 started to boo Budd incessantly who kept on running although her spirit was gone after her idol's fall. Maricica Puica from Romenia won the race effortlessly. Budd could only manage seventh place after she had been in third place only 200 m from the finish.[25]

Five Golden Rings

Ironically the decision to sell the five Olympic rings for commercial gain to the powerful multi-national corporations of the Western world was made in East Berlin in 1985, then in the throes of hard core communism. The announcement was made only a few hours after Monique Berlioux, the dominant Executive Director of the IOC was dispatched with a golden handshake. She was becoming an obstacle in the way forward for the Olympic Movement, as seen by Samaranch and Dassler. The decision to commercialise the Olympic ideal was a strategic one to counter the increasing dependence of the Olympic Movement on TV income.[26]

When Samaranch first mooted the idea of international marketing of the Olympics to Dassler, he was warned that it would be a time consuming and expensive process because 156 National Olympic Committees had to be approached, persuaded and paid to join The Olympic Programme (TOP) before Seoul in 1988. International Sports and Leisure (ISL), a subsidiary company of Horst Dassler's Adidas (51 %) and the Japanese advertising giant Dentsu (49 %) were given the marketing task at an IOC session in Delhi in April 1983.[27] The TOP was to simplify the task for large corporations to act as global Olympic sponsors. Before TOP was implemented in 1988 any company had to negotiate with each one of the National Olympic Committees before its products could be globally linked with the five rings.[28] But the negotiations with the NOC were complicated and expensive. Some had long standing contracts with sponsors which had to be bought out. Others had lucrative deals which they were not readily prepared to give up, and again the handshake had to be a golden one. For example the British Olympic Association had a thriving link with American Express, which had to be abandoned when Visa joined TOP.[29]

There was to be exclusivity in each category. For example Coca-Cola would be the only soft drink manufacturer worldwide to have Olympic connections. The Berlin session in 1985 finally approved TOP's operations with 154 NOC's and nine multinational corporations on board. Ironically Greece, the birth country of the Games, was one of the NOC's which declined to join the original TOP, although it later fell in with TOP II. The nine multi-national TOP I sponsors generated $95 million in the four years leading up to Seoul. This was as much as 35 sponsors brought in for Los Angeles in 1984. The IOC itself was taking 8 % of gross worldwide television rights and 3 % of the TOP programme.[30]

Not that Olympic marketing was entirely new. It was the immense scale and subsequent tremendous influence of the modern version of commercialism which threatens the inherent values of the movement. There are a number of examples of earlier efforts at commercialisation. In 1896 Kodak already advertised in the official programme of the inaugural Games. A century later Kodak was a TOP sponsor at Atlanta. Posters for Lipton's tea can be discerned in the film 'Chariots of Fire' which contains photographs that were taken inside the 1924 Paris Olympic stadium.[31] Today the Olympic stadium and the Wimbledon tennis final are about the only great sports events free from advertising in the stadiums, mainly because the television companies pay so much to screen these elite events that they demand all the attention for their programme sponsors. The 1920 Antwerp programme was full of advertisements and licensing of products started at Stockholm in 1912. At Tokyo in 1964 the organisers earned $1 million from a special brand of 'Olympia' cigarettes.[32] For the 1960 Rome Games Olivetti provided 1 000 typewriters, Omega the stopwatches and Zanussi 60 refrigerators for the Olympic Village. Fiat put 34 cars at the disposal of the organisers and popular Italian motorcycle company Lambretta made transportation available to journalists and photographers. By 1968 the organisers were making almost $9 million profit from royalties and the need to regulate sponsorships became apparent.[33] By 1992 the proceeds from sponsorships were equal to those from television rights with each of the two important sectors contributing about 28 % of Barcelona's total income. Previously the contribution from sponsorships was 8,6 % for Tokyo in 1964, 5,6 % in Mexico's case and 14,1 % of Munich's incomes.[34]

So TOP was clearly a successfully integrated international marketing programme. But it was not just the sponsorships that increased tremendously after 1984. The European television rights which had been undervalued for so long, were also due for some serious attention from the Olympic marketing brigade. For the LA Games ABC was paying $1,67 per television household in comparison with Europe's 17 cents per household. European television rights for 1984 were valued at $19 million and four years later at Seoul, $28 million came in via this source, in comparison to $300 million for US rights. No wonder Dick Pound said of the negotiations with the European Broadcasting Union, "There is always a great shredding of clothing and pouring on of ashes, quite a polished performance of how it is not possible for them to pay any thing".[35] At Barcelona the contribution from the European Broadcasting Union was already an impressive $90 million and for Atlanta this increased to a massive $250 million.[36] With the $456 million from the USA, TV rights amounted to $700 million in the Olympic kitty. It is no wonder the bid cities are proliferating.

Footnotes

[handwritten note: LA not first to use commericial]

1. Hill 1996, p 140
2. Hill 1996, pp 140, 141
3. Hill 1996, p 141
4. Hill 1996, p 142
5. Hill 1996, p 141
6. Miller 1992, p 107
7. Simson and Jennings 1992, p 268
8. Ueberroth (in Miller) 1992, pp 103, 104
9. Xth Olympiade Committee 1933, p 30
10. Hill 1996, p 139
11. Hill 1996, p 139
12. Miller 1992, pp 102, 103
13. Miller 1992, p 106
14. Hill 1996, p 141

15. Hill 1996, p 143
16. Hill 1996, p 142
17. Miller 1992, p 219
18. Miller 1992, p 219
19. Dong-Wook 1988, p 219
20. Miller 1992, p 103
21. Wallechinsky 1992, p 39
22. Wallechinsky 1992, p 19
23. Wallechinsky 1992, p 27
24. Wallechinsky 1992, p 151
25. Wallechinsky 1992, pp 155, 156
26. Wilson 1988, p 14
27. Hill 1996, p 80
28. De Moregas Spa et al 1995, p 28
29. Hill 1996, p 81
30. Miller 1992, p 46
31. Miller 1992, p 45
32. Hill 1996, p 80
33. De Moregas Spa et al 1995, p 26
34. De Moregas Spa et al 1995, p 17
35. Wilson 1988, p 23
36. De Moregas Spa et al 1995, p 19

CHAPTER 7

SEOUL 1988 -
A DIPLOMATIC TOUR DE FORCE

The Seoul Dynamo

Dr Un Yong Kim, "a shortish, thick-set man with glasses" was the driving force behind South Korea's efforts to host an Olympic Games. He first managed to get two Asian Athletics Championships for Seoul, then the shooting world championship in 1978, the first air rifle championship in 1979, the eighth woman's world basket ball championships and then the twelfth weight-lifting championships in 1980. Kim then felt confident to go to Baden Baden in 1981 to bid for the Olympic Games.[1] But Kim had much more behind him than just the successful hosting of a few championships. The South Korean economy had been growing at a vibrant 8 % per year on average since 1962 when the military government's new strategy of export-orientated industrialisation was launched. The strategy was to utilise South Korea's one competitive advantage "cheap but well educated labour".[2] The success of this policy over the long term can be illustrated by comparing South Korea's GDP to that of its equals in 1987, namely Austria and Mexico. All three of these countries had a GDP of under $200 billion in that year, with Mexico's the highest of the three.[3] Ten years later the Economist Intelligence Unit predicted a GDP of $544 billion for South Korea, $325 billion for Mexico and $226 billion for Austria for 1997.[4] During the same period the GDP per head for South Korea increased from under $5 000 to $12 000.

So economically speaking, South Korea was in an almost ideal position to host a successful event but politically speaking there were serious problems. The relatively highly educated population was not satisfied with low wages anymore and in political terms they demanded a larger slice of the action than the ruthlessly authoritarian government was prepared to give.

As far as its communist neighbour was concerned, "Korea was divided into Soviet and American zones of occupation and then in 1958 into two republics. The north's invasion of the south in 1950 led to three years of war, in which the UN saved the south and China the north from total defeat. The two sides were left glaring at each other across a cease-fire line not far from the original border".[5]

Seoul's Selection

It was already clear at the Moscow Games that Nagoya of Japan was the favourite. Not much opposition was expected from Melbourne, Athens or Seoul. London was initially planning to enter the race as well and a thorough feasibility study

considering either Wembley or the Docklands as the heartland of the Games was done in 1979. But Margaret Thatcher came to power and disbanded the Greater London Council and that meant the end of this effort. After all Nagoya was backed by the powerful Toyota car company. Japan already had a record of staging the Games successfully but the Japanese city was its own worst enemy as environmental protesters from Nagoya noisily paraded up and down the streets of the quiet Rhineland spa town of Baden Baden, where the selection was due, to demonstrate their opposition to the bid.

Seoul also had a powerful ally in Horst Dassler. Jennings quotes Nally, Dassler's erstwhile partner and marketing guru, "Firstly Horst couldn't control the Japanese. They were very independent minded ... they were too arrogant, they were always too confident that they would win the Games. Korea was different; they were co-operative and they manufactured nearly everybody's sports equipment and sports shoes. A lot of Adidas product was made there and Dassler knew the Koreans well. Politically it was an important country for him".[6] Yet it was observed by other participants that Horst originally backed the Japanese city and only 24 hours before voting changed his mind and asserted that Seoul was going to take the honours. Miller quotes Samaranch on the subject: "I had never thought to express reservations about Seoul before the vote in Baden Baden. My opinion had been that Nagoya was much the best, although the day before the vote I had asked close friends among the members what they thought, and they suggested Seoul was going to win. I was astonished".[7] Well Seoul trounced Nagoya by 52 votes to 27. Nally has no doubt as to the reason, "It was the first time that Dassler could prove to himself that he had been decisive in choosing an Olympic city".[8] But Hill offers another clue as to the likely reasons for the outcome when he quotes "Peter Ueberroth, the organiser of the Los Angeles Games and so an experienced, if jaundiced, observer, adds a down to earth assertion of corruption. Seoul also gave away, quietly, two first class roundtrip tickets to each IOC member. The tickets were easily redeemed for cash; many were".[9]

Impending embargoes

The announcement of the winner was almost immediately followed by threats of boycotts by North Korea. In fact North Korea tried to influence the other East bloc countries as well and there was always the possibility of terrorist attacks or sabotage. South Korea was relatively isolated from its western allies and relations with Japan were not good either considering the historical background of animosity between the two.

South Korea had almost no diplomatic relations with East bloc countries which in itself was already a formidable obstacle to the Games. The fact that many government ministers in eastern Europe were sports leaders as well as Olympic officials certainly compensated to some extent, and Olympic channels of communication developed out of necessity.[10]

But the official opposition from the Soviet bloc to the Games continued and even intensified with the boycott of Los Angeles. Horst Dassler again displayed his considerable international influence by arranging the first official meeting between the two sides at the LA Games. "Some of the USSR's concerns over Seoul were very similar to those which had bedevilled Los Angeles, but they seem to have been handled more effectively on the Korean side than they had been by LAOOC, and the Soviets also were probably more intent on achieving a satisfactory outcome than they had been in 1984".

The Soviets for example were keen to procure landing rights for Aeroflot and most East bloc countries wanted assurances that defectors would not be granted political asylum. Kim knew his government was opposed to most of the requests made by the Soviets and to refuse asylum would be against international law.[11]

Juan Antonio Samaranch probably saw the Seoul Games as his first, because when he was elected IOC President in 1980 Los Angeles had already been appointed as host city and besides the formidable Madam Berloux was there until 1985. Miller quotes Alan Coupat, his former chef de bureau: "The real change in him followed the removal of Berloux ... . He became much more active and assured; more willing to impose".[12] Well, a fourth successive Olympic boycott would have been a devastating blow to the Olympic Movement as well as to international sport, so Samaranch needed all the energy and assertiveness he could muster.

The Soviet Union was also in an awkward position in that it had to be seen to be in support of its more militant North Korean ally and yet did not really intend to boycott another Games. The USSR did not want its athletes to be relegated to also-rans and it was also wary of open discontent or outright disobedience among athletes or their governments in the member countries.[13]

North Korea made its demand to share the Games in 1985 as it suggested the "Pyongyang-Seoul Games" which would have meant a single team representing both countries as well as two opening and two closing ceremonies. Samaranch patiently travelled to and fro between the two Korean cities but eventually North Korea overplayed their hand and the IOC closed the door on further negotiations. But the serious negotiating role adopted by Samaranch was admired by the East bloc countries. "Samaranch's diplomacy over Seoul was masterful. South Korea in 1981 had diplomatic relations with only sixty countries, yet by the time of the Games there were more than one hundred and sixty there, and North Korea had failed to blow the Games out of the water".[14] Considering the prelude to the Games, security was, to say the least, tight. "Security was not only needed on the ground but also on the water, in the air and under the sea". The USA stationed two aircraft carriers in the vicinity and deployed 40 000 troops along the border, as a warning to North Korea. Seoul commissioned 81 630 military and police to guard facilities.[15]

Then there were the usual little irritations: the national teams of Iran and Iraq had to be kept apart; the Taiwanese could not use their national flag for fear of upsetting the Chinese from PRC; the electric scoreboard showed Jerusalem and not Tel Aviv as the capital of Israel and that had to be corrected; and Korean coaches vehemently protested against a decision where a Bulgarian beat one of their fighters and NBC gave the resulting rumpus live coverage for an hour.

Media Might

The major sports agreed to adjust the starting times of the events to 07:30 (Korean time). This was necessary to suit the all important American television audiences and for the same reason the Summer Games were moved forward by a week to avoid a clash with the important American baseball tournaments. But the Koreans, still smarting after their TV rights humiliation, made sure they got their pound of flesh for their inconveniences. The television rights scramble started after the Munich Games when the figure for American rights seemed to double every four years. For Munich the North American television rights were $12,5 million, of which $6 million was specified as a fee for technical services, which simply meant that the organising committee did not have to share this sum with the IOC. The value of the Montreal Games jumped to $25 million of which $12,5 million was again for technical services. The Moscow figure was negotiated at a high $72,33 million of which technical services, unbelievably, made out the biggest part, namely $50 million.[16] But it was the jump to $225 million for LA which really had the Korean expectations going. When the major US networks got into a showdown for the Winter Games of 1988, ABC paid an unrealistically high $309 million and realised it soon afterwards when the television market collapsed. ABC was publicly acknowledging a loss of between $50 million and $70 million and this set the tone for the Seoul negotiations. The Koreans were in a different frame of mind, they expected $600 million at least and based their optimism on the previous huge increases not realising the bottom had fallen out of the market. They were shocked when the bidding opened at just over $300 million for all three networks. Dick Pound, the IOC representative at the talks, expected at least $500 million for an opening bid and he relates the Korean response: "It was a big loss of face for the Koreans; they could not believe it".[17] The Seoul negotiators tried a hard line approach but in the end they had to make do with a best offer of $300 million from NBC, $25 million less than the first offer they had initially turned down. For a while a deadlock existed between the Seoul organisers and the television representative; this made the IOC realise that they have a different interest and approach from that of the organisers. The IOC felt quite rightly that every organising committee tried to squeeze every last dollar out of the networks, whilst the IOC was in favour of a more stable long term approach which would not kill the goose that lays the golden egg. So the rules of the bidding game were changed: from Barcelona 1992 onwards the IOC would conduct the negotiations with the city involved, merely being consulted instead of the other way around as it had been done previously.

Internal Battles

Internally the situation in South Korea was just as hectic and the run up to the Olympics involved the various political groups in constant confrontation. Unfortunately South Korea had a tradition of authoritarian rule and its ruler Major-General Chun Doo-Kwan was not very accommodating towards change. A student died whilst in detention and the obvious signs of an effort by the police at a cover-up led to considerable popular dissent. Many middle-class Koreans had now joined the widespread demonstrations and when Chun postponed talks with the opposition parties until after the referendum, things became worse and the anti-government rallies turned to violence. At the convention of the ruling party President Chun nominated Roh Tae Woo as his successor. By this stage the protests were even more widespread and getting out of hand. American influence was brought to bear, including messages from President Ronald Reagan urging Chun not to use troops against the protesters. All eyes were on South Korea because of the upcoming Olympics and this fact probably moderated the government's response to the riots and prevented martial law from being introduced. The rulers realised that the imposition of martial law might have caused the Games to be moved elsewhere. But it was mainly the intensity and scope of the opposition that persuaded first Roh and later Chun that it was time for serious reform. It was Roh, a retired four-star General with blood-stained hands, according to the London Sunday Times, who saved the 1988 Games from certain disaster with a short emotional speech in which he urged President Chun to either accede to the opposition's demands, including direct presidential elections, or Roh himself would resign. To everybody's astonishment Chun accepted all this in a statesman-like speech.[18] Roh promised more reforms during his election campaign and was elected in October 1979 when he received 37 % of the popular vote against 28 % for the closest other contender. But by April 1988 Roh's ruling party failed to gain an overall majority against the combined opposition and for the first time there was a real balancing force in the corridors of power which meant the entrenchment of democracy. It is interesting that the erosion of political restraints, according to Paul Johnson, was achieved by the freeing of markets in Thailand, Taiwan and South Korea. It proved that economic and political liberty were inseparably linked, as the acceptance of market economics inevitably involved a withdrawal by the state from important areas of decision-making, which then fell on the individual.[19] But The Economist warned that "The shift to democracy makes the technological priority inevitable, now that it is no longer politically possible to suppress workers' demands for a larger share of the new prosperity. South Korea's days as a cheap labour market are numbered; it will have to rely on nimble minds not nimble fingers".[20]

The Tokyo Mould

Lee Dong-Wook in his poorly translated 'How to prepare Olympics and its task' gives a detailed account of the total dedication with which the Koreans tackled their Games as well as how it was linked to widespread other infra structural developments and even to the industrialisation of attitudes.

In the foreword by the SLOOC President Park Seh-Jik it is stressed that, "One characteristic of the Seoul Olympic Games which distinguishes it from previous Olympic Games is that they were used as an ignition of national development". Not really a valid claim, since as one reads through this book it soon becomes clear that the whole approach to the 1988 Olympics was based on the developmental 1964 Tokyo Games. The Koreans and Japanese might have been arch enemies previously but it is clear from Lee Dong-Wook's detailed strategic explanations that the Koreans deeply admired Japan's industrial success and were intent on applying the same blueprints to their economic and consequent Olympic planning.[21]

It is also clear that the Koreans were determined to utilise the Olympics to get rid of their Korean war image. Lee Dong-Wook is adamant that, thanks to sport they, the Koreans, would introduce their country as "the country I'd like to visit because it hosted the historic Olympic Games" instead of, as he calls it, "a country of orphans" or amazingly, "a country of rapid economic development". (I can immediately name a few countries including my own which would not mind the 'rapid economic development' label in the least). Nevertheless one senses a deep urge for international acknowledgement: "it was essential that Korea be recognised for her competence and credibility in order that her people be acknowledged on the world stage".[22] Korea was determined to prove that developing countries could also host the Games successfully and it needed almost desperately to be recognised as a reliable mature trading partner and attractive international holiday destination.[23] With this in mind a policy was also adopted to give domestic firms contracts where possible. The aims were to enable Korean firms to internationalise their activities, to give priority to projects which could effect extra foreign exchange earnings and to stimulate tourism. LDW also specifically mentions the local production of sports products and specifies that "More than 70 % of the total Olympic Games products would be supplied from within the country".[24] Andrew Jennings however draws attention to the counterfeiting industry in Korea which churned out billions of dollars worth of imitations. Jennings quotes Howard

Bruns, President of America's sporting goods manufacturer's associaton: "Brand-name piracy has become highly sophisticated in South Korea. You can buy labels and identification tags for every well-known brand in the world". Apparently Bruns was backed up by the world federation of the sporting goods industry, which claimed "that Korea was the biggest single source of counterfeit goods in the world".[25] On the revenue side the first TOP (The Olympic Programme) was in operation with nine multi-national companies - Coca-Cola, Visa, Brother, Federal Express, 3M, Time-Life, National Panasonic, Kodak and Philips, contributing over $70 million to have the right to use the five rings anywhere in the world.[26] Seoul earned a smaller percentage of income from television rights or sponsorships than LA four years earlier (LA got 37 % of earnings from TV and 16,5 % from sponsorships while Seoul earned 25 % from TV and 8,2 % from sponsorships). LA managed a high 18 % of income from ticket sales which is amazing in this television age. Seoul in this respect could earn only 3 % of income. Where Seoul did well was in terms of earnings from subscriptions and lotteries from which 40 % of income was derived, against LA'S 8,6 % (LA had no lotteries). This also includes donations which made up 12 % of Seoul's 40 %. De Moregas Spa demonstrates how income from ticket sales gradually decreased with the ever growing importance of television rights, with the exception of the American Games: 16,5 % ticket derived income was forecast for Atlanta, where sport interest and purchasing power is strong.[27] During the Atlanta Games several journalists remarked how packed almost every event at the Atlanta Games was.

Steroid Sprints

Americans are great enthusiasts it seems, often attending international events like the Olympics or World Cup Soccer. Whether they appreciate these sports is another matter but the first step is surely to attend and that is where a lot of other communities fall short of expectations. The poor attendance at the recent World Athletic Championships in Athens comes to mind, as well as Barcelona which was criticised for empty stadiums at some events. The Koreans claim that over three million of their people attended Olympic events - the low revenue might be attributed to a deliberate policy to make entrance tickets affordable. As far as the actual sport was concerned, the Koreans certainly got value for money - how can they ever forget the colourful and swift Florence Griffith Joyner, who was as quick as she was eccentric. Joyner was once asked to leave a shopping centre because she was wearing a pet boa constrictor like a scarf around her neck. But at Seoul she proved that there was more to her performances than six inch long finger nails and extravagant attire. Although she originally started out as a 200 m specialist she studied video tapes of Ben Johnson's explosive starts intensely and stunned the world by breaking the world 100 m record at the US Olympic trials. Her new record was faster than the men's records in countries like Ireland, New Zealand, Norway, Iran and Turkey.[28] She surprised no one by taking both the 100 m and 200 m golds at Seoul, setting a new world record in the 200 m. In the 200 m even the second placed Grace Jackson came within one-hundredth of the pre-Olympic record, yet still finished a few metres behind "Flojo". The men's 100 m was the Ben Johnson affair, where Johnson beat Carl Lewis against expectations in the final, only to have his gold medal taken away when he tested positive for steroids. Three months later the IAAF invalidated Johnson's 1987 world record even though he had passed a drug test at that tournament in Rome.[29]

It is incredible that Johnson was not tested positive before Seoul. The sprinter admitted that he started taking steroids late in 1981, so his illegal habits remained undetected for almost seven years. The policy of in-competition testing, as it was then, was clearly inadequate and the Canadian investigation into the affair by senior judge Dubin proved as much. Johnson, by structuring his doping cycles and regulating clearance time according to meeting schedules, managed to pass 19 tests in the two years before the Seoul Olympics.[30] The suspicion even spilled over to Griffith Joyner when sceptics started pointing out how she suddenly improved when she developed more visible muscles. The rumours were strengthened when she retired in the beginning of 1989 just before the institution of random drug testing. But the fact remains that Flojo passed all the tests while competing. The first Olympic 10 000 m for women was held at Seoul. Alga Bondavenko of the Soviet Union, one of the pioneers of long distance running, took this special gold medal after the favourite Ingrid Kristiansen went out with a foot injury on the seventh lap. The second women's marathon was won by the tiny Portuguese Rosa Mota, whose career was going nowhere until she switched from middle distances to the marathon. In the swimming the diminutive Janet Evans took three gold medals. Her rare talent came to the world's attention when she broke both the longstanding 800 and 1 500 m world records at the tender age of 15. She only weighed 43 kg at that stage. It was certainly a sight as the tiny American stood on the starting blocks for the 200 m final between the 82 kg Astrid Strauss from East Germany and her 70 kg teammate Anke Möhring. But Janet beat them by more than three metres. She took gold in the 400 m and 800 m freestyle and in the 400 m individual medley.

All is Well

In 1981 when the Games were awarded to Seoul, South Korea did not even have colour television. By the late eighties it had become one of the ten largest exporters of tubes in the world.

The 1988 Seoul Games must have been one of the most risky undertakings ever by the Olympic Movement, with a hostile aggressive neighbour, a restive population, an unpopular indecisive leader, constant threats of a boycott by the massive Soviet bloc and an authoritarian history. That "The Olympic Games were a turning point for Korea to move into the ranks of the world's advanced nations"[31] was mainly due to the solid base supplied by a vibrant economy and a determined, educated and enthusiastic population.

Footnotes
1. Miller 1992, p 125
2. The Economist Atlas 1989, p 228
3. The Economist Atlas 1989, p 83
4. The Economist Publications 1996, pp 83, 88, 89
5. The Economist Atlas 1989, p 228
6. Simson and Jennings 1992, p 180
7. Miller, 1992, pp 128, 129
8. Simson and Jennings 1992, p 180
9. Hill 1996, p 168
10. Hill 1996, p 170
11. Hill 1996, p 171
12. Miller 1992, p 127
13. Hill 1996, p 171
14. Miller 1992, p 127
15. Hill 1996, p 175
16. De Moregas Spa et al 1995, p 19
17. Wilson 1980, p 20
18. Hill 1996, p 163
19. Johnson 1983, p 725
20. Economist Atlas 1989, p 229
21. Lee Dong-Wook 1988, pp 228, 229, 230, 231, 336
22. Lee Dong-Wook 1988, p 1
23. Lee Dong-Wook 1988, p 23
24. Lee Dong-Wook 1988, p 234
25. Simson and Jennings 1992, p 181
26. De Moregas Spa et al 1995, p 17
27. De Moregas Spa et al 1995, p 3
28. Wallechinsky 1992, p 147
29. Wallechinsky 1992, p 14
30. Simson and Jennings 1992, p 251
31. Hill 1996, p 178

CHAPTER 8

BARCELONA 1992 -
A GREAT BUT COSTLY GAMES

The Divisive Origins

Barcelona's intention to bid for the Olympic Games of 1992 was formally announced by Narcis Serra, Barcelona's Socialist Mayor, at a dinner in early 1981. Although the obstacles were nowhere as dramatic as those faced by Seoul, there were plenty of divisions in Spain itself. The Spanish Olympic Committee (COE) was headed by one Don Alfonso who had close ties with the previous Franco regime and whose relations with the Socialist Barcelona city authorities were stormy, until 1987 when a prominent businessman Carlos Ferrer Salat was elected in his place. Ferrer Salat also became Vice-President of the organising committee known as COOB '92. On a national level Barcelona could not count on much support from the Spanish capital Madrid, even though they both had socialists at the helm. There was intense rivalry between the two big Spanish cities and "Madrid's politicians played the politics of generosity, though with knives in their pockets".[1] When Serra first explored the Olympic possibilities for Barcelona he had to be very discreet so as not to let the Madrid authorities get wind of Barcelona's intentions.

In Catalonian terms the provincial authorities were clearly from a different political persuasion than those of Barcelona, being both conservative and nationalistic in Catalonian terms. But Serra was nevertheless convinced that a Barcelona bid would be the best way for the city and Spain to promote its newly established freedom and the continuing industrial growth. But there was to be formidable international opposition for the 1992 Games. Amsterdam, Belgrade, Birmingham, Brisbane and Paris were also in contention.

Pasqual Maragall became Mayor of Barcelona when Serra was promoted to the National Government as Minister of Defence and it was up to him to conduct Barcelona's international campaign. Early in 1983 the national government gave its full support to the bid as did the provincial government of Catalonia. The Catalonian leader Jordi Pujol and his parliament were "concerned about the place that would be accorded in the Olympic Games to the Catalonian language and national anthem". Maragall could only promise that these would be favourably treated within the framework of the regional and national laws.[2]

The Catalonian language by all accounts benefited substantially and was one of the official languages at the Games, often being given preference to Spanish. The "Television in the Olympics International Research Project" came to the conclusion that the objectives to project and promote the Catalonian culture were certainly

© 1988 COOB'92, S.A. All rights reserved TM

achieved as most international broadcasts referred to the inherent Catalonian heritage of, amongst others, the singers or actors taking part in the various ceremonies. Time Magazine's Rod Usher described the character of the opening and closing ceremonies as "all Catalonian to the core".[3] But television research project points out that the understanding of "Catalonia as a politically autonomous community within Spain" was not pursued by many commentators as it did not fit in with the central universal message of the Games as a force for harmony.[4]

A Bruising International Campaign

The international campaign for Barcelona ended in a classic confrontation with Paris, classic in terms of the unconventional games cities play to obtain the Olympic votes. By the time Maragall went to the 1984 LA Olympics he had the backing of all levels of Spanish society and he could concentrate on the international phase of the bid. Samaranch admitted that his heart was in Barcelona, his home town, but he obviously had to remain neutral as President of the IOC. Maragall got Julio Iglesias and Placido Domingo to perform at the reception for Barcelona's participants at LA. The public support for important figures in the sporting world started coming in. The first open declaration of support came from Primo Nebiolo, the powerful President of the International Amateur Athletic Federation (IAAF). His example was soon followed by Joao Havelange, the influential President of The International Football Association (FIFA). But the French were not idle: after Seoul was elected and the various threats and disputes flared up, Nelson Paillou, President of the French NOC suggested that the 1988 Games be taken away from South Korea and instead handed to Barcelona. This of course would have given Paris a clear run for 1992.[5]

When Havelange sided with Barcelona, Jacques Chirac, current President of France, the leader of the Paris effort and also former French Premier, "threatened to use his influence in Africa to ensure that Havelange is not re-elected President of FIFA".[6]

The solid Latin support for Barcelona's bid became apparent when Mario Vásquez Raña from Mexico and the President of The Association of National Olympic Committees admitted afterwards that he also helped to gather support for Barcelona; "my Games" as he called it.[7] But both Raña and Nebiolo had Samaranch to thank for their IOC membership so they owed him a favour. When the rich Raña was elected there were 13 votes for him, 10 against and 60 abstentions. It clearly indicated that a secret ballot might have provided a completely different result. But Samaranch, the diplomat by training, knew he had to get powerful figures such as Nebiolo and Raña on board of the IOC. After all, athletics is the very heart of any Olympic Games and the National Olympic Committees the one important part of the Olympic Family. Samaranch had Nebiolo appointed to the IOC without a vote being taken, under a new rule allowing the IOC President to install any two members of his own choosing.[8]

Both Barcelona and Paris spent lavishly on their bids. The IOC members who visited Barcelona were given lithographs of Salvador Dali's oil painting, "The Cosmic Athlete", signed by the artist himself. David Miller, prominent sports journalist, hinted at the shadow of Adidas when rumours of more extravagant gifts were heard.[9] A final reminder in the form of a personal letter from King Carlos himself was directed at each IOC member just before the decisive meeting. But the French were not idle: IOC members were wined and dined at the luxuriant Hotel de Crillon and the gifts included coats and perfumes from the best Paris boutiques. The Paris promotion campaign also tried to stir sentiment by constantly referring to the 1924 Paris Games. But the French had one strategic weakness - they had two candidates for 1992, Paris for the Summer Games and Albertville for the Winter Games. This tradition had changed in the meantime and currently there is a two year interval between the summer and winter affairs. Since the French cities of Chamonix and Grenoble had hosted previous Winter Games, the Albertville campaign was not viewed as particularly significant, especially since Falun from Sweden seemed to offer a much more viable and attractive alternative. Sofia (Bulgaria) also seemed an innovative alternative. But realising the impossibility of giving both the Summer and Winter Games to the same country, rumours of a Barcelona Albertville axis were emerging, prompting Norway's IOC member Jan Staubo to write a letter of concern to Samaranch, "There are now rumours of coalition and pre-arrangements being made between candidate city organisers and others, to get members to vote for a particular city for the Winter Games in order to influence the selection of the city to host the Olympiad".[10]

Samaranch continued to claim absolute neutrality as far as Barcelona's effort was concerned but, "He could afford to", claimed Dennis Howell former British Minister. "The longer he is in charge, the more the IOC members he appoints, and many of them feel a sense of obligation to him. This in itself is unhealthy. In my view, the way in which members are appointed to the IOC lends itself to a distortion".[11] But the French were not beaten yet. By all accounts Jacques Chirac gave a brilliant oration written by Madame Berlioux when he presented Paris' case and all but swept the IOC members off their feet. Miller's account showed they were very much on their feet afterwards applauding enthusiastically for a few minutes.[12] Barcelona's final presentation in contrast was rather dismal[13] but their footwork afterwards was effective, swift and clever.[14] Barcelona's backers rang up known supporters all night to tell them to support Albertville's bid for the Winter Games. Ex British Sports Minister Howell remembers; "It (Chirac's speech) had such a devastating effect that the decision was made by the Barcelona strategists to split the sympathy for France by supporting the French Winter bid for Albertville".[15] "Confronted by French candidates in both Games, the members awarded the Winter Games to Albertville - a decision that was to prove laden with hazards - and give Barcelona, making its fourth bid in sixty years, the Summer Games".[16]

Samaranch's former chef de bureau is of the opinion that the fact that there were four other cities, also favoured Barcelona's campaign. He felt that if there had been only two candidates, the membership would have polarised more around Paris. Both Olympic cities soon encountered difficulties: Albertville was criticised for changing the venues from the original proposal whilst Barcelona had to face an acute shortage in hotel rooms, plus unacceptable levels of sewage pollution in the water where the yachting was to take place.[17] COOB, the Barcelona Organising Committee were described in a 'Euroletter' as "a battlefield where problems quite unrelated to the Olympics were fought out". After the scale and success of the Seoul event Barcelona all of sudden realised how much work lay ahead. The organisers were irritated by Samaranch's constant involvement in Barcelona's arrangements and they often did not accept his proposals, and the central government was displeased by Maragall's bad relations with the Spanish Secretary of State for Sport, Gomez Navarro.[18] Security was also a serious challenge for the organisers: there were bombings in Barcelona the week before the voting and the Basque Seperatist Movement was at the back of everyone's mind. Even the cruise ships in Barcelona's harbour which served as extra hotel accommodation were subjected to underwater patrol by scuba divers. "For the second Games in succession, Samaranch would not be sleeping well until the flag was lowered and the flame extinguished".[19]

Real Local Support

In the meantime the Games were evoking a strong feeling of enthusiastic support right across Spain. As the Olympic torch travelled 5 000 km through the country, 35 million people had the opportunity to watch it go by. In September 1985 when the matter of hosting the Games in Barcelona was brought before the Catalon Parliament, 64 % of Spaniards were positive that the Barcelona Olympics would benefit the whole of Spain.[20] A year later just before Maragall was due to leave for the final vote, 40 000 volunteers had already signed. Alfred Bosch, who was involved with the preparations for Barcelona for six years in different capacities and eventually as head of the Secratariat of Miquel Abad, the Chief Executive, reckoned that this obvious groundswell of popular support was one of the main reasons Barcelona was elected. He saw the Parisians as indifferent to the Games, whilst in Amsterdam's case there was a very vocal extremist lobby against it, and with Birmingham the problem was the Thatcher government's lukewarm support.[21]

After the Games a newsletter of the City of Barcelona under the heading of 'What the Citizens thought' quoted the findings of a telephonic public opinion poll that was carried out to discover what the city's residents thought of Olympics. It indicated that more than 90 % were satisfied with the way the Games went. This survey also provided another important fact, that the majority of those interviewed were of the opinion that the general standard of services improved noticeably.

Public co-operation was essential in temporary measures such as the usually unpopular policy to restrict the use of private cars, in order to encourage increased use of public transport and to establish exclusive Olympic lanes for Olympic traffic, mainly spectators. Just under 90 % of those polled indicated that they were in no way inconvenienced by these measures.[22] The extent of co-operation is clearly illustrated by the fact that the amount of traffic on Barcelona's roads actually decreased by 20 % while the Games were on. The other interesting aspect is that crime actually decreased during the Olympic period in spite of the huge influx of visitors. The huge visible security presence contributed to a 32 % drop in the number of crimes reported. The total number of people detained in connection with suspected criminal activities increased by 12 % - indicating a pro-active approach by the security forces. In our interview in the hectic central Barcelona a year after the Games, Miquel Botella, the Deputy Director General of Resources, unequivocally stated that the aspect of the whole process that had left the biggest impression on him personally, was the tremendous sense of pride and social involvement that took hold of the city during those last few seemingly chaotic weeks before D-day. (We were sitting in a large dusty office where all the files and papers were packed in boxes and the table and two chairs were the only pieces of furniture left so I could well imagine the chaos before the Games Botella was referring to). As an example Botella mentioned that in order to complete projects on time, some companies had to ask their workers to put in stints of 12 to 14 hours a day. Yet the organising committee did not receive one claim for overtime.[23]

Numerous Strategic Objectives

When Serra was elected as mayor of Barcelona in 1979 he was the first after almost half a century of unelected councils. He was confronted by the task of urban renewal after decades of uncontrolled growth and property speculation as well as the effects of social and infra structural inequality in most parts of the city.

The main impetus behind the idea to host these Games was to utilise the whole process as a springboard for huge investment to effect widespread development and to rejuvenate Spain's international image at the same time. Alfred Bosch in our interview emphasised that urban renewal was the first and main objective behind the Games. Linked to the enhanced image was a comprehensive plan to increase tourism by widening Barcelona's scope of attractions, as well as to improve facilities. Barcelona was well known as a cultural destination with the medieval art of the Gothic Quarter, the work of Art Nouveau Architects like Gaudi and museums with art works by Picasso or Miro. In Spanish terms Barcelona was also considered an industrial centre and was popular for conventions and congresses. For the period 1989 to 1992 the yearly number of conventions, courses and congresses ranged between 310 and 373. The number of delegates attending these events ranged from 95 426 in 1989 to 168 966 in 1991. So Barcelona was clearly established as a reasonably popular destination for congresses and the like. In order to establish a solid base for the expansion of tourism, two improvements were considered essential: the hotel accommodation in central Barcelona was inadequate and a 43 % increase took place from 9 500 rooms in 1989 to 13 500 rooms in 1992 (the total number of hotel rooms for Catalonia was 106 136 in 1993 and 41 278 for the greater Barcelona according to the Secretaria General de Turismo).

The second aspect that was also linked to the urban regeneration theme, was the construction of the Olympic Village in an old and derelict industrial area close to the sea. This operation resulted in the transformation of this decaying area into an attractive residential area with five kilometres of recovered seashore for public use.

The idea was for Barcelona to become the only large European city able to offer, besides the cultural and architectural attractions, the traditional attractions of sun and sea.

This strategy certainly paid off handsomely as the number of delegates to congresses, conventions and so on increased from 95 426 in 1989 to an impressive 213 086 in 1996. The number of international delegates increased from 36 155 in 1989 to 118 899 in 1996. The total number of these events also more than doubled during the same period.

The number of tourists also grew impressively. In 1990 the total for local and international visitors stood at 1,7 million, by 1992 this figure was 1,87 million, 93 saw a jump to 2,45 million and in 1995 the three million mark was reached. The visitors from Europe more than doubled from 57 7022 in 1991 to 1,23 million in 1995. Visitors from the USA, Japan and the rest of the world also showed significant increases from 1991 when just over 300 000 visited, to 1995 when 707 604 came, saw and enjoyed. The total number of international visitors declined slightly after a peak in 1995. As far as specific nationalities are concerned, it seems that the 1992 Games created a strong awareness of Barcelona's attractions with the North American. In 1992 when the Games took place they constituted 4,9 % of visitors, in 1996 this group made up 9 % of all guests. Japanese tourism in 1996 showed the opposite trend with the figure being only half of what it was in 1992. The only other national group to increase interest after the Games is UK and Ireland whose figure rose from 6,8 to 8,8 in 1996. The number of hotel beds kept on increasing after the Games albeit at a slower pace, so that the 25 055 beds in 1992 became

28 040 in 1996. The average bed occupancy remained much the same, with 58 % in 1990, 54 % in 1992, 46 % in 1994 and 61 % in 1996. So the massive increase in the number of tourists was almost equalled by the growth in accommodation capacity. If the impressive increase in overall tourism had not occured, there would have been a huge oversupply in hotel accommodation. The other factor was the deep worldwide recession in the early nineties, the end of which coincided with the after-Games buildup in tourism traffic.

How much of the increased tourism traffic is due to the Olympic Games and how much to the switch from recession to an upturn in the economy? The lesson for bidding cities is clear - the extra accommodation facilities cannot be created just for the Games; it has to be tied to a well planned tourism strategy. If one takes the national figures for Spain into account it is clear that Barcelona's growth was well above the national average. **So it is clear that in tourism terms the Barcelona Games were a resounding success.** The fact that the five star establishments suffered lower occupancy after 1992 is explained by the fact that from 1993 five-star hotels were VAT rated at 14 % whilst all other hotel grades only paid 7 %. So quite a few five-star establishments downgraded to four-star to remain competitive in the market for conventions.[24]

Total number of visitors to Barcelona

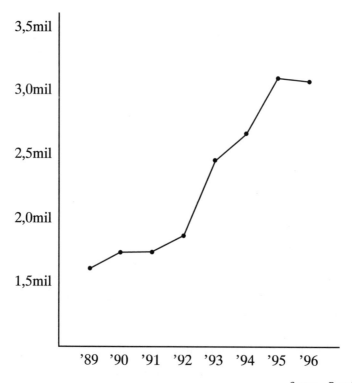

Source – Barcelona Bureau de Turisme

Number of delegates participating in meetings and congresses

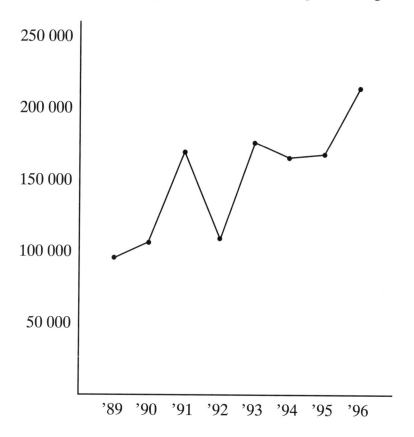

Source – Barcelona Bureau de Turisme

Urban Renewal

The appointment as Olympic host in October 1986 meant that the far reaching 'Economic and Strategic' plan could be implemented. The Olympic Games presented a golden opportunity as it not only virtually forced all levels of authorities to co-operate in a process which normally might have taken more than a decade for such a large undertaking, but it also simplified the all important access to finance. The encompassing plan evolved around three main strategic areas.

Strategy A

This section was about setting up Barcelona as one of the main driving forces within the macro region. The aim was to strengthen communications and transport on a national, local and Metropolitan level. In order to achieve this, Barcelona airport was remodelled, rail links with the rest of Europe improved, port activities increased and a network of large projects in Catalonia concluded.

Strategy B
This evolved mainly around improving the quality of life of the inhabitants and ensuring progress to improve the environment, strengthen specialisation and research, and increase social activities.

Strategy C
This was aimed at improving industry and advanced services in companies, the creation of support infrastructures for advanced services, road systems and telecommunications, and the conversion of Barcelona into an important area for economic and cultural development, with the incorporation of institutions of a European nature, such as the European Central Bank or the European Agency of Medical evaluation amongst others.

In 1991, the Strategic Plan was awarded the special prize for planning by the European Communities, for: "the high level of public/private co-operation and consensus, the internationalisation of the city, and the first European city to develop this concept of a strategic plan, thus serving as a future model for its application by other cities".[25]

It is this breadth of vision that enabled the planners of the city's future to link urban renewal to internationalisation, to commercial expansion in order to eventually achieve long term improvements in the quality of life of all its citizens.

 The City Council was quick to establish its own priorities: "Faced with the slowness and complexity of sticking to an overall development plan, the City Council decided instead to adopt specific measures in the areas of greatest need and to stimulate development based around local centres. The combination of a politically favourable climate, a group of very good architects, and the idea of creating a new urban environment through local individual projects produced some exceptional results. By taking advantage of old factory sites, railway stations and even disused quarries, new public spaces were created throughout Barcelona". As Rowe, Dean of the Harvard Architecture School, pointed out, this was achieved without distinguishing between rich and poor areas. In all cases the same levels of quality were applied. In 1990 Barcelona's urban development effort was recognised when it was awarded the Prince of Wales Urban Design Award by Harvard University.[26] The restructuring and remodelling of the road network was one of the great challenges that faced the densely populated Barcelona (with almost 17 000 people per square kilometre, the highest of any European city). Two new ring roads were built, 40 km in length. The first one, with a capacity of 130 000 vehicles per day, serves to link together all the access roads of the Metropolitan area. The second ring road has a capacity of 90 000 vehicles per day, and the function of the Ronda Litoral is to distribute traffic inside the city and to serve certain particular areas. The result of this excess capacity is that the previous limit of 590 000 vehicles per day has gone up to 900 000 per day.[27]

Airport reforms, consisted of the building of a new international terminal, the enlargement and refurbishing of the existing main passenger terminal, the construction of links with the cargo terminal, a new computer system (the only other airports in the world with this specific system are Dallas and Stuttgart), as well as landscaping and the improvement of access roads. These changes enable Barcelona's airport to cope easily with 12 million passengers per year.[28]

The city's hotel facilities were improved: in the five years preceding the Games the number of hotels increased by almost 37 % - from 96 to 132.

Erection of the Olympic Village in the transformation of an obsoléte and decaying area signified the city's principal urban development and is one of the largest of its kind in Europe. "It has meant the creation of a completely new district in an area previously ignored, reclaiming Barcelona's waterfront, building a new housing area, a sports marina, its connection with freeways, the cleaning up of 3 km of beaches, creating new parks and gardens and a network of sanitation systems".[29]

Before 1988 the telephone services in Barcelona were distinctly inferior to those in the majority of European countries. In the six years since 1988 the growth in telephone services came to 70 %. The total investment made by Telefónica in Barcelona from 1988 to 1992 was $3 170 million of which $650 million corresponded to investments made directly in the Olympics. In 1992 Spain had the ninth largest telephone network in the world.[30]

Starting in 1988, nearly 220 km of new sewers were installed. This increased the old network by 20 % to a total of 1 050 km. This was done to bring relief to a total of 31 zones which were prone to flooding.[31]

A network of service galleries was constructed, conducting electricity, gas, water and telephone supplies under the major roads built in Barcelona. Similar operations have been carried out in Madrid, London, Vienna and Helsinki.[32]

Barcelona's nomination in 1986 as Olympic host gave a substantial boost to the expansion and development of public sports facilities. New installations were built and many existing facilities were enlarged, modernised and remodelled. The total investment in sports installations between 1982 and 1992 came to about $385 million - which represents 20 years of development in the region's sporting needs.

135

When one looks at the totality of the above projects, it is difficult not to agree with Usher's verdict in Time Magazine:[33] "Since winning its bid for the Games six years ago Barcelona has done a stunning amount of remodelling. About $7,4 billion has gone into Olympic facilities, roads and other public works". Declares the socialist mayor, Maragall: "Never has so much been done in so little time".

A Complex Socio-economic Legacy

The overall effects of the massive total expenditure of $10 billion ($8 billion capital costs, $1,8 billion budget of the Organising Committee plus visitor spending) is difficult to determine. Much more comprehensive efforts have been undertaken by inter alia Prof Ferran Brunet. It is without doubt that the overall impression is a favourable one, although critics like Professor Zarnowski ask how much the quality of life has improved in Barcelona and to what extent employment opportunities have been enhanced?[34] So the question is simply: could the massive investment have been utilised more effectively? As soon as that type of argument is pursued the relative importance and contributions of quantitative and qualitative factors begin to intermingle and make it almost impossible to draw a single comparative conclusion in terms of conventional opportunity cost methods. How do you measure the pride of a community in acting as a host to the world? How much is the Catalonian culture enhanced and how would that be measured in terms of improved quality of life? What are the tangible benefits in terms of an enhanced Spanish image? So figures can give definite guidelines but there is an intuitive side as well which is important in deciding whether the effort was worth while.

An opinion poll would also provide an important clue as to the measure of overall success and would, especially now after a few years, be able to assess whether the locals really felt that it was worth the effort and the expenditure.

But the Spaniards have every reason to look back on 1992 as a remarkable year. It was the completion of the transition period of Spain's EC membership. Spain hosted the Olympic Games in Barcelona and the International Expo in Seville. It also coincided with the 500th anniversary of the discovery of America by Christopher Columbus.

To quote Miquel Abad: "People are only the anecdotes of history, only events really count, and they have to be seen in the context of the time".[35] Undoubtedly Barcelona will be seen by future generations as an important chapter in Olympic history.

Footnotes
1.   Hill 1996, p 182

2.   Hill 1996, p 183
3.   Usher July 1992, p 13
4.   De Moregas Spa et al 1995, p 184
5.   Hill 1996, p 188
6.   Simson and Jennings 1992, p 8
7.   Hill 1996, p 188
8.   Simson and Jennings 1992, p 347
9.   Hill 1996, p 189
10. Jennings 1996, p 128
11. Simson and Jennings 1992, p 322
12. Hill 1996, p 99
13. Miller 1992, p 231
14. Hill 1996, p 191
15. Simson and Jennings 1992, p 322
16. Miller 1992, p 231
17. Miller 1992, p 232
18. Hill 1996, pp 186, 187
19. Miller 1992, p 233
20. Hill 1992, p 228
21. Bosch Interview 28 May 1993
22. Newsletter of the City of Barcelona 1992:7, pp 6, 7
23. Botella Interview 14 July 1993, Barcelona
24. Rojas 1993
25. City of Barcelona Press Communique 1992 JG 0103A
26. City of Barcelona Press Communique 1992:0608A MDF
27. City of Barcelona Press Communique 1992:0103A JG
28. City of Barcelona Press Communique 1992:0201A JM
29. Press Dossier COOB '92 SA 24
30. City of Barcelona Press 1992:0405A AB
31. City of Barcelona Press 1992:0309A JMC
32. City of Barcelona Press 1992:0202A JH
33. Usher July 1992, pp 12, 13
35. Hill 1996, p 195

CHAPTER 9

ATLANTA 1996 -
THE SECOND BEST GAMES?

"These Olympics are going to be gigantic and the problems a nightmare. Can Atlanta for all its facilities, friendliness and foreplanning, pull off the Games?"[1]

In 1990 when Atlanta was chosen above Athens, Melbourne, Manchester, Toronto and Belgrade, the event was immediately labelled "the Coca-Cola Games" by the disappointed actress Melina Mercouri who expressed the Greeks' anger at losing out on the Centenary Games.[2] The 1996 Games were certainly unique in a number of aspects apart from the fact that it was 100 years since the first modern Olympic Games were hosted in Athens in 1896. These were to be the first Olympics where every nation on earth took part, thanks to Jimmy Carter who persuaded the North Koreans to be number 197.[3]

The opening ceremony of the largest Games ever entertained 3,5 billion viewers worldwide. The number of available entrance tickets to the 271 events came to a huge 11 million, which is almost three times the number offered by Barcelona and double Sydney's intended five and a half million entrance tickets.[4] No wonder the Atlanta organisers referred to the 1996 Games as the largest peacetime social event in human history! They had to contend with 2 million visitors after all, and had to house, feed and transport 15 500 athletes and officials for 16 days; that is apart from the rest of the Olympic family and VIP's. The Olympic Games staff numbered some 99 000 and consisted of 1 400 ACOG employees, 45 000 volunteers, 48 000 contractors and 4 600 temporary staff.[5] A record cumulative worldwide viewer audience of 19,6 billion watched the celebration of the XXVI Olympiad for at least a couple of minutes.[6]

Not that the organisers were reticent about the prospects beforehand. ACOG President and CEO William Payne confidently predicted "the most memorable Games ever". Marketers promised advertisers $6 for every $1 spent. The more timid amongst the would-be spectators were reassured that "Atlanta will be the safest place in the world this summer" during the Olympic Games.[7] And the IOC were assured that "Atlanta's Olympic Ring will be the scene of the most compact Games in history".[8] A substantial financial surplus was confidently predicted by the organisers which they intended to distribute to the international sports community.

The 1996 Games were after all due to be held in the United States of America, the only country with an economy so powerful that the government does not have to underwrite the finances of an Olympic Games. That the Americans are more than superficially aware of this would become only too apparent in the sixteen days from 20 July to 4 August. In fact, this all pervasive sense of self-importance irritated the visitors no end. It compelled columnist Tony Parsons to write in Britain's Daily Mirror that: "The self-obsessed hosts proved themselves incapable of recognising greatness unless it came with an American passport. Atlanta was awash with boorish crowds, bad losers and patriotism so cheap ...".[9] The Russians saw it only slightly differently: the daily paper Sevodnia reckoned: "We can't accuse the Americans of being inhospitable, it's simply that they are so full of themselves that they don't even notice their opponents".[10] It seemed to foreigners as though the Americans behaved accordingly and acted out the words of 1831 Liberator newspaper which arrogantly pronounced: "Our country is the world - our countrymen are mankind".[11]

The Security Set-up

Then things started to go awry: firstly security. In spite of a comprehensive security plan involving more than 40 regional and local law enforcement agencies, as well as the US Dept of Defence and support from the US Coast Guard, the Federal Drug Agency, the FBI and Interpol, the first warning signs appeared at the opening ceremony. Newsweek reported that "Security was capricious ..." four Newsweek photographers waltzed into the opening ceremonies, before the presidential presence itself, lugging their large ominous work bags without so much as a hi y'all!".[12] Indeed a gun-toting intruder without a ticket managed to sneak into the Olympic stadium, despite very tight security arrangements which meant it took the 83 000 spectators, some of whom paid over $600 for tickets, three hours to fill the stadium.

Then on day 9, Saturday 26 July, the first terrorist attack at the Olympics since the 1972 Games in Munich, occurred. A crude pipe bomb exploded inside Atlanta's Centennial Olympic Park area, killing two people and wounding about another 100.[13] If Atlanta was "a city too busy to hate", unfortunately there were individuals or groups who were not. The world at large reacted with horror and revulsion. The intensity of this reaction demonstrated once again how special the Olympic Games are to most people.

ACOG and the law enforcement agencies were responsible for securing the Olympic Games in Atlanta. ACOG security was responsible for providing a secure environment for the staging of the Games. Whilst law enforcement retained its traditional responsibilities for handling issues relating to general law and order, the absence of an overall joint command centre resulted in ineffective communication and a lack of co-ordination.[14]

The Joint Co-ordinating Centre: this was designed to be the place where all information concerning public safety came together, but it was not a command centre.[15]

The various law enforcement agencies maintained their individual command centres. The novel idea of using active and retired law enforcement or public safety officials from all over the world in its volunteer programme seemed a good one. They were called the Security Team Programme Volunteers or STP's. But again the general organisation was well below expectations - the reception and accreditation of these STP's were chaotic, accommodation was poor and the run down Morehouse College in which they stayed was in an unpleasant and dangerous neighbourhood. The STP's were assigned to specific venues or positions without taking individual skills or experience into account at all. Top police officers were to guard staircases and an Indian bomb disposal expert had to direct traffic! Small wonder that 300 of these experienced volunteers quit Atlanta halfway through the Games. Of the 33 volunteers from South Africa only one quit and the two most senior officers actually took the lead when things went wrong and ended up in much more responsible positions.[16]

The local ACOG volunteers actually fared worse. Most of them only worked so that they could watch the Games and were not keen to be assigned to security anyway. The result was that only about 62 % of them turned up for daily duty, and after the bomb explosion fewer than 30 % reported for duty.[17]

The Transport Mess

It is interesting to note that the name Atlanta comes from the Western and Atlantic railroad that ran from Atlanta to the coast.[18] Colin Bryden of the Johannesburg Sunday Times was very forthright at this stage: "Frustrations of transport seem limitless, security is tight to the point of the ridiculous ... some teams spend many hours in the accreditation process, there were not enough beds and in newly built facilities numerous cases of lights or plumbing that did not work".[19]

There were many comments of this kind. The Hong Kong Standard stated in an editorial: "... Atlanta which ought to have been a showcase for American know-how and efficiency has become instead a byword for American bungles, bloopers and botched opportunities".[20] The London Daily Telegraph described it as the "cock-up Games" instead of the "can do Olympics" it should have been. Kate Battersby of the London Evening Standard got the impression that the organisers were content to cover up the mistakes simply by smiling and saying; "Gee, we've never hosted the Olympics before. It'll all be fine by the time the Games are over" and just ignored the fact that it was supposed to be fine on the day the Games began.[21]

Richard Palmer, Secretary General of the British Olympic Association simply denounced the Atlanta Games as "being cheap and tasteless".[22] Prince Alexandre de Merode, the IOC member for Belgium was convinced that the organisation in Seoul and Barcelona had been significantly better.[23]

When an Austrian Judo Heavyweight, Eric Krieger, with suspected neck injuries had to wait almost an hour for an ambulance, because of battery problems, this shortcoming took on a new dimension.[24] In fact Rezzo Gallor, the Vice President of Hungary's NOC was convinced that he had never witnessed "such chaos" in the three decades that he had been attending the Games.[25]

But why all this chaos when so much was expected and promised beforehand, one might ask? Is it really just the fault of the organisers or are there problems inherent in the way the Olympic Movement is heading? Let's try and find out where the Olympic Games were supposed to fit into the city of Atlanta's bigger scheme of things.

The Successful Partnership

Atlanta's progress from an ordinary medium-sized city to a world-class destination started 22 years before the 1996 Games when the alliance between business and the black city government took shape. According to Dr Nash of Boston University, the key aspects of this "informal partnership between the city hall and the downtown business elite" consisted of, firstly, a "concern for image and a propensity for **grandiose hype** that pushed a vision of Atlanta as the world's next great metropolis!" Secondly, that a respect for **economic pragmatism** was required in order to get things done. Thirdly, a "**tightly knit network of business elites**" which could stimulate growth and also participate in the organising of business/community partnerships. Lastly, the existence of "**historically strong, segregated black higher educational institutions** which defied federal government attempts at desegregation and which produced Atlanta's elite group of black educators, religious leaders and business executives".[26]

Obviously Atlanta's urban and racial problems did not just disappear overnight. Sadly its murder rate is still the third highest in the US, but the progress was impressive and is illustrated by the fact that between 1985 and 1994 Atlanta attracted 1 561 new companies, 360 of which were international corporations. From 1988 to 1992, the metropolitan region's economic growth rate was nearly twice as high as in the rest of the USA. It was also the number one US city in terms of net employment growth in 1992, 1993 and 1994.

Atlanta possesses one of the technologically most advanced, fully integrated transportation systems in the world. Hartsfield International Airport handles over 2 000 flight operations per day and 51 million passengers pass through the 146 gates annually. Atlanta has become one of the three leading conference and exhibition centres in North America which on average attracts about 600 000 conference attendants per year. No wonder Fortune Magazine ranked Atlanta as the fourth "Best City in the World for Business".[27] It indeed seemed as though Atlanta was ready to turn its struggle into a dream and the Olympics was to be the crowning glory of its achievements and an important stepping stone to its ultimate goal of world-class city status.

According to Stephen Roulac, an international strategic advisor, Atlanta was poised to benefit particularly from investment in information and communication capabilities and was strategically positioned before the Games to emerge as a leading player in the frontier of worldwide communication technologies.[28]

It was over to IBM, the mighty International Business Machines Corporation with an annual budget larger than some of the nations participating, to take up the role of flagship in communication terms. Before the Games, IBM Chairman Louis Gerstner said: "We both have a lot on the line. It's a chance for your city and our company to show their very best on a world stage. I don't need to tell you there's an element of risk in stepping onto that stage". This proved to be sadly prophetic.

The harsh reality was that 12 international news agencies paid $10 000 each for the privilege of receiving the results instantaneously and ended up with such "beauties" as an athlete of 21 being described as 97 years old, a report of a French fencer beating the 400 m world record, one of a boxer being two feet tall, and another 21 feet high. Unfortunately athletes had to rely on this system to provide starting times and sadly some missed the events and were disqualified. It was not that IBM did not do their homework. They had observers at Barcelona and appointed a specialist team to prepare for Atlanta.

In the end, one has to conclude that they simply did not run enough simulated tests of a system that was to represent "the most ambitious exercise in integrated communications ever attempted by a computer system". What is even more worrying is the fact that this embarrassed company has won the contract to build a supercomputer to monitor America's nuclear arsenal: a fact to keep you awake at night![29]

Atlanta 1996 and Los Angeles 1984 - Different Eras, Strategies and Results

The fact that Atlanta is further from Los Angeles than Barcelona is from Moscow, is indicative of how vastly different these two Olympic Games were. Atlanta was the first US city to actually win the Games against competition from foreign cities. Los Angeles was handed the Games on a plate, both in 1932 when there was depression worldwide and in 1984 when no other city wanted it, following the huge losses incurred by Montreal in 1978 as well as the massive government investment required by Munich in 1972.[30]

Los Angeles had to contend with East/West tension, subsequent international boycotts and extreme scepticism from local citizens. The result of these tensions was that Los Angeles could not send representatives to study the hosting of the Moscow Games and the local voters managed to preclude any access to public city funds by the passing of a charter. In contrast, Atlanta's organising committee could revel in initial local euphoria and relative international harmony and stability. The 1992 Barcelona Games was attended and studied in detail by numerous Atlanta experts. The other obvious differences are that Los Angeles is situated on the West coast of America, whilst Atlanta is the first East coast city to have hosted the Olympic Games (if the farcical 1904 St Louis Games is discounted), that for Los Angeles it was the second time around after the 1932 Los Angeles Games, whilst Atlanta was very much a "Johnny come lately", because it had never even bid for the Olympics before.[31]

Before its Olympic escapades, Atlanta was mainly known for "Gone with the Wind" whilst Los Angeles was, even before 1984, a more mature city and better known internationally. The Olympic legacy of 1932 also gave Los Angeles a definite advantage in terms of existing sports infrastructure, just three new competition sites needing to be built, while 24 sites from the 1932 Games including the Olympic stadium simply needed refurbishing. Atlanta required $600 million for new sports facilities. Los Angeles' Games were spread over a vast area in order to utilise existing facilities. British journalist, David Miller described how he rented a car for flexibility and in two and a half weeks covered a distance of 2 400 km (1 500 miles) without ever leaving the Olympic circuit.[32]

Atlanta, on the other hand, was able to offer a much more compact Games: sixteen of the 25 sports could be held within the Olympic ring, a circle with a 2,5 km radius encircling the Olympic village. Atlanta also had the advantage of a rapid rail network with a peak capacity of 96 000 passengers per hour, serving more than 39 stations as well as the airport, which was only 16 km away.

Of course the scale of these two Olympic Games also differed: Atlanta sold more tickets than Los Angeles and Barcelona put together. Los Angeles' Olympic celebrations attracted half a million visitors, whilst Atlanta's organisers had to cope with the better part of two million enthusiasts.

In 1984 the security threats were somewhat more predictable: apart from the prevailing international tension between the superpowers, which incidentally contributed to a more patriotic and united USA, the organisers only had to contend with terror groups advocating independence for Puerto Rico. ACOG on the other hand had to take into account possible attacks from dozens of domestic right wing movements (like the Aryan Nations, The Unorganised Militia of the US and the White Aryan Resistance Movement), and international terrorist groups of every persuasion.[33] After Oklahoma City, Long Island and Atlanta, Americans realised that they were living, suddenly, in a Northern Ireland or an Israel. Even before the

1996 Games a poll of downtown Atlanta workers indicated that 71 % were concerned about terrorism.[34] These security contrasts between Los Angeles and Atlanta signify increased cultural and racial tensions inside the USA as well as the ever changing face of international terrorism.

Even the two reigning US Presidents treated these two Olympic Games differently. According to Peter Ueberroth, Los Angeles' Olympic supremo, President Ronald Reagan instinctively realised that he should not try to upstage the athletes during the 1984 Games. Subsequently, he refrained from attending any Olympic events apart from the opening ceremony. President Bill Clinton on the other hand could not resist hitching an Olympic ride in a big way. His wife and daughter flew to Greece for the lighting of the Olympic torch in April before the 1996 Games, his Vice President opened the new Olympic stadium and Atlanta scored $230 million in federal grants. President Clinton opened the Summer Games as well as the Paralympics for the disabled, he entertained the American competitors and tolerated the Olympic flame on the White House lawn for one night.[35]

It's clear that Los Angeles had to struggle for recognition until ironically the Soviet boycott stirred American patriotism. On the other hand Atlanta latched on to an Olympic movement in full swing after the triumphs of Seoul and Barcelona. In the case of Los Angeles the commercialism was seen and portrayed as inventive, entrepreneurial, and as an indivisible part of Los Angeles' overall managerial competence. Christopher Hill described it as "the origin of the 'private enterprise' Games, from which the Olympic movement drew so much of its inspiration for the Games' wholehearted commercialism under Samaranch." By the time Atlanta came round, the overt Olympic commercialism had become an offensive threat to Olympic values as perceived by the public at large. Reuters News Agency: "Every tale of transport hell and logistical confusion can be matched by another of naked greed and opportunism. If the Olympic spirit does still exist, it can only be a matter of time before it is bottled and sold alongside the official Games' cuddly toys and fridge magnets."[36]

Paradoxically, Los Angeles projected success overall in spite of serious traffic problems, almost intolerable smog, rampant drug-taking, strained race relations and threatening crime whilst Atlanta's apparent failures tended to overshadow significant achievements.

Conclusions

Why the mess? The overseas press could not resist using the ACOG acronym to express their frustrations by stating "Atlanta could not organise a garden party ...".[37]

Was it such a mess after all when one looks at the enormous scale of the whole organisation? There are many who feel, with good reason, that this event has simply grown too big for almost any city to handle. "There is a body of opinion that Atlanta simply drew the short straw in bidding for a global event which has grown too big for any one city to stage comfortably".[38]

The first crucial mistake that Atlanta made was simply to talk too big too soon. They certainly managed to oversell themselves and created unrealistic expectations of an "end all Games". This "grandiose hype" is probably part of the Southern culture, and it seems to be an integral part of Atlanta's growth strategies as defined by Dr Laura Nash.

The overseas media are convinced that the Games bring out the worst in the Americans. But it also has to be borne in mind that the Olympics are special to the Americans because their biggest sports (baseball, football and basketball) are domestic in orientation and almost shun foreign competition. The Americans are not part of a football World Cup or similar events in cricket or rugby. So the Olympics is where they really can prove themselves internationally.[39]

The second crucial setback was to make mistakes that directly affected members of the international press - the transport problems and information glitches made life very difficult for reporters and they of course had the power and means to convey very eloquently their frustrations to just about the whole world. There can be little doubt that ACOG tried too hard to emulate Los Angeles' successful low-cost strategies: for example a contingency fund of less than 1 % of the Games' budget severely limited the capacity to react quickly to unforeseen problems.

The Atlanta organisers were also much too dependent on volunteers who were often ill-informed and inexperienced. This severely hampered the standard of service and organisation. For example, ACOG press chief, Bob Brennan admitted that it was quite possible that some drivers on the transport network during the Games may never have been behind the wheel of a bus before.[40] Germany's Suddeutsche Zeitung summarised this aspect of the Games quite well: "Thousands of volunteers who are as friendly as they are clueless are baffled over what their job actually is".[41] The over-complex security plan involved too many unco-ordinated agencies, command centres and inexperienced local volunteers. In the report by the South African STP's the security was described as superficial: "It appeared that the Director of Security was given a mission to provide the appearance of a very secure event, but with greatly reduced costs." For instance, even the inexperienced volunteers were dressed up in serious looking uniforms.[42]

The IBM mess could not really be laid at the door of the Organising Committee and as such it was simply unforgivable for such a prestigious firm in their own backyard. At least now they had a proper trial run for Sydney in 2000.

Looking at the sheer size of the Atlanta event, it is clear that very few cities world-wide would have been able to cope any better. The Olympic Movement is simply too massive and the IOC would be prudent to realise it before the Olympic Games gets crushed by its own weight.[43] Sadly two more sports events have already been added for Sydney. Surely the Olympics should be about sports where the Olympic victory is seen as the pinnacle of achievement such as the 400 m or gymnastics where an Olympic medal is really the ultimate. Other sports such as tennis, where Wimbledon or the US Open reign as the supreme goals, or football where the World Cup is the major title, do not really belong in the Olympics. Surely the Olympic Games is a sports event of unequalled stature. Is this really the place for beach volleyball, tae kwon do and the like?[44] Apparently second hand gold medals for some of these lesser events were readily for sale in Atlanta.[45]

At least the spirit of the Olympic Games successfully survived the blatant commercialism in Atlanta. From an American point of view the celebration of Americannes at least acted as an antidote to the process of fragmentation and provides a common bond to a nation threatened by a multitude of cultures and values.[46] Surely Atlanta's greatest achievement was the way the Games rebounded after the terrorist attack and actually gelled into a very successful final week.[47]

Footnotes

1. Doust, April 1996, p 84
2. The Star 8 March 1996, p 15
3. Wulf 29 July 1997, p 54
4. Miller 5 May 1995, p 18
5. Nel 16 September 1996, p 2
6. Mc Mahon April/May 1997, p 5
7. The Star 5 August 1996, p 23
8. Doust April 1996, p 84
9. Parsons 6 August 1996, p 18
10. The Star 24 July 1996, p 23
11. The Sunday Independent 14 July 1996, p 17
12. Deford 29 July 1996, p 41
13. Newsweek 5 August 1996, p 15
14. Nel 1996, p 4
15. Nel 1996, p 9
16. Fabricius 10 August 1996, p 3
17. Groenewald 12 March 1997. Interview
18. Doust 1996, p 87
19. Bryden 1996, p 30
20. The Star 6 August 1996, p 18
21. Battersby 25 July 1996, p 12
22. The Star 14 November 1996, p 26

23. Die Beeld 5 Augustus 1996, p 19
24. The Daily Telegraph 23 July 1996, p 8
25. The Star 6 August 1996, p 18
26. Bernstein 26 February 1997, p 21
27. Bernstein 26 February 1997, p 21
28. Roulac 1993, p 11
29. Carlin 5 August 1996, p 10
30. Roulac 1993, p 12
31. Roulac 1993, pp 3, 4, 5
32. Miller 1992, p 107
33. Martz 10 July 1996, p 15
34. Martz 10 July 1996, p 15
35. Lexington 20 July 1996, p 52
36. The Star 25 July 1996, p 20
37. The Economist 3 August 1996, p 81
38. The Star 25 July 1996, p 20
39. Lexington 3 August 1996, p 52
40. The Star 31 July 1996, p 27
41. The Star (BR) 24 July 1996, p 3
42. Nel 16 September 1996, p 28
43. The Star 25 July 1996, p 20
44. Bryant 26 June 1996, p 16
45. The Star 5 August 1996, p 23
46. Lexington 3 August 1996, p 52
47. Smith and Springen 5 August 1996, p 19

CHAPTER 10

SYDNEY 2000 - CAN THEY "HACK" IT?

"Australia won tonight, that's the most important thing. It shows we can hack it in the big swim".[1]

Where do you find Ollie the kookaburra, Syd the platypus, Millie the echidna, Homebush Bay, Darling Harbour, Pyrmont, Rushcutter's Bay, Holsworthy and Parramatta? All connected to Sydney's 2000 Games of course. Ollie, Syd and Millie are the charming mascots and they make for an interesting and informative combination. Did you know that the platypus and echidna are mammals that lay eggs? That Ollie the kingfisher has a raucous call that sounds almost like human laughter. Homebush Bay is where the main Olympic action is going to be, in other words the Olympic Stadium, the Velodrome, Aquatic centre, the Olympic Village and the Main Press Centre which are all part of the Sydney Olympic Park. The Sydney Harbour Zone is where Darling Harbour (basketball, weightlifting, table tennis, boxing and judo) Rushcutters Bay (yachting) and Pyrmont (Media Village and International Broadcast Centre) are situated.[2] The 2000 "down under" Games is the first occasion since Melbourne in 1956 that the Olympics venture south of the equator. Each Olympic Games has its own character and ambience quite apart from any sporting achievements. Barcelona was as different from Atlanta as Seoul was from Moscow. Just imagine the vast and delightful contrasts between Tokyo's chopsticks Games in 1964 and Mexico City's tortilla Olympics four years later.

The fact that an Olympic host can imbue its Games with its own specific feeling and flavour is part of the marvellous Olympic heritage. Berlin in 1936 was vibrant with the grandiose pomposity and military precision of a powerful dictator with a limitless budget. Munich in 1972 also had the benefit of a large state-sponsored budget but by now the vibe was a friendly inviting one from a newly industrialised and innovative West Germany.

What will Sydney be like? The same unpretentious cordiality of a Melbourne? What will organisation be like? As near chaotic and blatantly commercial as Atlanta?

Let us first take a look at the unique aspects of these Games and interesting developments since Atlanta.

Inventions, Innovations, Interesting Facts and Unique Features

Australia and Greece are the only two nations to have competed in every Summer Games since 1896.[3] The Organising Committee claims that for the first time in modern Olympic history all the athletes will live in the one Olympic Village and will be able to walk to events. After all, the Australian bid became known in the international press as the one that intended to give the Games back to the athletes. Sydney's bid for 2000 was the third consecutive bid by an Australian city: Brisbane was in the running against Barcelona, Paris, Birmingham, Belgrade and Amsterdam. Then Melbourne competed against Atlanta. Another unique feature is that the Sydney 2000 organisers offered to pay round trip fares for all accredited athletes and officials in 2000, as well as round trip freight costs for sailing craft, horses, canoes, kayaks and rowing shells.[4]

Two new sports events, triathlon and tae kwon do will be part of an Olympic Games for the first time and it is possible that softball and beach volleyball might also be included in the programme for the Sydney Games. The IOC's Programme Commission is constantly reviewing existing and potential Olympic sports and can advise changes to the programme for 2000. If softball and beach volleyball are included, the number of sports events for 2000 will rise to 29.[5]

On the cycling front, the Sydney Games might be the first Games where new restrictions on the design of bicycles will be enforced to make sure that the cycling medals go to the ablest athlete and not the most ingenious designer. Plans are to limit the bicycles to the same size of wheels and basic design.[6]

On the accreditation side there is a "revolutionary plan" to avoid the accreditation disaster that occurred at Atlanta. Sydney might be able to accredit athletes and officials in their home countries in the month before the Games take place. This system will be applicable to athletes and officials from the European Union, the USA and Canada.

An innovative three tiered screening system is to be introduced at all Australian international airports. The upside of this new Advance Passenger Clearance scheme (APC) is to cut waiting times for passengers by doing the customs and excise computer checks while they are still in the air. The details are supplied by the authorities when they check in overseas. Australia is currently receiving about three million visitors per year and the expectations are for about 6,9 million by the year 2000.[7]

If Lyall Munro, the NSW Aboriginal Legal Service former chairman has his way, another unique feature to the Sydney Games will be an Aboriginal tent embassy in view of Sydney's Olympic Stadium. The idea would be to attract worldwide attention to the plight of these native Australians.[8]

The choice of Sydney's mascot for 2000 was quite a difficult one since Australia is blessed with an abundance of wildlife. Suggestions for a mascot ranged from the frill necked lizard to the echidna, the goanna, cockatoo, platypus, kookaburra, dingo and the rather obvious and well-known koala and kangaroo. Luckily the choice fell on the kookaburra bird, the shy platypus and the strange echidna. Three relatively unknown creatures will be introduced to the world stage and renew the public's focus on the marvellous heritage of wildlife worldwide and consequently also on the fact that there is a great deal to lose if some of these species become extinct.

It is the first time that a Summer Olympics will feature more than one mascot and one of them a female to boot: Millie the echidna, after Millennium, Syd the platypus after guess-which-city, and Ollie the kookaburra after a certain four yearly sports event of some importance.

The announcement of these mascots has already given the Wilderness Society the opportunity to draw the public's attention to the plight of Australian wildlife: "Australia has the highest rate of mammal species extinction in the world" said society spokesman Kevin Palmer. "Hundreds of plants and animals unique to the continent are on the brink of extinction".[9]

The three certainly make for a weird and wonderful blend, since the platypus lives in remote freshwater streams and features a bill and webbed feet like a duck, but a furry body and flat tail like a beaver. When settlers originally sent a platypus carcass back to Europe some two hundred years ago, many scientists considered it a hoax, a fictitious creature stitched together from different spare body parts. The echidna has spiky quills like a porcupine and burrows in the ground. The extrovert kookaburra is the largest of all kingfishers.[10] The only problem is that an internationally renowned mammal expert, Dr Peggy Rismiller described the depiction of Millie the echidna and Syd the platypus as "worryingly inaccurate in the fingers and toes".[11] It is definitely not a case of just picking the cuddliest animal available as Penny Baker, group manager for consumer products at the SOCOG explained: "Mascots have to satisfy the world's expectations of what Australia is without incurring the wrath of the people who live here. To work, a mascot needs to have a personality which can be animated and taken into a three dimensional image".[12]

Of course the selection of a mascot is a serious business these days as The Australian explained: "Regrettable as it may be in the minds of purists the staging of the modern Olympic Games is as much about marketing as sporting prowess, and hence the choice of mascot is an important business consideration". The Winter Games first departed from the single mascot in 1988 with Hidy and Howdy, two polar bears that served as mascots for the Calgary Winter Games. They were followed by Hakon and Kristin, two Viking children for Lillehammer in 1994 and in 1998 Nagano will feature two owls as its mascot.[13]

Of Sydney's outstanding features right from the beginning of its bid, was the commitment to the environment, to a "Green Games". Rod McGeogh, the leader of the successful bidding campaign and one of the directors on SOCOG's Board motivated this aspect: "As the 2000 Games are the first major event of the next century, it is fitting that the Olympic Movement leads the push to protect the environment".[14] That the Aussies are serious about this is already apparent in the design of the Olympic Village. The features make up an impressive list of pointers for future Games and indeed urban planning: Features include improved energy efficiency, passive solar design and solar street lighting. Recyclable and recycled building materials will be used wherever possible, avoidance of materials that are toxic in production, recycling of waste for garden irrigation and maximised public transport opportunities.

The Bid Company's Environment Committee developed the guidelines for this important aspect and just about anybody with a tinge of green was represented on the committee. This included independent environmental organisations like Green Peace Australia, Ark Australia, Clean-up Australia, the Australian Centre for Environmental Law, and also government authorities and the business sector. The guidelines cover five major areas: global warming, ozone depletion, biodiversity (living species), pollution (air, soil and water) and resource depletion. These guidelines are available to any city undertaking major residential, sporting or cultural projects, according to the OCOG.[15]

The water reclamation scheme for the Homebush Olympic site is an extensive multimillion dollar project that will be awarded to a private concern by the New South Wales Government. The use of reclaimed water for toilet flushing and irrigation should substantially diminish the need for fresh water in the Homebush development area. According to a water treatment specialist representing a company that might be in the competition, there is so much infrastructural development in the South East Asian region that according to the Sydney Business "the Sydney Olympics are a perfect chance to say to the developing countries that reclamation systems are the future".[16]

The Harsh Realities of the Costly Environment and the Precious Bottom Line

President of the IOC, Juan Antonio Samaranch is quoted as saying "The Olympic Games in 2000 were awarded to Sydney partly because of the consideration they gave to environmental matters". And the world was keen to learn about how Homebush Bay was being transformed from a neglected landfill site described as "the most polluted place in Australia" ten years ago, to quite a pleasant place with a rural feeling to it, teeming with birds and wildlife. The organisers were proud to point out that when one of the last remaining colonies of the green and golden bellfrog was discovered in an area that was destined to become part of the

Olympic tennis courts, the courts were simply moved. The frogs now have access to their own highways underneath the roads that would otherwise have been between them and their favourite breeding grounds and wetlands.

Greener than Thou

But now the locally based Games' environmental watchdog reckons that the organisers' green is not quite the shade they had in mind. The OCOG received its first environmental report card on the construction activities at Homebush Bay and five out of a possible ten is certainly not in keeping with the expectations of a "Green Games". The Green Games Watch 2000 (GGW) rated pollution control in terms of air and water quality as well as the control of waste, as poor. GGW chairman Jeff Angel stated: "This audit certainly displays to us that the government has reached an environmental slump, a slump in its environmental credibility, and certainly there is a major warning in this audit for the government to lift its game". Peggy Jones, the GGW convenor added that design codes and compliance plans agreed on in 1995 need to be effected on Olympic developments. She also warned that the promises made by the organisers in terms of protection of the rare green and gold bellfrogs were not being kept.

The Olympics Minister Michael Knight's response was that the NSW government disputed some of the assessments and that he believed that the guidelines were being adhered to. The Olympic Co-ordination Authority Director General David Richmonds also felt that the organisers were on the right track since they received a positive rating by the GGW in 49 out of 59 provisions of the environmental guidelines.[17]

Costing the Bottom Line

While Michael Knights predicted a neat $38,75 million profit, the opposition leader Peter Collins claimed that the Auditor General had discovered that the Olympic budget had escalated from $1,55 billion to $3,87 billion.[18] Indeed the NSW Auditor General Tony Harris warned the state government that it is facing a financial time bomb if it continues to link major building projects to the Olympics. Apparently the government tried to label a $31 million overhaul of roads as part of the Olympic development. Harris said that if it is the case, the project should also be reflected as part of the Olympic costs. It seems the government is using an "Olympic excuse" to get projects approved in double quick time without necessarily adding it to the budget.[19]

This is the complete opposite of the policy of the original bidding committee, which tried its hardest to disconnect as many projects as possible from the Games. In Rod McGeoch The Bid it is stated: "Let's take out of the budget the cost of the permanent facilities that Sydney's going to have for the next 100 years and leave only the cost of converting existing facilities at Homebush Bay. That's what the Olympic Games budget ought to bear. We all agreed. If you have a facility like Darling Harbour, you don't expect to pay for it in one year. You have to look at it in the context of its useful life. Any company looking at investing in a fixed asset, always assesses the cost over its useful life. Berlin was planning to use the stadium which was used for the 1936 Olympics in its proposals for the 2 000 Games. So we drew up a smaller budget for the organising committee of the Games and it was that which was included in the Bid Books".[20] No wonder the budget is ballooning.

As early as May 1995, Michael Knight accused his predecessors of underestimating costs.[21] There are already signs of an effort to cut back on the capital expenditure side: the original plans for two media villages of permanent housing have been abandoned and the SOCOG is now considering the extensive use of temporary housing similar to plans for the athletes' village.[22] A year later Knight had to admit that costs had risen by another $300 million.[23]

The $515 million Olympic Stadium is a private sector effort and the contracted firm Stadium Australia believed it devised a novel way of obtaining finance when its platinum and gold packages were to be sold to the public in advance. The 600 platinum packages were going for $26 400 each for which the buyer received prime seats in the Olympic Stadium plus an impressive list of perks for 30 years. The 34 400 gold packages were available at $7 750 each which also included two lesser Olympic tickets for all prime events, plus the two seats for all stadium events for 30 years. The idea was to get buyers to snap up these packages and then if they so wished sell the package devoid of the Olympic tickets on the stock exchange (an equity investment plus stadium club membership made up the rest of the package). The floating turned out a $178 million flop with the gold packages especially failing to maintain their value, or in more formal language, an underwriting disaster to the tune of $178 million which indicates the shortfall on capital raising.

This was a serious setback and especially disappointing after the initial response of a flood of enquiries. Weaknesses were subsequently identified and it turned out, firstly, that the prospectus was "boring, legalistic and unsuitable for the product". The second problem was that the timing was out - the issuing should have coincided with the Atlanta Games; instead it only materialised before Christmas, a bad time for any new product of this nature. Thirdly there were no details of the long-term sport that was to take place at the stadium simply because of the failure of the organisation to tie up a single sport. Stadium Australia could not tell prospective buyers if they would have access to Australian rules, rugby league, rugby union or soccer or any combination of these sports.[24]

The Inevitable Power Struggles

On 28 March 1997 Dr Mal Hemmerling, the Chief Executive of OCOG resigned. He was the third casualty of this nature in 14 months. The first Executive President was Gary Pemberton, a highly regarded businessman; he was Quantas' chairman, after all. Pemberton left in March 1996, replaced by John Iliffe, chairman of the huge retailing concern Woolworths. He in turn resigned only six months later to be replaced by Minister Michael Knight, ostensibly as a reaction to the Atlanta debacle where, according to Knight, "there was a lack of closeness between private enterprise and government at Atlanta and ... difficulties flowed from that". According to the Sydney Morning Herald, the SOCOG was set up initially as "an independent body, free of government shackles".

After Hemmerling's departure and Sandy Hollway's appointment as CEO (Hollway, a former diplomat and advisor to former Prime Minister, Paul Keating), Olympics Minister and Executive President, Michael Knight and John Coates, president of the Australian Olympic Committee, as well as Graham Richardson, a former federal Labour senator in the Hawk and Keating governments, seem to have seized almost total control of the Sydney Games. Initially Coates had a deal with the NSW government for all profits to go to the AOC, apart from the 10 % which is always earmarked for the IOC. Coates also had veto rights over SOCOG decisions. Knight at that stage felt the situation untenable. A deal was brokered between Coates and Knight by mutual friend, Graham Richardson, whereby the AOC was guaranteed $77,5 million from the Sydney Games (courtesy of NSW tax-payers if the Games show no profit) and Coates' veto was narrowed down to matters of sport.[25]

For an outsider, it's not easy to discern the implications of such complex power struggles. The best way is simply to reflect the different opinions as published in the Australian media:

• Sydney's Sun Herald newspaper made the biggest issue a monetary one with its heading "When the A$500 000 a year executive asked his A$135 000 a year boss for a big pay rise, it began his downfall". The report acknowledged that Hemmerling had performed "brilliantly in selling rights and finding sponsors". But it stated that Michael Knight was concerned about the slow pace of selection of key personnel and its handling of core operational issues such as transport, accommodation and sports venues.[26]
• The Sydney Daily Telegraph reflected the opinion of one of the staff: "We have record TV rights, the marketing is on track and the Olympics are on time and on bloody budget. What more does the chief executive have to do?"[27]
• The Courier Mail from Brisbane was of the opinion that the writing was already on the wall in 1996: "The SOCOG board leaks like a sieve: Several members were

actively briefing journalists that Knight wanted Hemmerling out of the job and wanted his own man - for that, read Richardson's - in the job".[28]

• The Sydney Morning Herald emphasised that the Knight/Coates relationship is the dominant force in Olympic politics. "The two fell out a year back over power. Coates the person most responsible for winning Sydney the Games, had obtained a diamond studded agreement from the Fahey government that he still blushes about".[29]

• The Canberra Times discerns an electioneering plot in all these machiavellian moves: "The latest upheaval also comes amid claims that the NSW government is attempting to stack the SOCOG board with political mates, that SOCOG is being used to help re-elect Labour in 1999 as well as organise the Olympics".[30]

• The Sun Herald's prediction about the likely outcome: "It is a high risk business. Winning the Olympic Bid did not secure a second term for John Fahey. Will the electorate be any kinder to Premier Carr?"[31]

Areas of Agreement

There seems to be general agreement in these various newspapers on a few cardinal issues: firstly that the original intention was for SOCOG to be an independent organisation; secondly that there were power struggles from the beginning and that the Knight/Hollway/Richardson labour combination in alliance with Coates of the Australian Olympic Committee have taken over total control of the SOCOG. They are all agreed that the staff at the SOCOG's headquarters were extremely loyal to Hemmerling and were impressed with his abilities. There is certainly no doubt that Knight is very ambitious in a personal sense: the Courier Mail of Brisbane expressed the aspect when it quoted "one SOCOG insider": "Knight can't help himself. He's a media junkie, loves to see his face on television and (is) determined to take all the credit that's going". The Courier concluded, "And in the run-up to the Sydney Olympics, there is a lot of credit to be taken".[32]

The upside of all this is that the damaging power struggles should be over and the homogeneous group can get on with the enormous task of organising the 2000 Games. With the local Labour Movement family in control, co-ordination and co-operation between the four crucial organisations - the State Government, SOCOG, the Olympic Co-ordination Authority and the Olympic Roads and Transport Authority - should be enhanced.

On the downside, losing business figures such as Pemberton, Iliffe and Hemmerling means tremendous experience and skills are simply thrown away in crucial areas such as marketing and cost containment. If one looks at the Stadium, Australia's setback and the overall increase in the construction budget, these are skills that SOCOG certainly need. Why could the dynamic Hemmerling, for example, not have been retained in a marketing capacity where he is obviously skilled and experienced? The fact that three executives from three prominent business concerns: Quantas, the Australian Airline, Woolworths the retailing giant, and Hemmerling's Grand Prix Australia, were pushed to resign, does not augur well for relations between SOCOG and big business in general.

Apart from anything else, just imagine what SOCOG had to pay in golden hand-shakes. In Hemmerling's case alone it amounted to $420 000. The Australian public at large also cannot be very impressed with these barely concealed power games and the subsequent image of instability created by it. After all, people just want to see a successful Olympics and if there is a major mess-up the NSW tax-payers in particular are going to be hard hit.

IOC Reaction

A few weeks before Hemmerling's resignation, Jacques Rogge, the IOC Co-ordination Commissioner for the Sydney Olympics, was quoted by Reuters as saying: "We plead for stability now in all aspects of the Olympic Games ... I don't think SOCOG can afford too many changes in key positions now".[33] When the IOC was confronted with a fait accompli there was not much it could do. The IOC's Director General, Francois Carrard, was reported in The Sydney Morning Herald as saying: "From a preparation and operation standpoint for the Games we do not think that, in spite of his qualities, his departure is a major concern for us for the success of the Games".[34]

Lessons from Atlanta and Pointers for 2004

Scale of events: in the original Bid Books 5,6 million entrance tickets were con-templated for the various events and the Olympic Stadium was planned to accom-modate 80 000 spectators; by 1997 the number of tickets has increased to 8,8 mil-lion and the capacity of the $515 million Olympic Stadium to 110 000. Atlanta sold about 8,5 million tickets from the 11 million available and its Olympic Stadium was smaller at 85 000 seats. Will Sydney, with fewer hotel rooms, be able to cope with the expected masses - provided they manage to sell enough tickets? Sydney is obviously not part of densely populated North America or Europe.

As far as the IBM's Atlanta debacle is concerned, the Sydney organisers have made provisions for nine months of simulations before the start of the Games. On the security front there will be one police force under one commander with an easier task than their Atlanta counterparts because of a much lower prevailing crime rate and no history of local terrorism.

Finances

In the bid, Rod McGeoch described how conservative the bidding committee was in terms of expected income in comparison to the other contenders: for example

Sydney budgeted for $297 million from international and local sponsorships, whilst Berlin was looking at $455 million, Manchester at $478 million and Beijing at $630 million! Perhaps they deliberately followed Ueberroth's strategy for Los Angeles when he said in 1984: "We made a conscious decision to underestimate projected revenues as this was our only protection against unknown cost factors ...".[35] This policy certainly paid dividends for on 30 March 1997 the Sun Herald quoted confidential figures that demonstrated an increase of $500 million in income from original estimates as a result of greater than expected revenue for TV rights and marketing deals. This was good news for Sydney and it added a lot of value to Knight's deal with Coates, which in effect meant that instead of 90 % of profits going to the AOC, the NSW government would inherit all the profits after the AOC $84 million is paid.[36]

But will it be sufficient to cover all the unexpected cost increases, especially on the construction front? In the Australian Financial Review, for example, it is reported that the construction programme at Homebush Bay alone is in the order of $2,5 billion. In June 1997 it was reported that the NSW state government was planning to introduce an Olympic bed tax from September to contribute to the massive infrastructure costs in preparing for the Games. This led various sponsors to threaten to withdraw about $250 million in sponsorship. The whole row was about the fact that the Olympic organisers have managed to secure only one third of the 25 000 hotel rooms they need in central Sydney.[37]

Strategic Contrasts with Atlanta

Instead of constantly trying to impress the world, as Atlanta did - they intended hosting "the best Games ever" - the Australians settled for saying: "What we are planning would be wonderful for the whole Olympic Movement". Payne's bidding effort for Atlanta had no official backing from local authorities; indeed he was shunned by the establishment until of course the Games were awarded to Atlanta. By contrast the NSW Government and the Sydney City Council were involved in Sydney's bid from the beginning, much the same as Barcelona where the city authorities actually led the bid.

In fact, there are many similarities between Sydney and Barcelona - both beautiful harbour cities blessed with unusual architectural designs. The bids in both cases involved the rejuvenation of neglected areas: in Barcelona's case of a derelict industrial area near the sea, and in Sydney's case of a polluted disused landfill site. In both cases the taxpayer has to bear the brunt in case of financial losses. But in Barcelona there was a deliberate and strategically planned redevelopment of parts of the city, whilst in the case of Sydney the taxpayers might still be in the innocent stage where they hope that they will not need to contribute. However, the signs on the costs side are ominous. Barcelona's expenses ended approximately 40 % higher than anticipated and Sydney will inevitably have to face much higher costs.

What Will the Games be Like?

Sydney has so much going for it: scenic beauty, distinctive architectural designs, a vigorously healthy economy, excellent infrastructure, a strong sports culture, an extensive range of sports facilities to start with, and last but by no means least, a population with a strong desire to prove that they can be among the best. One can only guess of course, but no one should be surprised if it's a totally marvellous occasion. The potential for a new-world Barcelona is certainly there, with added exuberance and vitality instead of Barcelona's old-world charm. If only the bureaucrats don't make a hash of it!

Footnotes

1.   The Observer 24 September 1993, p 21
2.   SOCOG (Sydney Organising Committee for the Olympic Games) Fact sheet 1995, p 2
3.   SOCOG Fact sheet 1995, p 1
4.   SOCOG Fact sheet 1995, p 15
5.   SOCOG Fact sheet 1995, p 2
6.   Jefferey 16 April 1997. (In Comité International Olympique N72), p 7
7.   Mc Kenzie 28 January 1997. (In CIO N17) p 15
8.   Dasey 26 January 1997. (In CIO N17), p 11
9.   Spencer 24 January 1997. (In CIO N15), p 47
10. Spencer 24 January 1997. (In CIO N15), p 47
11. Innes 28 January 1997. (In CIO N17), p 9
12. Moore 22 January 1997. (In CIO N13), p 3
13. The West Australian 22 January 1997. (In CIO N13), p 4
14. Sydney Olympics 2000 Bid Ltd 1993, p 6
15. SOCOG Fact sheet (Environment) 1995, p 7
16. Pavlovic 14 April 1997. (In CIO N72), p 10
17. The Citizen 29 May 1997, p 30
18. The Daily Telegraph, Sydney, 18 April 1997. (In CIO N74), p 8
19. Chulov 30 March 1997. (In CIO N61), p 12
20. McGeoch 1994, p 187
21. Galvin 26 May 1995 , p 8
22. Moore 28 January 1997. (In CIO N17), p 13
23. The Star 24 May 1996, p 18
24. Moore and Korporaal 29 March 1997. (In CIO N61), p 27
25. Moore 29 March 1997, pp 19, 22
26. Mitchell 30 March 1997. (In CIO N61), p 4
27. Porter and Mc Dougall 27 March 1997. (In CIO N61), p 6

28. Charlton 29 March 1997. (In CIO N61), p 7
29. Moore 29 March 1997. (In CIO N61), p 8
30. The Canberra Times 28 March 1997. (In CIO N61), p 10
31. Mitchell 30 March 1997. (In CIO N61), p 5
32. Charlton 29 March 1997. (In CIO N61), p 7
33. Galvin 27 March 1997. (In CIO N61), p 76
34. The Sydney Morning Herald 28 March 1997, p 11
35. McGeoch 1994, p 189
36. Dasey 30 March 1997. (In CIO N61), p 12
37. The Citizen 17 June 1997, p 15

CHAPTER 11

CAPE TOWN 2004 -
THE AFRICAN DILEMMA

The greater the absence of meaning in the life of the individual, the more violent and disordered his life becomes.

Laurens van der Post

Africa - the Have-not Continent

In Olympic terms the absence of an African Games is the missing link. On the sporting side, the Africans are winning more and more medals - altogether 31 at Atlanta (10 gold, 9 silver and 12 bronze). But on the organisational side, no African city had ever put in a bid for an Olympic Games, whereas the first South American bid came from Buenos Aires as early as 1936.

To try and grasp why Africa has lagged behind the rest of the world and what to expect in the immediate future, consider some qualified international opinions: in 1993 The Economist carried a comprehensive report on sub-Saharan Africa which conveyed a sombre message: "To grasp the scale of Africa's poverty, consider this statistic: the combined GNP of the entire continent south of the Sahara is less than that of Holland." The Economist report continued by quoting a World Bank report predicting that "... sub- Saharan Africa is the only region in the world likely to experience an increase in absolute poverty over the next decade".[1]

The Third World Finance Survey gave a variety of reasons for Africa's economic predicament: "The reluctance of the private sector to invest in Africa is understandable. Much of the region suffers from bad (though improving) government, pitifully inadequate infrastructure, an under-educated and often under-nourished labour force, and a burden of debt that, despite the restructuring of recent years, remains insupportable". The ominous consequences of these debilitating weaknesses were eloquently depicted: "When an economy in the third world fails to grow as fast as it might, the harm is much greater than in a rich country. Even where the shortfall between actual and potential output is not literally a matter of life and death (as it often is), the result is poverty of a breadth and depth that the industrial world has long since forgotten". Figures were supplied via a graph that demonstrated that the annual average growth of GNP per person for the whole sub-Saharan Africa for the 11-year period 1980 to 1991 was in the region of -1,6 % in contrast to the East Asian and Pacific group which registered a 6 % growth over the same period.[2]

Closer to the world of sport but still staying with Africa, David Miller wrote in 1992 in The Olympic Biography of Juan Antonio Samaranch: "You hear it said that

Africa is a lost cause. In Nairobi in 1987 such cynicism was energetically dismissed. The opening ceremony of the fourth All-Africa Games, and the ten days of events that followed were a heartening festival of pride and opportunism. They proved that black Africa is able to stage major public events with some style". Then he describes how the Kenyan Organising Committee might have lived close to chaos up to the last minute and how the Games had "been postponed three times whilst awaiting the completion of another gift of China". "The worst African problem," Miller went on, "any European resident there will tell you, is corruption. Consignments of toilet paper to tanks, simply go missing. A dozen Mercedes-Benz limousines, the manufacturer's gift to the Games, were still untraced in Nairobi a year later. In the long term Africa has a bright future, if and when it can fully get its act together and if it is not betrayed by those current leaders who claim to be rescuing it. To achieve this, Africans need progress, self-discipline and diplomacy, none of which regularly comes easily to many of them".[3]

Why has Africa always been in such an economic mess? It is beyond the scope of this book to try and analyse likely causes in depth, but it is nevertheless interesting to look at a few varied opinions on certain aspects that contributed to this parlous state of affairs. Peter Drucker, for 20 years Professor of Management at the Graduate Business School of New York University and author of many international bestsellers on management, in his book New Realities, lays the blame squarely at the door of socialist planning; "Fashioned primarily in England during the thirties and forties at the London School of Economics, it has been the main cause of the catastrophic decline in production and productivity in the former British colonies in Africa. They were major food exporters before; all of them now have huge deficits in agricultural trade and would starve without food imports".[4]

Africa's failure in terms of food production is illustrated by the fact that since 1960 the production per person has decreased by 11,6 % whilst the food production for Latin America for the same period, 1961 to 1995 grew by 31,4 % per person, and Asia's increased by an impressive 70,6 % per person.[5]

Paul Johnson, well known British historian, blamed the policies adopted by the colonial powers in his book A History of the Modern World: "The biggest mistake by the colonial powers ... and it had political and moral, as well as economic consequences - was to refuse to allow the market system to operate in land. Here they followed the procedures first worked out in the British colonies in the seventeenth century, elaborated to develop the American Midwest and West (to the destruction of the indigenous Indians) and refined, on a purely racial basis, in South Africa. It involved human engineering, and was therefore destructive of the individualistic principle which lies at the heart of the Judaeo-Christian ethic"[6] (human engineering comes down to shovelling people around like concrete, Johnson explains elsewhere).

But there is at least a ray of hope on the horizon. The Economist, 14 June 1997, found enough evidence of an economic revival in Southern Africa to publish "An African Success Story" in which it describes the "turnaround in economic think-ing" which is characterised by the now prevalent concepts of: "luring in the foreign investor" (World Economic Forum in Harare), "ambitious privatisation schemes" (Mozambique and Zambia), "more prudent economic management" and in the case of South Africa, "new financial conservatism". The article describes the 6 % growth rate achieved by this region in 1996 as "a rate more often associated with Asia than sluggish Africa".[7]

Weaknesses that remain are the fact that Africa "still depends heavily on selling what it can dig out of the ground or pluck from the trees", Southern Africa's growth prospects remaining shackled, not least by the region's relatively small market and the fact that the region has not yet managed to form an integrated market. The dominance of South Africa's economy is also emphasised by the fact that this country's GDP accounts for four-fifths of the region's GDP.[8] The Economist "The World in 1997" discerned another negative aspect: "Africa's eco-nomic life will improve in 1997, but its political life, alas, will shift a notch further to authoritarianism. The gap will grow in 1997 between Africa's richer and poor-er and sometimes collapsing nations".[9]

South Africa's importance to Southern Africa and indeed the whole of sub-Saharan Africa can be demonstrated clearly by comparing South Africa's GDP of $136 billion with that of Nigeria which is only $32,9 billion. In terms of population Nigeria is the African giant with over 105 million inhabitants, South Africa with a population of approximately 40 million is relatively affluent if one looks at the average number of cars and telephones per member of the population, which is at least five times higher than that of other leading African economies.

Zimbabwe, whose economy is growing well at 6 % per year can only manage an average production of $690 per head per year compared with South Africa's fig-ure of $3 130 and oil rich Nigeria is lagging behind with a pitiful $310 per head per year, according to Economist Intelligence Unit as published in The World in 1997.[10] Peter Hawthorne, of Time Magazine, in an article captioned "From Pariah to Powerhouse" supplied South Africa's trade figures with the rest of Africa, which jumped from $926 million in 1987 to $3,65 billion in 1995.[11]

In Olympic financial terms, the African continent hardly features. The combined television rights income from Africa for the 1992 and 1996 Olympic Games was just over $13 million, of which South Africa contributed $12,75 million compared to the $64 million income from the Australian continent for the same Games.[12] So, clearly South Africa is important in every socio-economic sense to the rest of Africa and to Southern Africa in particular. It is thus no wonder that Africa's first

Olympic bid was from a South African city. But this bid symbolised much more than a mere sports event, albeit one of unequalled excellence.

The First African Games

The first African Olympic Games is bound to be a special and unique occasion for the world in general and Africa in particular, but the success and the outcome of such an occurrence would be even more critical than usual. Firstly the symbolism for Africans attached to an original African Games would be one of displaying their real independence from the rest - in a sense, a coming of age - and their being able to compete with the world's best, as African athletes have proven themselves of being quite capable. In the second place the possible socio-economic implications are simply much more drastic in a less developed society. There has been so much gut wrenching hardship in Africa over centuries, which is still a reality as we approach the 21st century. For example, in May 1997 the UN Food and Agricultural Organisation warned that many people were dying of starvation and disease in sub-Saharan Africa while tens of thousands were severely malnourished. The criticism of unnecessary spending, or of perceived expensive white elephant sports infrastructure is bound to be more severe.

Make no mistake; the first African Games can count on the world's goodwill and best wishes but it would also be under a very large magnifying glass as far as transparency by the organising committee, promises of job creation and the likely resultant burden on taxpayers are concerned. The modern Olympic Games viewed simply in an operational context is a huge, complex and extremely costly undertaking. And the smaller the economy and lower the productivity, the more drastic the potential positive or negative impact.

The per capita income is indicative of the relative productivity of an economy and according to Pareto's law the more productive the economy, the less the inequality of incomes. This of course means that less productive economies have a greater distribution of incomes leaving more people vulnerable to the outcome of large socio-economic decisions such as an Olympic Games. The overall size of an economy is a rough indication of how large the tax base is, for ultimately the host government (taxpayer) has to foot the bill.

As a practical example one can compare the relative impact of the developmental efforts by Barcelona and those proposed by Cape Town. Chris Ball, the Cape Town 2004 leader, in the September 1995 issue of Project Pro declared: "The Spanish government decided to rebuild the city of Barcelona and they dropped the Olympic Games into the equation, using the Olympics as an excuse for the rebuild. We, on the other hand, are not planning to rebuild Cape Town".[13]

Well, when looking at the comparative size of the Spanish and South African economies, it is clear that Cape Town's capital budget of $2 billion is placing the same burden on the South African economy and taxpayer as the $8 billion undertaking by the Spanish with a GDP almost five times larger both in absolute and in per capita terms (GDP - SA $136 billion, Spain $611 billion; GDP per capita - South Africa $3 130, Spain $15 522). Even if one takes into account the cost of staging the 1992 Games and the resultant direct visitor spending, the $10 billion Spanish Games is still directly comparable to a $2 billion South African Games in an economic sense. (As we shall see in the next chapter there is every likelihood that a Cape Town Games would be much more costly).

And it is in an economic sense that South Africa is having to face up to international reality after the remarkably peaceful transition to a democracy. Christopher Ogden of the American Time Magazine illustrated the extent of the challenge: "The most pressing reality is sheer economic survival. South Africa is battling with 40 % unemployment, suffers a budget deficit amounting to 5 % of its $118 billion gross domestic product, and must compete for business in the international marketplace with the likes of Brazil, Chile, Indonesia and South Korea, where economies are growing at warp speed. Four decades of international disinvestment, coupled with political and economic mismanagement by the pro-apartheid National Party, has left South Africa ill-prepared for the challenge".[14]

The British Economist just a month later (Oct '96) under the heading, "How Wrong is it Going?" emphasised the fact that South Africa's post-apartheid self-confidence has crumbled because of "three new anxieties: lawlessness, unemployment and political accountability".[15] The effect of crime and the resulting fear is also emphasised in The Economist's "The World in 1997", where it states: "But more important is the need to cut crime - killing, burglary, violence and fear must be reduced, otherwise all the effort of the past few years will be blown away".[16]

Crime, Grime and Sleaze

When South Africa became the "New South Africa" in 1994 and entered the world arena and an era of unlimited opportunity, it was unfortunately not just those with honest intentions that jumped aboard the golden opportunities bandwagon. The Economist compared the situation with that of Russia: "As in Russia, the collapse of the authoritarian state in South Africa has unleashed social and political freedoms - and with them controversy and criminality. The reasons are the same: the end of the old order dramatically increased the number of new commercial opportunities, but did so at a time when the criminal-justice system (designed for the old regime) had changed comparatively little. Organised crime has filled the "resulting gap".[17] The report quotes a Nedcor study which exposed serious weaknesses in the criminal justice system that resulted in just 36 imprisonments from 100 prosecutions for 450 crimes reported! The symptoms of this ineffectual criminal justice system are also listed: poorly paid policemen who accept bribes to drop charges; excessive bureaucracy; public mistrust; ineffective prosecutions; loose conditions for bail; and overcrowded prisons.[18]

It is no wonder the Western Cape's murder rate is a shocking 85,5 per 100 000 of the population in comparison to its 2004 competitors where the IOC report states Sweden's (Stockholm) equivalent figure as 2, Athens' as 2,14 and Buenos Aires' figure as 3 homicides per 100 000 of the population.[19] Unfortunately Rome as well as Cape Town preferred to use nonsensical "violations" statistics in their Bid Books which can be very misleading because a violation can be anything from a traffic offence to smoking in a forbidden area.

Maybe the Cape Town bid company was not too keen for the world to know that 165 women out of 100 000 were raped in the Western Cape area in 1996. This is worse than the 152,7 figure for 1995 and the already terrible 147,8 statistic for 1994. In the case of murder and rape the Western Cape figure is higher than the national average which for murder was 61,1 and for rape 119,5 in 1996.[20] The comparative statistics for other contender countries for the 2004 Games (also for rape incidences but in 1994) were 0,14 for Argentina, 2,47 for Greece, 20,56 for Stockholm and unfortunately again nothing available for Rome or Italy from the SAPS.[21]

One can scarcely imagine what a terrible effect this constant physical threat must have on the psychological well-being of women in general. When you look at these figures and read about real cases in the daily press, the often quoted ideal of sexual equality almost sounds like a sick joke because there can be no real progress to equality before women are free to move around as they please, free from the fear of being physically harassed or assaulted. South Africans like all other civilised people have a basic human right, namely to be free from fear. Freedom from fear incidentally was one of Franklin Roosevelt's famous four freedoms.

A newspaper report that revealed the ridiculous side of this sad situation appeared in The Star of 27 February 1997: "Tourists who want to brave the larger centres are advised that they should keep their eyes downcast in case of an armed robbery while they are sightseeing and also that they should carry enough money to satisfy the armed robber". This advice was given to tourists at various travel agencies throughout Europe and is an elaboration on guidelines set out by the SAPS tourist assistance unit in Johannesburg.[22]

The onslaught of crime on the South African society covers a wide front, encompasses many facets, and also elicits unexpected reactions such as when a Cape drug baron was burned to death in full view of TV cameras and policemen. Thami Mazwai, a black writer, told The Economist "I and several friends watched with undisguised admiration".[23] This aspect of South African society was a particularly awkward issue for the IOC to digest in terms of Cape Town's bid. Would crime be likely to decrease in the years leading up to the Games?

The constitution might also limit the extent or even the effectiveness of any type of emergency measures or curfews that might be required. Curfews are temporary steps to limit the theft of building materials during the huge construction processes before Olympic Games. In Atlanta's case, a temporary curfew was deemed necessary. What would the costs of securing a South African Games be, given all the prevailing uncertainties? The serious problem of visitors' physical safety must be a constant worry for IOC decision makers. After all, overseas visitors want to move about freely to explore as they wish. In South Africa's case, sadly, the likelihood of visiting spectators being hurt or killed was just that much greater. To pretend otherwise would have been blatantly dishonest.

The Different Strategic Approaches

The modern Olympic Games has become a major socio-economic event and just to illustrate the sheer size of the present Games, let's begin in London in 1948, where 541 competitors represented 59 nations. By 1960 in Rome, the number of athletes and officials increased to 6 460 and the participating nations to 84. The Mexico City Games had to cater for 16 158 accreditations which consisted of 8 500 athletes and team officials with the members of the IOC representatives, International Sports Federations, National Olympic Committees and media observers making up the rest of the numbers. In 1992 the Catalonians prepared for 10 000 competitors and 5 200 officials representing 164 nations and territories. Atlanta played host to 195 countries in 1996, many of whom do not have athletes that qualify for the Olympics but they all have NOC's and subsequently the representing officials have to be accommodated by the host nation. The growth in spectators over the years has also been impressive to say the least:

Helsinki	1952 sold 1,2 million tickets,
Melbourne	1956 sold 1,34 million,
Rome	1960 sold 1,44 million,
Tokyo	1964 sold 2,11 million,
Barcelona	1992 sold 3,14 million and
Atlanta	1996 sold 8,5 million.[24]

It is clear that the Games have enjoyed almost constant growth, but alas not constant success, at least as far as finances are concerned. Montreal's citizens needed 20 years to pay off the $1 billion debt incurred by the 1976 Games, and that happened shortly before the Atlanta Games. If Montreal is seen as a big flop in a financial sense, then surely Los Angeles 1984 is known as the "Big Success Games" with

a reported profit of $215 million. Los Angeles of course was blessed with a sophis-
ticated infrastructure, it could use huge university buildings as Olympic villages
and it also had the benefit of a legacy of extensive sports infrastructure from the
1932 Games.

The South Koreans through Seoul in 1988 spent a lot of money but also seemed to
benefit from it in more ways than one. David Miller in Olympic Revolution reckons: "The Koreans had the organisation of the Germans, the courtesy of the Orient
and the financial sense of the Americans".[25]

The Spaniards, or should we rather emphasise "the Catalonian section of the
Spanish nation" managed to spend even more than they originally expected: about
30 to 40 % on top of the original estimate. This was partly due to demand-driven
inflation because of the huge construction projects taking place in and around the
city before the Games. The citizens of Barcelona were given $8 billion of roads,
telecommunication towers, storm water drains, new buildings and a reclaimed
beach front that normally would have taken about 20 years to deliver if the normal public programme was being followed. But they also ended up with a higher
cost of living and higher business taxes than the rest of Spain according to
Jennings.[26]

Nonetheless, on the whole the positives from the Barcelona Games seem to out-
weigh the negatives. Christopher Hill in Olympic Politics quotes Prof Zarnouski
who reviewed Prof Brunet's Economy of the 1992 Olympic Games and comment-
ed: "There is no doubt that the legacy of the 1992 Barcelona Olympics is a better
quality of life for its residents, more employment opportunities and greater
accrued capital. The question is, how much better? how much more? how much
greater?"[27] Perhaps the main reason that Barcelona came right in the end despite
the huge overrun on expenditure was the well co-ordinated and publicised strategic planning that was implemented at the right time. Consequently the public
knew what to expect.

If one examines the various approaches to the Olympic Games adopted by the different cities, it is clear that there are two basic strategic options: if the city and
region are highly developed with a sophisticated infrastructure, including sports
facilities, a low-cost approach with minimum construction and development can
be followed. If the city or region is reasonably developed and managed, with adequate infrastructure and services, but with some remaining weaknesses that can
be improved by Olympic development, the developmental approach can work.

Steven Roulac, an international strategic consultant, is of the opinion that before a
city can hope to benefit from Olympic developments, the city should be a pleasant
place to live and work in, with an educated and motivated work force that has

access to affordable housing and effective transit systems. The prevailing government of such a region should also be a responsive one that does not impose undue restrictions and burdensome taxes on business in general. Overall Roulac contends that any city wishing to host the Olympic Games successfully should already be able to offer its citizens a good quality of life.[28]

When Johannesburg was in the running against Cape Town, Swilling of the School of Public and Development Management at the University of the Witwatersrand stated: "Johannesburg should not even entertain the thought unless the Olympic Games form part of a comprehensive developmental strategy for the entire region".[29]

Patrick Troy, Head of the City Research Programme for Social Sciences at the University of Australia in Canberra is of the opinion that these "signature" events do not produce the advantages that are claimed for them. Prof Troy is quoted in Insig Magazine as saying that the number and duration of job creation affected by such an event is usually vastly exaggerated, that the construction and hamburger selling type of job is usually very short-lived, and that a lot of big undertakings are by international companies like Coca-Cola who are likely to take their profits out of the country anyway. He also states that the skills demanded are often too sophisticated for those underprivileged locals who need jobs most and that the construction or renovation contracts often go to the international companies with proven records. If there is a regulation that enforces a minimum number of contracts being given to companies representing underprivileged communities, the end product is often exorbitantly expensive because this process inhibits free competition. Troy emphasises another aspect, the fact that standards set by the IOC are of such a nature that the housing can be sold afterwards; it is designed for middle income group use and is too expensive for the lower income section where the need is usually the greatest.[30]

It is clearly not a simple task to tackle an Olympic bid. Atlanta tried to emulate Los Angeles' low-cost strategy, with some elements of development included and it fell between the two stools, even though its notable economic successes and social achievements of the past 20 years meant that Atlanta was definitely equipped to host a Games. Even with adequate infrastructure, an educated population, a strong local economy and reasonable government in place, the Olympics can go wrong if the strategic planning and managerial execution are not of the highest order. In the case of an African host, the challenges would be much more daunting and the risks that much greater.

Footnotes
1.   The Economist 1993, p 53
2.   The Economist 1993, p 53

3. Miller 1992, p 170
4. Drucker 1989, p 139
5. Sachs 29 June 1997, p 27
6. Johnson 1983, p 159
7. The Economist 14 June 1997, p 53
8. The Economist 14 June 1997, p 53
9. Smith 1996, p 79
10. The World in 1997, 1996, p 89
11. Hawthorne 16 September 1996, p 56
12. De Moregas Spa et al 1995, p 19
13. Project Pro September 1995, p 33
14. Ogden 16 September 1996, p 49
15. The Economist 12 October 1996, p 21
16. The World in 1997, 1996, p 80
17. The Economist 12 October 1996, p 21
18. The Economist 12 October 1996, p 22
19. Report of the IOC Evaluation Commission January 1997, pp 120, 121
20. SAPS January 1997, (Annexure A), p 2
21. SAPS 21 April 1995, p 10
22. The Star 2 July 1997, p 9
23. The Economist 12 October 1997, p 22
24. Information from the various Reports of the Organising Committees
25. Miller 1992, p 142
26. Jennings interview June 1996
27. Zarnowski (In Hill), 1996, p 195
28. Roulac 28 May 1993, p 10
29. Swilling (In Myburgh) 1993, p 15
30. Olivier May 1997, p 24

CHAPTER12

CAPE TOWN 2004 - THE BID

Nothing which is truly done, nothing which is truly conceived, nothing which is matched to the living word and the true word is ever vain.

Laurens van der Post

The Philosophical Approach to Cape Town 2004

The elections of 27 April 1994 catapulted South Africa into a different league: the uncharted territory of **unlimited opportunity.** The election process might have been imperfect but the results changed this country forever; it first brought dignity and then opportunity to the patient masses and resulted in increased uncertainty for beleaguered bureaucrats of previous decades.

Global developments such as the drastic decline in the belief of salvation by society which led to the widespread collapse of socialism, a gradual decline in heavy industry, the vigorous growth of the service sector, the general downsizing of corporations, and generally, the effect of the knowledge society have also impacted on the tremendous changes in South Africa.

The climate is one in which opportunists thrive, but those who try to maintain the status quo, fall further behind. It is in this new uncertain, **extremely competitive world**, situated on a continent that was described as "The Bleak Continent" by The Economist when it predicted that the Africa of 2020 might well be as dirt poor as it then was in 1989, that South Africa must lead the way to increased enlightenment and prosperity. Indeed there are signs that Africa is ready to enter into a renaissance era. The Director of External Relations of the IMF forecasted the best economic growth for two decades in 1996, combined with the lowest inflation for six years. The expected progress is attributed to the adoption of sound economic policies by many African countries.

But this precarious window of opportunity brought about by the new democratic order in a world where change has become the norm, also implies a **tremendous responsibility**, not to squander our precious few competitive advantages for the sake of short term opportunism, but to apply the relevant lessons of international experience to our particular situation in order to achieve sustainable long-term growth, which of course is the only realistic way of combatting endemic poverty.

It is within the context of our new-found experience of freedom of expression, the all important spirit of reconciliation, a still pervasive urge to conform, which often finds expression in a shallow political correctness, a realisation of crushing economic realities and of the importance of facing up to it, that this critique of Cape Town's bid for the 2004 Olympic Games is made.

To Support or Not?

South Africans are usually a very loyal lot on whom the national teams can rely for unwavering and enthusiastic support whether they be the Bafana Bafana or the Springboks, but more and more people are becoming aware of the fact that planning and organising this huge socio-economic event is very far removed from supporting your national side in any sporting contest, simply because demands are much greater and more complex and the socio-economic consequences can last for decades, as in the case of Montreal where the taxpayers had to carry an extra burden for 20 years.

The potential for hardship is much greater in a less developed country where there is a much greater disparity of incomes. Let us examine Cape Town's weaknesses. The Bidding Committee was very forthright in their articulation of the bid's potential advantages, but less so about some serious and potentially crippling weaknesses.

The Debilitating Weaknesses

The weaknesses mostly had to do with:

• Where Cape Town is Situated
Cape Town is on the most Southern point of the continent, far from the core of the South African population and the rest of Africa.

• What Cape Town Is
Cape Town is a medium-sized city with an underdeveloped infrastructure and huge socio-economic problems.

• Where Cape Town is Heading
The first democratic local elections only took place in May 1996, so Cape Town cannot yet be sure where it is heading in terms of political management. Still many poor South Africans are heading for the Cape, and this relentless migration naturally places an enormous extra load on resources, making responsible long-term planning even more vital.

• A Total Lack of Long-term Direction for Cape Town's Tourism Industry
Cape Town is presently occupying a profitable niche in the tourism market, but the massive building programme required to erect the extensive infrastructure for the Olympic Games would have placed Cape Town irrevocably on the highway to

mass tourism. This enforced strategy would then have placed great strain on its limited resources and endangered the exceptional natural beauty, and subsequently threatened the very basis of Cape Town's unique appeal.

• Strategic Faults Displayed by NOCSA
In the quest for a first African Games, the most obvious fault was the ousting of the original bidding committee, which led to the loss of the services of experienced international consultants, and the support of powerful sponsors. This also left the new team with precious little time to get their show on the road.

• The Lack of Transparency Concerning Costs and Jobs
The fact is that the Bidding Committee was not open and forthright about the potential for cost increases, as well as the likely number of jobs created by such an event. The cost increases were implied in the developmental approach which obviously is the opposite of a low-cost strategy. You cannot have a lean and light developmental Games; it is a contradiction in terms because development costs serious money as international experience has amply demonstrated. The jobs issue is an emotional one in a South African context and one cannot avoid the feeling that Chris Ball and his team were guilty of exploiting this to promote the bid.

A Population in Isolation

Cape Town's relative isolation can best be demonstrated by the fact that it is situated on the coast, which limits access, that the Western Cape is not densely populated (the population density for the Western Cape is 30 people per square km, the Northern Cape 2 per square km, Gauteng 350 per square km and Catalonia Spain 200 inhabitants per square kilometre), that the neighbour with which it shares the longest border, the Northern Cape, is the most sparsely populated region in the country with only 2 % of the population, and that the nearest urban area Port Elizabeth is more than 700 km away.

Compare that with Barcelona, the 1992 host which is situated in densely populated Catalonia with a population of over 6 million. Barcelona is also within 90 minutes driving distance of the French border and 50 minutes by plane from Madrid (4 million population). Atlanta, the 1996 host, is within a two hour flying distance of 210 million Americans. Sydney, the 2000 host with a population of 3,7 million, is situated in New South Wales where over 6 million people reside.

In developed countries, with a much higher per capita income, more people can afford to fly relatively long distances in order to attend sports events. The Australian GDP is $22 115 per head, the US equivalent is $29 600, whilst the Spanish figure is $15 522, compared to South Africa's $3 130.[1]

The Relative Isolation of Cape Town Counted Against it in Terms of:

• The Potential to Sell Entrance Tickets to the Various Olympic Events Over the Two Week Period

In the case of Barcelona, over three million tickets were sold, 80 % of them in Spain, contributing 8 % of the revenue. A total of 5,6 million entrance tickets will be available for the 16 days of competition in Sydney, contributing an expected 14 % of revenue. Atlanta had 11 million tickets available. The first African Games would have had 6,2 million tickets printed and was expected to sell about 4,7 million (where and how I just do not know, especially after the empty stadiums of the Rugby World Cup and the African Nations Cup when South Africa was not involved).

• The Number of Prospective Bed-and-breakfast Type of Accommodation Units Potentially Available in Private Homes

With between 200 000 and 400 000 visitors per day expected during the Olympic period, Cape Town was bound to have more than a slight accommodation problem. The city's number of hotel rooms is only a tenth of that of Atlanta.

• The Levels of Utilisation of the Various Stadiums and Sports Facilities

The IOC is very critical in its analysis of the long-term needs for expensive sports infrastructure. With such a relatively small accessible population, there had to be a serious question mark against a capital outlay of R2 billion on sports facilities.

List of New Competition Sites which Cape Town Would Have Had to Build:

Olympic Stadium	- $78 million (R351 million)
Olympic rowing and canoeing course	- $24 million (R108 million)
Philippi East Baseball Centre (finals)	- $8 million (R36 million)
Cape Town Exhibition Centre (handball finals, basketball finals, gymnastics and volleyball preliminaries)	- $53 million (R238,5 million)
Philippi East Basketball Centre (basketball preliminaries)	- $11 million (R49,5 million)
Mew Way Community Centre	- $13 million (R58,5 million) (boxing)
Slalom Course	- $4 million (R18 million) (canoeing)
Archery Centre	- $3 million (R13,5 million)
Cape of Good Hope Agricultural Society Showgrounds (equestrian events)	- $16 million (R72 million)

Indoor Arena	- $14 million (R63 million)
(handball preliminaries)	
Cape Town Convention Centre	-$9 million (R40,5 million)
(wrestling and weightlifting)	
Cape Town Aquatic Centre	- $26 million (R117 million
Metro Entertainment Centre	- $29 million (R130,5 million)
(indoor volleyball finals)	
Total	- $288 million (R1 296 million)[2]

The Cape Town Bid Books listed the above 13 new competition sites, the IOC report mentioned 16 new sports venues, but in both cases the bottom line was $444 million that would be required for altered and new sports sites. One cannot justify this huge expenditure on sports infrastructure in a relatively isolated city, especially if one looks at international experience - The Economist reports: "A study of nine cities over 1965 - 1983 found no significant relationship between economic growth and the arrival of new teams or stadiums". This was a United States based study by Andrew Zimbalist, an economist at Smith College.[3]

• A Distant African Host

A glance at any map will confirm that the expensive and extensive sports facilities would not have been very favourably situated for would-be spectators and future participants from the rest of Africa. The figures confirm this - the aggregate distance from Zimbabwe, Swaziland, Mozambique, Lesotho, Botswana and Namibia is just under 10 000 km in the case of Cape Town, while for Johannesburg it would be under 4 000 km. It would have been almost impossible for hundreds of thousands of sports enthusiasts from these countries, with a yearly per capita income of less than $500, to attend the first African Games in significant numbers if these were to be held in Cape Town - just as well, because the average projected price was almost R200 per ticket. In Barcelona 85 % of the tickets sold for less than R100 each. The average ticket price for the Atlanta Games was R280.

Underdeveloped Infrastructure

A serious analysis soon demonstrates that in terms of required infrastructure, Cape Town's shortcomings were obvious and fundamental to the requirements for a credible Olympic host, mainly in the areas of accommodation and transport.

Accommodation

An obviously confidential Executive Summary reached me by post. The name of the firm or organisation was erased, but people in strategic positions must have been worried about Cape Town's ability to provide accommodation, and the conclusions of this study justified their concern. We quote from page 1 of this study:

"The purpose of this investigation was to determine whether Cape Town has the potential to provide sufficient accommodation to host the 2004 Olympic Games"

And on page 19:

"CONCLUSIONS

The first is that this report believes that other studies and estimates of present and future accommodation stock in Cape Town are optimistic.

The report has also shown that it will be an enormous task for Cape Town to provide enough accommodation to host the Olympics, and that Cape Town will have to double its stock of suitable accommodation in the space of 9 years in order to host the 2004 Olympic Games. The use of ocean liners will not solve the problem. It was also demonstrated that Cape Town falls short of Seoul, Barcelona, Atlanta and Sydney in its ability to provide sufficient quantities of suitable accommodation.

Finally, this report draws attention to the dangers of lowered hotel room occupation after an Olympic event as a result of an oversupply of accommodation and cites Barcelona as an example where occupancies have dropped by approximately 20 %". (Rumour has it that this was a Southern Sun report).

In this investigation "Cape Town and environs" actually meant that all commercial accommodation within a 200 km radius from the main stadium was taken into account. If one considers the potential for huge traffic problems, then this was almost unrealistically generous. The Bid Company applied this same over-optimistic interpretation in the Bid Books. That is probably why the author of this study applied this unconventional methodology.

This study also assumed that 30 % of visitors could be accommodated by family and friends, which does not tie up with the "Rugby World Cup Assessment Survey (City of Cape Town)" which showed that nearly 85 % of visitors stayed at hotels and guest houses.

This research came to the conclusion that <u>Cape Town was still short of 71 500 rooms!</u>

The IOC's requirement of 6 800 "superior category" hotel rooms is a formidable one indeed. Just to keep the pampered sponsors happy, 5 000 luxury rooms are required exclusively for them. The influential IOC members and all the presidents and secretaries general of NOC's need a further 1 200 rooms, and then the representatives of the various sports federations also require an estimated 600 luxury rooms.[4]

Comparisons with other Olympic hosts reveal that Cape Town was simply not in this accommodation league:

City of Cape Town	4 718 hotel rooms (Financial Mail, 12/4/96, p 49)
City of Seoul (1988)	15 726 hotel rooms (OC Report)
City of Barcelona (1992)	13 590 hotel rooms (OC Report)
City of Atlanta (1996)	42 089 hotel rooms (OC Fact sheet)
City of Sydney (2000)	40 000 hotel rooms (OC Fact sheet)

(These figures are for the metropolitan areas alone. In a densely populated, highly developed area such as Barcelona's environs, the number of available hotel rooms within a short distance goes up to 40 000).[5]

Interestingly, the official report of Rome's 1960 Games listed 19 418 hotel rooms for the city, which was three times Cape Town's capacity. Rome sold 1,44 million tickets in 1960 and was packed to capacity. Cape Town hoped to sell almost five million tickets. Where would all these people have been accommodated? To simply embark on a massive building programme would also have been unwise.

The danger for Cape Town lay in the fact that at R850 000 per room, a five-star hotel's construction is extremely expensive. One cannot erect such expensive infrastructure merely to conform to IOC standards - what if there were an international recession or a slump in international tourism? South Africans would certainly not be able to afford the rates that this type of investment would require.

Other Relevant Comments

Kessel Feinstein, Tourist and Leisure Consultant, Delano Caras said: "Twice the required amount of hotel accommodation for Cape Town is in the construction pipeline". But Caras and Southern Sun Operations Director Helder Pereira were concerned that most of the planned development was in the four- and five-star, not the three-star category where it was believed tourism demand lay.[6]

Even the IOC's big boss Juan Samaranch cautioned Cape Town to erect infrastructure and facilities which the country required anyway. Beeld's Arrie Rossouw reported on 22 July 1996 that Samaranch told Vice President Thabo Mbeki that nothing should be built just for the Games.[7]

The Rugby World Cup Tournament served as a warning that South Africa was ill-equipped to handle the 200 000 daily visitors for the Olympic Games. "World Cup expectations were exaggerated: a year ago 50 000 rugby related tourists were expected; we think 18 000 actually came in. The hype scared away normal business travellers - it is possible that we had fewer tourists than normal".[8]

Cape Town had been experiencing excellent growth in tourism for some time, but one could not rely on this to continue unabated. With the current vigorous growth in virtually all sectors of the economy in the Western Cape, the question had to be asked: does Cape Town really need the Olympics that South Africa cannot afford?

Transport

Because it is the area in which development was to be focussed, it is also the section where budget overruns were most likely to occur. It is a technical and complex issue but again a few debilitating weaknesses were conspicuous - the lack of a central transport authority, the absence of a rail link with the airport, no metro or underground rail system, no reliable widespread taxi service, poor managerial control over existing commuter stations where fare evasion was often the rule rather than the exception. Varied opinions were offered as well as widely differing figures; it often seemed as though the millions or billions of rands in expected expenditure on transport were confused or exploited by various spokesmen. Let's take a look at the published specialist views:

From the original Ackerman committee:

"Cape Town has budgeted R5,4 billion for these projects. The airport will need to be upgraded as will the road and rail networks. Forty year old rolling stock will have to be replaced. These costs will be picked up by private and related industries, as well as local and national governments. Cape Town bid consultant Des Correia says R3 billion will be spent on capital projects in the city before 2004 anyway, therefore 'R2,4 billion is the real cost '".[9]

Clive Keegan, the then Chairman of the Executive of the City of Cape Town Municipality, named the key elements in the programme: "... improvements to the road, rail and harbour infrastructure at a cost of R3 103 million, and sports facilities costing R979 million" (1993 base date).[10]

The Ball Committee

In a Sunday Times interview (3 March 1996), Chris Ball quoted much more modest figures. He envisaged the total spending on infrastructure such as road and rail network as well as sports facilities at an estimated R1,76 billion.[11]

By April 1996 Business Day reported that <u>sports facilities alone</u> would amount to R1,92 billion against previous forecasts of R1,25 billion.[12] Later various members of the Bid Committee (Bidco) were quoted as saying that <u>accelerated transport</u> expenditure by government would amount to R979 million. But the Argus was adamant that "upgrading Cape Town's transport system to an acceptable level for the 2004 Olympics will cost a massive R5,6 billion."[13]

Nevertheless, the South African Transport Magazine of August 1996 was optimistic "<u>because additional expenditure of no less than 'R7,5 billion' will be allocated to improving Cape Town's transport infrastructure by 2004</u> if South Africa were awarded the Games. This was classified as <u>accelerated expenditure</u> to cope with growth forecasts to 2010 without the Games. Some billions of this would be for improvements to Cape Town International Airport while the remainder would be allocated to a variety of road and rail upgrading programmes".[14]

In October 1996 the Cape Town city planners' department produced a scathing report which amongst other things stated "<u>that the transport system envisaged for the Games has massive financial implications</u>". The report also mentioned growing frustration among city planners at their exclusion from key aspects of the Olympic bid - a point which, according to the Sunday Times (20 October, 1996), was acknowledged by Peter de Tolley of the Bid Company.[15]

Numerous comparisons were made with Atlanta during the first half of 1996:

JR Kingwill, Bidco:
<u>Cape Town's rail is larger than Marta in Atlanta</u>, which only has one third Cape Town's rail capacity.[16]

J Robbie Stewart, Bidco:
"<u>Our planning's better than Atlanta's</u> which has some venues 40 minutes away by train, and another 40 minutes by bus" (According to the IOC report, Cape Town had two competition sites over 50 km away from the Olympic Village - slalom canoeing and yachting, and four football venues in other cities which are at least 700 km away).[17]

J R Proctor Sims, Editor of South African Transport Magazine:
"<u>The city's present transport capacity is no more than 40 % of Atlanta's or 20 % of Sydney's</u>. More serious is the unrealistically low budget presented in conjunction with the Cape bid. This would need to be trebled for Cape Town to cope efficiently with the transport requirements of competitors, managers, media teams and spectators". He continued: "On current evidence, therefore, the best thing for South Africa would be for Rome or one of the other contenders to win the 2004 bid".[18]

The following transport "pointers" were included in an excellent article by Rollo Dickson in the South African Transport Magazine of August 1996:

- "A single highly computerised operations control centre in Atlanta, where there were no minibuses, monitors and co-ordinates trains and buses - both owned and run by the same authority - as well as road traffic. There has also been substantial investment in 'incident management'. Had this not been the case, there is little doubt that the 'chaos' imaginatively reported by certain impatient reporters might actually have eventuated. Similar unitary central transport direction exists in Sydney as well as Barcelona and other past Olympic host cities ...
- The fragmentation of authority (Cape Town) is the most disturbing aspect of the situation. Trains are run by Metro, buses by golden Arrow ... Not only does Cape Town lack an executive metropolitan transport authority, which is widely recognised as indispensable and long overdue, but the current White Paper foresees further devolution of management - bus routes and rail operations worked by smaller entities which tender for the right. It is difficult under conditions like these to imagine a city the size of Cape Town successfully co-ordinating and directing transport on an Olympic scale.
- Unlike Barcelona and Atlanta, Cape Town will have no rail link to its airport. Sydney is currently spending R2 billion on a 10 km rail connection to Kingsford Smith Air.
- Cape Town which was famous for its superb public transport system 40 years ago, paid a heavy penalty for concentrating on freeways and cars, for giving away much of what remained to the unpredictable minibus taxis.
- The role played by the minibus mode in the Olympics has yet to be defined. So far, and no doubt in deference to the AK-47, nobody has ventured suggestions".

According to Dickson the message for Cape Town was straightforward:

- Strictly exercised control and security were the deciding factors if crowd management was not to get out of hand; critical issues here were adequate footbridge capacity between platforms, the limiting of informal sidewalk trading, and the alarming extent of fare evasion which was 70 % in some areas.
- According to him, the challenge was that tens of thousands of Olympics-related visitors to Cape Town would expect accessible public transport (reliable, fixed fare, fixed route, round the clock availability) as a basic metropolitan facility. And the problem: "The likely lifespan, under South Africa's conditions, of bulging public area money boxes seem somewhat uncertain, judging by the rate at which vandals help themselves to the contents of kerb-side parking metres in Cape Town".
- He highlighted another disturbing aspect: "The covering of public transport operating costs escapes mention in contemporary estimates at Cape Town, which is busy enough putting together a R6,5 billion construction bill".

- Also "Cape Town's transport is limited as much by the city's geography as by the money it would need to build enough infrastructure in time".[19]

The fragility of Cape Town's transit systems was again emphasised when The Star of 22 May 1997 reported: "Bid to end attacks on 'Cape Hell Run'. The N2 highway into Cape Town, especially the stretch of road near the airport, will be patrolled on foot by police and soldiers with immediate effect, Western Cape Safety and Security MEC Gerhard Morkel said in Cape town yesterday". Apparently in some of the attacks boulders were rolled onto the road to force motorists to stop when they were subsequently robbed.[20]

A prominent figure in Olympic circles told me that when the three so-called experts visited Cape Town in 1994 to determine which South African city was best suited to bid for the Games, the hosts had to draw away the visitors' attention every time they approached a bridge so that they wouldn't notice the armed guards.

A Tale of Two Studies (and a Multiplicity of Figures)

The first impact study was the well-known report by KPMG supported by Gobodo and Co. This was also part of the documentation that was submitted to cabinet when they had to make the all important decision regarding governmental financial guarantees for Cape Town's bid. On the other hand there was the "Impact Study of the 2004 Olympic Games compiled by Chief Directorate Regional Development, Central Economic Advisory Service. March 1996" (which for some reason disappeared into thin air or dusty cabinets and was never referred to or even acknowledged).

For reasons of brevity the first well-known study will be referred to as KPMG and the second rare one with nocturnal habits as CEAS.

Introductions to the Studies

KPMG: "The aim of the study is to attempt to measure the economic impacts of Cape Town hosting the Olympic Games in 2004. The impacts are to be measured for the Western Cape, and for South Africa as a whole, and are to cover both anticipated quantitative and qualitative impacts."[21]

CEAS: "The Ministry of Finance requested the Central Economic Advisory Service (CEAS) to make an assessment of the possible contribution the 2004 Olympic Games could make to the economic and socio-economic activity in the Western Cape as well as in the RSA as a whole".[22]

Both were impact studies, in other words they were instructed to calculate the likely economic impacts of the huge sums of television and other revenues expected to be generated by a Cape Town Games. These figures were supplied by the Bidco and the studies went through reasonably standardised calculations to arrive at expected benefits. <u>It is important to note that these were not feasibility studies; in other words no critical analysis was executed in terms of likely levels of expenditure or of possible benefits derived from similar sized investments applied in more conventional economic terms.</u> It has to be recognised that the mere measurement of an increase in GDP has serious limitations when used as the sole indicator of economics excess as applied to a project. A natural disaster such as Damoina with the consequent insurance pay out, spent on clean-up operations and rebuilding of facilities, can be deemed a regional economic success if accelerated economic activity in terms of GDP is accepted as the only barometer. Likewise the funding of a project by taxpayers can also be labelled as positive growth if GDP expansion alone is considered.

Then both studies described in more detail what they actually measured and the methodology that was applied, and followed pretty much the same route except for KPMG's time span, which was from 1995 to 2010 unlike CEAS' 1997 to 2008.

Let us first take a look at the findings that <u>coincided</u>: The CEAS calculates the effect on Gross Geographical product as an annual average of between R1,4 and R1,9 billion. The KPMG referred to the total direct and indirect economic impact on GDP and expected it to vary between R1,1 and R1,9 billion for the slightly extended period. That's about the same in anybody's language and both studies agreed on the fact that roughly 60 % of the benefits would be outside the Western Cape area. So these two studies followed roughly the same number-crunching routine measuring likely outputs, inputs and so on.

But where these two studies <u>differed markedly</u> was on the potential for job creation. This was probably where the death knell for the CEAS sounded, because its expected figures for job creation were much lower and in true scientific style the CEAS study cautioned: "Cognisance must, however, be taken thereof that these unemployment figures are not indicating that this number of jobs will be created permanently and continue to exist after the Games. The number of permanent working opportunities that could be created was not calculated in this study but could be assumed to be much lower". Clearly the figures were too low for the Bidco's purposes as well as the fact that they were not deemed to be permanent. This meant that the CEAS study could not be used as a selling document to impress the cabinet and the eager nation.

Compare the figures for likely job creation in terms of average annual jobs: (In both cases it is assumed temporary employment).

KPMG:
Average annual jobs (1995 - 2010)

	low	high
South Africa	77 734	143 804

CEAS:
Effect on employment (numbers) annual average 1997 - 2008.

	low	high
Total RSA	24 391	32 740

The KPMG figures were between 300 and 400 % higher. It was clear to anyone why the CEAS document was not quoted by the bid proponents or laid in front of cabinet meetings. The KPMG document again stressed the job creation in section 1.3.2 under "Direct Benefits of Winning the Games" where it stated: "The capital investment, operating and visitor spending, could have a total impact on the GDP of between R17 billion and R29,9 billion and could create an annual average of between 77 000 and 144 000 jobs."

If any Olympic Games had ever produced an annual job creation figure of between 77 000 and 144 000 jobs over a period of 15 years, it would have been hailed as an economic miracle of unequalled proportion. Even if these were meant as person years it would still be totally unrealistic. If this wonderful news were a scientifically derived figure, why did the bid company only enter "90 000 person years" in its Bid Books to the IOC, while to Cabinet and the nation as a whole it's a highly unlikely 90 000 - 120 000 permanent jobs? After all 90 000 "person years" would in effect mean only about 9 000 permanent jobs.

The international convention of interpreting 10 person years as a permanent job, was first explained to me by Manchester's Bid Committee's Financial Director, Bill Enevoldson and, ironically, Manchester's Economic Benefits and Opportunities of the Olympic Games was done by none other than KPMG Management Consulting. Their figures in approximate person-years for previous Games were Los Angeles 1984 76 000, Barcelona 128 000 and Atlanta 84 000. Manchester's expectations were 110 000 person years which they then clearly defined as 11 000 full time jobs.[23] Steven Roulac writes that the Los Angeles 76 000 figure was for temporary jobs of which some were so short lived that the person year figure is only 25 000. It is clear from the widely differing figures produced by the two studies, as well as the huge variations in job creation figures attributed to previous Games that these figures had to be treated with some circumspection to say the least.[24]

A List of Pronouncements on the Job Creation Aspects of a Cape Town Games

"The work leading up to the bid would create 55 000 new jobs of which 80 % would be permanent" - Clive Keegan, Project Pro: Sept 1994, p 27.

"By 2008...160 000 new jobs would have been created" - Clive Keegan, Project Pro: Sept 1994, p 27.

"75 000 permanent jobs will be created out of tourism alone" - Chris Ball, Project Pro: Sept 1995, p 33

"Creation of 110 000 permanent jobs in tourism alone" - Chris Ball, Star: 11 Jan 1996, p 6.

"115 000 jobs" - Chris Ball, Beeld: 26 Jan 1996, p 2.

"110 000 sustainable jobs will be created - of which 85 000 will be outside of the Western Cape" - Chris Ball, Sunday Times: 3 March 1996, p 22.

"More than 110 000 job opportunities" - Beeld, 'Sake': 6 March 1996, p 20.

"We are looking at the creation of 110 000 sustainable jobs outside semi- permanent jobs" - Paul Johnson, Press Officer for Cape Town 2004: interviewed 17 April 1996

"Cape Town can expect between 77 000 and 144 000 new jobs to be created if the bid succeeds" - Sunday Times: 24 April 1996, p 24.

"125 000 additional job opportunities" - Chris Ball, Beeld 'Sake': 8 May 1996, p 5.

"Over 30 000 permanent jobs would be created" - Gill Marcus, then deputy Minister of Finance: The Star (BR), 6 June 1996, p 1 .

"The Cabinet. ...decided yesterday to support Cape Town's bid for the 2004 Olympic Games...it would create more than 90 000 permanent jobs" - Star: 6 June 1996, p 1.

"Half the expected 90 000 full time job opportunities to be created in the Western Cape" - Dr David Bridgman Wesgro, Beeld 'Sake': 11 June 1996, p 6.

"Games would add 336 000 new jobs" - Kevin Kilroe, TA Securities, The Star Business Report: 19 August 1996, p 5.

"Creation of at least 110 000 jobs (70 % outside Western Cape)" - Smith Borkum Hare, Sunday Times: 8 Sept 1996, p 3.

"Games could create 45 000 jobs in the Western Cape alone" - Time Magazine: 16 Sept 1996, p 63.

"...the 100 000 jobs that will be created" - Paul Johnson, Press Officer Cape Town 2004, Mail and Guardian: 6 Dec 1996, p 11.

"more than 90 000 sustainable jobs will be created" - from Cape Chamber of Commerce and Industries monthly bulletin, Sunday Finance: 7/8 Dec 1996, p 2.

"90 000 jobs created by Games" - Development Bank, Financial Mail: 13 Dec 1996, p 18.

"90 000 permanent jobs will be created, either directly related to the Olympics or as part of the ripple effect created by the Games" - Equinox: issue 1 1997, p 85.

IOC Pronouncements - on the basis of information supplied by Cape Town's Bidding Committee

Cape Town 2004 Bid Book, Vol 1, p 36: "It is estimated that a Cape Town Olympic Games will increase employment by <u>90 000 person years</u> as a result of job creation."

Report of the IOC Evaluation Commission, p 29. "It estimates the Olympic Games will increase employment by <u>90 000 person years</u>"

Olympic Review (Official publication of the Olympic movement), p 39. It estimated the Olympic Games would increase employment by <u>90 000 person years</u>.

This hard sell approach can be construed as extremely cynical in view of the fact that many thousands of rather desperate people would probably have flocked to Cape Town in the hope of sharing in these often promised job opportunities, had Cape Town be awarded the Games.

Why the enormous difference between the job creation figures laid on the table for the cabinet decision and those entered in the Bid Books for the IOC's perusal? The answer is probably that the cabinet's decision was crucial and job creation was a pivotal part of the argument in favour of the Games. In The Star's report where the cabinet's support for the Games was announced, the <u>"90 000 permanent"</u> jobs were mentioned in the first paragraph. The Financial Mail of 13 December 1996 referred to "hard won financial guarantees from government which were obtained based on Development Bank growth projections".

The Jolly Jumper

Playing around with figures is nothing new for Cape Town's Bidco or other bidding committees. (Billy Payne of Atlanta admitted that they entered Atlanta's average 24 hour temperature as the average day temperature in their report to the IOC, to conceal the worst of the searing summer heat.)

The problems with Cape Town's figures began with the fact that this was South Africa's first bid, that both Bidding Committees had insufficient time to tackle this massive task and that they were under enormous pressure to supply a viable bid. The first Bidding Committee's consultants, Ove Arup, were experienced in the matter of Olympic bidding, since they had been involved in Birmingham's efforts. Maybe that explains why some of their earlier figures were relatively higher (more realistic?). The Ball Committee started out by quoting some very low figures for, for example, sports infrastructure, which soon had to be revised. Let's take a look at some interesting published figures:

Telecommunication

R2,1 billion ($475 million) - Des Correia (first bidding committee), Project Pro: May 1995, p 19.

R1 billion - Chris Ball, Business Report: 2/10/95, p 5.
R1,2 billion - The Argus: 11/4/96, p 1.

Security

R200 million - Chris Ball, Sunday Independent: 24/9/95, p 1.
R300 million - Chris Ball, Sunday Times: 3/12/95, p 28.

Sports Facilities

R0,9 billion - Beeld: 26/1/96, p 2.
R0,918 billion - Chris Ball, Sunday Times: 3/3/96, p 22.
R1,25 billion - Business Day: 12/4/96 (up from 1,25 to 1,92billion), p 1
R1,92 billion - Business Day:12/4/96, p 1.
R1,7 billion + R141 million - Argus: 11/4/96, p 1.
R1,998 billion - Cape Town Bid Book (Vol. 2), p 22.

Transport Infrastructure

R5,4 billion - Des Correia, Ove Arup, Sunday Times: 25/9/94, p 9 (R2,4 billion accelerated spending)
R0,969 billion - Chris Ball, Sunday Times: 3/3/96, p 22 (accelerated spending)
R0,8 billion - Chris Ball, Beeld: 26/1/96, p 2 (accelerated spending)
R5,6 billion - Argus, 18/4/96, p 1 (total transport bill)
R7,5 billion - SA Transport Magazine: August 96, p 15 (accelerated spending)
R0,9 billion - Mail & Guardian: 6/12/96, p 11 (accelerated spending)
R3,3 billion - Ronnie Kingwell, Bidco, 28/6/97 (accelerated government spending for infrastructure)
R8 billion - Ronnie Kingwell, Bidco, 28/6/97 (transport plan for Western Cape until 2010)
(R21 billion was Ramsamy of NOCSA's estimate of total infrastructural costs) Sunday Times: 12/3/95, p 3
The R7,25 billion capital budget would be shared between state R3,3 billion and private sector R2,4 billion, local government 10 % and OCOG 10 %. Financial Mail of 13/12/96, p 18.

Comment

Accelerated spending for a private individual would mean spending tomorrow's earnings today - for a Bid Company it can be spending future taxpayers' money (with resultant interest payment cost implications). It has to be borne in mind that with huge amounts of accelerated spending, the Western Cape would have had to be able to survive in a relative vacuum of state spending after an Olympic Games and since capital is a finite item some other regions would have had to wait longer for their share of the cake.

The Capital Cost Conundrum

On 3 March 1996, Chris Ball wrote an article for the Sunday Times in which he described the "move in international Olympic circles towards lighter, leaner Games without extravagance". (The statement is hardly credible since it was made a few months before the Atlanta Games which was the largest event ever; Sydney is building an even larger Olympic Stadium and all the finalists of 2004 intend printing and selling at least 30 % more tickets than Barcelona, the 1992 host.) In this article Ball stated: "We are now putting together the Bid Books which we have to submit to the International Olympic Committee by 15 August". He then again stated the specific figures for transport and competition facilities: Of this total of R1,7 billion, R843 million would go towards transport infrastructure and R918 million would be spent on competition and training facilities.[25]

Then came a bit of a shock - Massive bill for 2004 Olympics, revealed Andrea Weiss of The Argus on 11/4/96 - Bidco estimates R1,7 billion is needed to build sporting facilities. Sporting facilities alone were now estimated at R1,78 billion and with training facilities added, the figure suddenly came to over R1,9 billion. And this just a month after Ball wrote in the Sunday Times that "R918 million will be spent on competition and training facilities".[26] The next day in a Business Day report Michael Fuller, the "Bid Spokesman" stressed that the aim was for "low-budget Games".[27]

Well, this low budget was rising on a steep curve. In The Argus of 18 April 1996 Andrea Weiss reported that "Upgrading Cape Town's transport system to an 'acceptable' level for the 2004 Olympics will cost a massive R5,6 billion". She could not get any bid spokesman to confirm or deny this. In her report however she did mention the fact that at the time the Cabinet Sub-committee was meeting prior to its report to the full cabinet the following week.[28]

The by now defunct R1,7 billion capital cost figure was mentioned a few times more: in the American Time Magazine of 16 September 1996 [29] and in Colin Bryden's Sunday Times column of 19 May 1996.[30] Then on 6 June 1996 we were informed by The Star and others that "cabinet supports Cape Town's bid for 2004 Olympic Games" and that "the total capital cost of staging the Games is estimated at R7,5 billion, half of which would be accounted for by the private sector".[31] Surely the chief executive had known all along. Why did he only mention the relatively paltry figure of R1,7 billion in all those interviews? Was it a deliberate ploy to placate the public before the crucial cabinet meeting so as to prevent a huge public reaction to the figures, that might have influenced cabinet?

In the Sunday Times of 27 October 1996, the Olympic Bid Company's Financial Director Michael Fuller said: "The government will assume, in the place of Cape Town, financial responsibility for the organisation of the Games ... the undertaking would come into effect only if other financial shareholders could not meet their commitments". According to Charl de Villiers of the Sunday Times, the private sector would contribute 35 % of the capital budget.[32]

The Capital Budget (Vol 3 of the Bid Books)

The capital budget consisted of:
Airport $155 million (R697,5 million),
Roads and railways $211 million (R949 million),
Visitor accommodation $453 million (R2 035,5 million),
Sports venues $261 (R1 174,5 million) - the balance reflected in the operating budget,
Olympic Village $269 million (R1 210,5 million),
Media $60 million (R270 million),
Bulk services $153 million (R688,5 million),
Land costs $58 million (R261 million) and
Contingencies $357 million (R1 606,5 million).[33]

A Comprehensive Strategic Environmental Assessment, involving inputs from various disparate experts, was released in July 1997 - sketching the extent of the bid's threats and weaknesses.
The Strategic Environmental Assessment Report's Overall Conclusion pointed out:"*South Africa has a relatively small, developing economy with a limited fiscus on which there are diverse demands*".

"*It would be unrealistic to expect the hosting of the Games to solve all developmental problems of the region and the country*".

The 90 000 person years is deemed unrealistic by this report, because Barcelona, the only city to achieve this type of result, invested five times more than Cape Town intended to.

"*Total public sector investment will increase to R8 680 million if all the metropolitan transport needs are met.*

Total private sector investment will increase to R4 015 million if all the metropolitan transport needs are met.

The possibility of the Government failing to keep in line with GEAR targets.

The possibility of significant cost overruns relating to operations and capital expenditure.

The likelihood of increased government borrowing to fund the commitment given to the Games. "This is likely to increase interest rates and reduce local government incentives".

The possibility of the OCOG being unable to mobilise the minimum level of required private sector funding.[34]

A CSIR study which served as an input to the Strategic Environmental Assessment: The Impact of the Olympics on the Construction Industry, pointed out the risks of huge increases in building costs. (20-30 % per year). The scale of Olympic construction would expose serious capacity constraints in the South African building industry.[35] (It was interesting that Andrew Merrifield in private conversation seemed much less convinced of Cape Town's ability to cope than his report's conclusion).

After elucidating all these looming threats, the Strategic Environmental Assessment nevertheless fell meekly in line with the prevailing mode of collective thinking: "On balance the Olympic Assessment Team is cautiously confident that the Games will not pose an unmanageable burden on the economy and public finance system, and are likely to be affordable and beneficial to South Africa and the Cape Metropolitan region".

Private Sector Load

If Cape Town had been awarded the Games, the "poor" private sector would have had to carry the brunt of the burden. Let us take a look at all the items that the private sector would have been expected to carry:

Local sponsorship	$114 million (R513 million)
Licensing	$19 million (R85,5 million)
Official suppliers	$38 million (R171 million)
Olympic villages	$269 million (R1 210,5 million)
Visitor accommodation	$453 million (R2 038,5million)
Sports venue	$92 million (R414 million)
Total	$985 million (R4,4 billion)[36]

That is 0,75 % of South Africa's yearly GDP. What if there is a recession, a permanent slump in the gold price or a downturn in international tourism for whatever reason? Of course if the private sector cannot perform, the government in the form of the suffering taxpayer, will be the last refuge.

Odds and Ends

Land claims

Wingfield is where the main Olympic action was due to take place. The Olympic stadium and the athletes' village as well as the 100 m rowing venue would have been situated there. It is the site of an old Second World War airfield in an unattractive and rather barren area. Apparently it was the windiest airport under Allied command in the Second World War. The land belonged to the <u>Graaff Family Trust</u> and they "sold" the land cheaply to the South African government "with the proviso that the government had to sell the land back to the trust the moment it was no longer needed for defence purposes. Taking into account a set interest rate of 3 % a year laid down in the original deal, the trust would have to pay the government approximately R255 000 to buy back the land - but stand to sell it for 500 times that price". The commercial value attached to this prime commercial land of 259 ha is a conservative R129 million, according to the Sunday Times.[37]

The problem is that the 1995 preliminary operating and capital budget review was done with a major assumption that "there would be no capital outlay for the acquisition of land".

Indeed the original Basic Information Package on Cape Town 2004 Bid stated: "One of the most important features of Wingfield is that the land is effectively state owned and its management and control can be managed in the most appropriate way to suit the Olympics".[38] In Vol 2 of the Bid Books, the current owner of the Olympic Stadium site was given as Republic of South Africa (Department of Public Works) and the future owner was described as the Central Substructure.[39]

Regrettably for the bidding effort, there was another claim against Wingfield. On 15 March 1996 The Star reported: "The planned erection of an Olympic Village in a prime Cape Town industrial site is set to clash head-on with land claims by people removed from the area in 1924".[40] A few months later Business Day reported: "Government officials will meet the Ndabeni Restitution Committee today in a bid to compromise on land claims they have lodged on the main site for Cape Town's Olympic bid". The report went on to say that up to 5 000 families could seek restitution.[41] During our last interview, Bidco Spokesman Paul Johnson was very vague on the land claims issues, but it is noteworthy that a land cost provision of $58 million (R261 million) was brought into the capital budget.

On page 40 of volume 3 of the Bid Books it was stated that "The national government has guaranteed the building of the Olympic Village. The documents with respect to the purchasing of the land have been received from the Department of Public Works". So it was very likely that the taxpayer would be buying the land on behalf of the bidding committee, but surely then we, the taxpayers, had a right to be informed about it.

One could presume that the claims by the Ndabeni Restitution Committee would be stalled until the IOC's decision, and if Cape Town was elected, this issue would be very prominent, unless of course secret financial deals had been concluded with both the Graaff Trust and the Ndabeni Restitution Committee. (I questioned Bidco's Paul Johnson on the issues, but his response was to refer me to the Department of Public Works and the Land Claims Court.)

In April 1996 Paul Johnson told me "Essentially those families are going to be looking towards financial compensation." A year later Paul simply referred me to the Department of Public Works when I asked the same question.

"Cape Town loses international scouts conference". This was the heading of The Star report that described how the three-yearly international conference had been awarded to Cape Town in 1993 after an impressive video representation. When on-site inspections were done in 1996, the promised conference centre was not even built yet, and visitors likened the existing Good Hope Centre to a "urinal". The 1999 conference is particularly important to the World Organisation of Scout Movements "because it will be 100 years after the siege of Mafeking where Lord Baden-Powell used young boys in non-combative roles and in the process developed a concept which led to the launch of the scout movement in 1907". Durban is now due to host the 1 800 delegates from 1 500 centres which will include the king of Norway.[42]

Bidco's relations with local and regional authorities were anything but rosy. In July 1996 The Star reported that the "city's Olympic Bid Company wants local authorities in the area to put up big money to sponsor the 2004 bid, but that they infuriated the Eastern substructure by failing to arrive for a meeting to explain the pleas for cash. A delegation was scheduled to address the full council at its monthly meeting on Tuesday night, but they did not turn up". The amount in question was R14 million. According to The Star, the Olympic Bid Company could not be reached for comment.[43]

In October it was the turn of the Cape Town city planners to turn the heavy artillery on the 2004 Bid Company, and it was management of vital issues that came in for flak. Firstly the planners questioned the possibility of raising R3,5 billion in private sector funding that would be required. Secondly their report stated that the transport system envisaged for the Games had "massive financial implications". Other problems raised in this report include: concern about the event's environmental impact, "not enough planning for the supply of bulk services". (I presume that means all the water, sewerage and electricity installations and connections at the sports venues), "the marketability of Olympic housing units after the Games ... concerns about the viability of a 6 000 seat indoor stadium ... a proposed tennis venue that is contrary to developmental principles ... serious concern with the proposed rowing site".[44] (The IOC report also raised concerns about "security, noise, access and accreditation" with regard to the rowing and canoeing course) ... "Concerns about the ownership and maintenance of facilities and no clear understanding of the national government's role".

In reaction the Head of the Bid's Planning Department, Peter de Tolley, stated that the document displayed a "staggering ignorance" of the company's operations. But De Tolley did acknowledge the fact that the city planners were frustrated by their exclusion from key aspects of the Olympic bid. In the interview with Alderman Clive Keegan this tendency of the Bidco to reinvent the wheel as it were, was also mentioned when Keegan recalled instances where the city's existing long-term plans had been ignored and the planning resources not utilised by the Bid Company.

Public Support for Cape Town 2004

The IOC report maintained: "The extent of public support for the candidature is difficult to assess". Project PRO's Terry Deacon noted: "Western Cape support for Cape Town's 2004 bid has dropped dramatically from 80 % during 1996 according to polls conducted by Market Research Africa. If hosting the Games is as beneficial as the Cape Town 2004 Olympic Bid Committee says it is, then they have failed to communicate this to the Capetonians".[45] This view was reflected in a 32 200 vote survey by Cape Community - 76,67 % of readers of Cape Town newspapers voted a resounding "no" the previous week to whether the city should bid. The Citizen also mentioned another survey in which 62 % of 2 800 people in the country's metropolitan centres were in favour of the government's providing funds to support Cape Town's bid for 2004.[46]

It is not difficult to understand the Capetonians' lack of enthusiasm for their city's bid. They had been exposed to both sides of the arguments to a greater extent, because of the wide exposure Olympic matters enjoy in the local press. The problems between the Bidco and the city planners, for example, enjoyed detailed coverage in the Cape Town newspapers. Also Capetonians instinctively realised that they had a lot to lose if the mother city actually had to host the Games; the pervasive laid back atmosphere which contributes to the absence of that big city urgency would certainly be threatened by the massive building programme that the vigorous IOC standards would necessitate.

The consequence of this massive artificial expansion of accommodation, transport and sports infrastructure would have been to adopt an aggressive mass tourism strategy in order to utilise all these added facilities. A practical example of the unnecessary expansions that would have been required: the Cape Town 2004 Bid Books transport section stated that the airport expected to handle up to six million passengers per year in 2004 (normal demand), that Olympic demand would necessitate a 14 million per year capacity (130 % excess) and that the difference could be made up by a combination of extra permanent and temporary facilities, which in turn would mean tranquillity lost forever. The other perhaps even greater asset, the natural beauty, would also be endangered. Unfortunately the natural beauty and the unique atmosphere are two precious assets which cannot be retrieved once scarred. It would be like trying to recreate the incomparable District Six.

Lastly there was the not unreasonable fear of the <u>region's being inundated by desperate people</u> from other regions looking for the thousands of jobs liberally promised by Bidco. After all it happened in first-world Atlanta: Bill Bolling who heeded the Atlanta Food Bank was quoted in The Star as saying: "Many people came from all over the South for the Olympics, thinking we had unlimited employment opportunities". Instead of finding jobs they had to join the already long lines at churches or city shelters where food was handed out.[47]

Prof Spies, a futurologist formerly attached to the Institute for Future Research at Stellenbosch University, predicted that the Cape Town Games could end up as a "disaster" because the huge temporary spurt of growth would lead to an influx of people from the Eastern Cape and transfer many of the Eastern Cape's problems to the Western Cape.[48] Spies pointed out that balanced development is the answer, in other words more emphasis on development in the Eastern Cape to minimise the existing differential in opportunities between the Eastern and Western Cape.

These comments of Prof Spies were in line with the advice offered by Prof Troy, the Head of the City Research Programme at the University of Australia in Canberra; namely that Cape Town or any other region presumably should go for a long-term development plan with widespread impact, "The incoming tide thesis" as he called it, which would lift all the boats instead of just one.[49]

THE BATTLE OF THE BID

"There were several changes in senior positions for the Barcelona Games and the top job in the Seoul Olympics changed so many times we lost count". (The Sydney Morning Herald quoting an IOC source).[50]

In Cape Town's case it was much worse than just losing a chief executive, because virtually the whole team including most consultants and some sponsors had to be replaced when Raymond Ackerman, owner of Pick'n Pay and the driving force behind Cape Town's original bid, was ousted.

A Chronology of Events

2 July 1992: South Africa's return to world sport is secured by an ANC decision to withdraw its call for the reimposition of the international boycott. This call for a boycott is made after the Boipatong massacre and the suspension of the Codesa negotiations.[51]

4 April 1993: Johannesburg, Cape Town and Durban hand in their respective proposals with NOCSA as to how each city would propose to host the 2004 Olympics.

28 January 1994: NOCSA appoints Cape Town as South Africa's candidate for 2004.

25 September 1994: Cape Town's bid is given provisional government backing.

20 November 1994: J A Samaranch visits Cape Town and suggests Cape Town has "plenty of work to do in upgrading the city's infrastructure". Samaranch also emphasises the importance of public support for the bid.[52]

20 November 1994: Muleleki George, head of NSC criticises Antonio Samaranch for not consulting other heads of sport before South Africa's first IOC member is nominated.[53]

11 December 1994: China's bid suffers a serious setback when 11 Chinese athletes are tested positive at the Asian Games.[54] This no doubt spelled the end of Beijing's aspirations for 2004.

20 February 1995: Four officials of the Cape Town City Council leave for Barcelona and Lausanne to gain more information regarding the implications of Cape Town's bid.[55]

22 February 1995: National Olympic Congress of South Africa refuses to sign interim agreement with the bidding committee, which would have freed much needed sponsors' money.[56]

26 February 1995: The headline of The Sunday Times shouts "Massive clash of two egos threatens Cape Olympic bid". Martin Gillingham also writes that "The knives are out for Raymond Ackerman in South African Olympic circles".[57] NOCSA said the Olympic Charter required that the application to organise the Games must be made by the official authority of the city with the approval of the

National Olympic Committee. Mr Ackerman retorted that "All we were interested in was a marketing agreement, which would allow us to continue our fundraising efforts. All parties, including NOCSA and the former city council, had decided that a formal host city agreement would be signed only after a legitimate local authority was in place". The Sunday Times reported that "NOCSA has given the council a new draft contract to sign - but some counsellors say they are horrified by some of its financial implications... Under the new management the council would have to pay NOCSA R200 million - R140 million more than it originally agreed to pay".

27 February 1995: Die Beeld reports on the dinner held by President Mandela to try and solve problems between NOCSA, the City Council and Raymond Ackerman. In this report it is stated that the Mayor of Cape Town, Rev William Bantam walked out.[58] This is not correct, as the interviews later prove.

7 March 1995: Raymond Ackerman, Co-chairman of the Cape Town Olympic Bid Committee announces his resignation.[59]

10 March 1995: "Minutes of the Cape Town 2004 Olympic Bid Trust show how it was plunged into a crisis when sponsors held back. They put the brakes on the agreement between the City Council and the National Olympic Committee of SA". On 10 February the Trust's deficit was R8,6 million.[60]

12 March 1995: NOCSA president Sam Ramsamy warns that hosting the 2004 Olympic Games can cost South Africa R21 billion. Ramsamy is quoted as saying the proposed R5,6 billion expenditure by the former Cape Town Bidding Committee "could only include the cost of facilities and the direct expenditure in relation to the Games" and not the cost of upgrading the city's infrastructure.[61]

15 March 1995: Cape Town city council executive and Bid Committee member Clive Keegan says Ackerman's return is essential and adds that a newspaper poll has indicated that most Capetonians believe the city should abandon its bid to host the 2004 Games.[62]

23 March 1995: Sam Ramsamy, President of NOCSA is awarded the Murray and Roberts/Jack Cheetham award at a function at the Wanderers Club in Johannesburg.

25/26 March 1995: "Supermarket tycoon Raymond Ackerman has confirmed that he will return to the Cape Town Olympic bid committee because conditions he set for his return are to be met"..."It will be the bid committee running it with the city council".[63]

31 March 1995: The Cape Town City Council accepts a proposal to go ahead with the bid to host the Olympic Games in 2004.[64]

6 April 1995: Raymond Ackerman is temporarily installed as the chief executive officer of the bid until a replacement is found.[65]

30 April 1995: The Olympic bid contract between Cape Town City Council and the National Olympic Committee of South Africa is signed, but not sealed yet as Raymond Ackerman of the Interim Steering Committee for the bid accuses NOCSA and the council "of breach of contract".[66]

7 May 1995: "South Africa's Olympic movement gave its backing to Cape Town's bid for the 2004 Olympic Games but heavily criticised the bid's interim chief executive Raymond Ackerman". Ramsamy is quoted as saying NOCSA has been "denigrated in the media by some clever manipulation and misinformation by a private individual".[67]

18 May 1995: A statement that NOCSA would not allow review of its Olympic bid agreement with Cape Town is rejected by Western Cape business leaders.[68]

19 June 1995: Sam Ramsamy elected as an International Olympic Committee member.

25 June 1995: Business Times reports "Cape Town's Olympic Bid to Play Ball" after the appointment of ex-banker Chris Ball as Chief Executive.

25 June 1995: "Pay row mars Olympic bid" writes Charl de Villiers in The Sunday Times over the controversy stirred up by newly appointed Chris Ball's reputed R1 million a year salary. Cape Town City Councillor Arthur Wienburg demands full disclosure of all benefits being paid to bid company members.[69]

12 September 1995: Raymond Ackerman, Pick-'n-Pay Chief Executive and former leader of Cape Town's bid, to be repaid millions to reimburse him for the money he spent on Cape Town's 2004 Olympic bid, but the new Olympic Bid Company will not divulge the exact amount.[70]

4 October 1995: Cabinet approves a process which involves government and the private sector to keep the bid on track. The final decision regarding Government support is postponed to 1996.[71]

24 December 1995: Chris Ball, Chief Executive of Cape Town 2004, hands a letter to Juan Antonia Samaranch, President of the IOC, formally proposing Cape Town's candidature. Ball is accompanied by Cape Town's Mayor Rev William Bantam and NOCSA President Sam Ramsamy.[72]

31 March 1996: Twenty Executive Members of the IOC attend a meeting at Sun City in South Africa and Juan Antonia Samaranch warns that the support of the South African government is crucial if Cape Town's bid for 2004 is to be successful. Samaranch reiterates the importance of an African Games because in Olympic terms Africa is the missing link.[73]

10 April 1996: Clive Keegan, Deputy Chairman of Cape Town 's Bid Company resigns because of what he terms undemocratic and unprofessional behaviour and a lack of transparency from Ball and his management team.[74]

6 June 1996: "The Cabinet - citing a R30 billion boost to the economy between 1997 and 2006 - decided yesterday to support Cape Town's bid for the 2004 Olympic Games. It decided at its regular fortnightly meeting to back the bid, saying it would create more than 90 000 permanent jobs with substantial gains for other provinces".[75]

12 June 1996: Robin Lee, head of the management faculty at Wits University warns that "South Africa is in serious danger of slipping into a culture of crime". Lee says that it is the first time in 20 years that "surveys had reflected crime to be a greater problem than unemployment, education and housing". He emphasises that the estimated cost of crime last year could exceed the projected benefits of the Olympic Games to South Africa over the next 10 years.[76]

9 December 1996: "National Sports Council Chief, Muleleki George, suggests Sam Ramsamy is becoming dictatorial in his management of South African Olympic sport. He even accuses Ramsamy, South Africa's only "lord of Lausanne", of actively lobbying opposition to Cape Town's Olympic bid".[77]

Crucial Issues Brought up in Interviews - These comments are important in so far as the whole culture of South Africa's bid is reflected.

Role players

Wendy Ackerman, wife of the Co-chairman of the original Bidco and Pick-'n-Pay supremo, who was the driving force behind Cape Town's original bid. Wendy was also a member of the original Bidco.

Clive Grinaker, MD of Grinaker Sports Management, the official marketing agents to the National Olympic Committee of South Africa.

Sam Ramsamy, head of NOCSA and South Africa's only IOC member.

Clive Keegan, then Chairman of the Executive of the city of Cape Town Municipality, represented the city on the first Bidco. He was also part of the Ball Bidco, by then as Deputy Chairman.

General approach by the Ackerman Committee as described by Wendy Ackerman: "We did this bid very professionally. We did it, my husband and I, with a great passion because we believed in what we were doing. The city didn't pay us, we were not employed, we did this of our own but we financed it ourselves. We got a committee together and we put out tenders for consortiums; we got 32 replies. Ove Arup won and were entrusted with the task of putting the bid together. Their top economist came out and did an economic feasibility study ... We were not a fly by night thing, we spent a lot of money on it, and when we put our books in, we were really professional ... The weather: for a whole month on the site where we planned the Olympics, someone photographed twice a day and did a wind reading. The last two weeks in September and first two weeks in October we had very little rain ... Our window of opportunity is now 2004. South African sports people are riding high in the world, South Africa is the place where people want to be".

Clive Grinaker - In our conversation he clearly indicated that he believed Ackerman did not fulfil his obligation to enter into contract with NOCSA in terms of the agreement under which he was appointed in February 1994.

Wendy Ackerman: "The three way contract was overdue to be signed. We needed the sponsor's money to continue and he (Ramsamy) told the sponsors not to pay us the money until the contract was signed. We had more sponsors than we needed at R10 million a throw. We had six major sponsors and various smaller ones - so we had R75 million that would have taken us through to 1997 which is what we needed. Ramsamy then sent us a contract that we had to sign, which we could not sign, because their demands for NOCSA were enormous and just plain greedy. They did not justify or show us why they wanted all these hundreds of millions of rands that they were calling for. The IOC just sets down parameters; they don't want to get involved. We did not want the city of Cape Town's ratepayers pouring out all these millions to NOCSA. First class hotel accommodation and air tickets, etc. After Samaranch's visit, we were going to Atlanta to represent, to be observers at this major conference in Atlanta. Ramsamy was going with NOCSA and they said you have got to have an official letter appointing you from the city of Cape Town giving you the appointment of the Bid Committee. My husband went to the City Council and they gave him a letter signed by Keith Nicol, stating: 'This is to introduce Raymond Ackerman, Chairman of the Bid Committee, Raymond and Wendy have the city of Cape Town's blessing.' When we came back they (the City Council) said it (the letter) was only for the conference and Raymond said it was not for the conference. Ramsamy had three people on the Council who were obviously on his side. Keith was one of them, as well as Jill Bolton. This letter and the contract was the cause of the conflict."

A copy of a letter signed by town clerk Keith Nicol dated 9 December 1994 was published in the Weekend Argus of 25 February 1995. It read as follows:

TO WHOM IT MAY CONCERN

Cape Town 2004/Mr Raymond Ackerman

A trust was created with the full blessing of the City of Cape Town on 22 January 1993 and Mr Raymond Ackerman is presently a trustee of this trust. The mayor of Cape Town is, ex officio, also a trustee of the trust and chairs all meetings of trustees.

The objects of the trust are, inter alia:

1. As its mission to support financially and materially and endeavour to secure for the broader Metropolitan area of Cape Town, its appointment as host city for the holding of the 2004 Summer Olympic Games;
2. To raise funds and collect contributions for the purposes of the trust, from the private and public sectors by grants, donations, loans, subscriptions or otherwise by inviting and accepting gifts, whether from corporate entities, natural persons or by will and whether or not subject to conditions, provided that the area in which such contribution shall be col-lected in which the trust shall carry on its business shall be the Republic of South Africa subject only to any statutory limitations which may apply from time to time.

This trust and its various committees have, since that date, vigorously pursued those objects and have been supported in all respects by the City of Cape Town.

It has been the responsibility of Mr Ackerman as Chief Executive Officer of the Bid Committee of the trust, to report the activities of that committee to the trustees of the trust and to date, this has been duly done and reported to the City.

The Council and the trust are continuing in their serious commitment to secure the host-ing of the Olympic Games in Cape Town in the year 2004.

Yours faithfully,
Keith Nichol
Town Clerk[78]

Clive Keegan: "The Ackerman committee and more specifically Mr Ackerman's marketing advisors Corporate Image were very keen for the City Council to play a minimal role in this whole exercise, because this was the period before the first democratic elections locally and the political scene was very uncertain. The city was not seen to be a reliable partner because of political chaos and because there had been professional friction in the past between Corporate Image and the City

Council and they had problems with certain personnel in the city. Corporate Image was to keep it to themselves as a private sector thing because of professional jealousy. I served on that committee and together with others such as Ngconde Balfour, we kept reminding them of the provisions of the Olympic Charter. Any contract or bid put in with the IOC had to be lodged by the city. They (Ackerman) kept on telling Ramsamy that the city was on board while resisting the requests. This is not true. The city was sent a contract by the end of 1994, the so-called NOCSA's City Council contract, but for the first time they (the city) realised that Ackerman was to sign a document binding the city without the city's full involvement in the whole thing. And this is when all the conflict between the city and Ackerman started. They kept on telling Ramsamy that there was a formal resolution by the City Council, giving Ackerman the permission to go ahead and sign the contract on behalf of the city. Now that was not true. They were relying on the resolution by the city giving its support to the bid. It was a very vague kind of thing, giving symbolic support. But certainly nobody had any legal authority to sign documents on behalf of the city. Ramsamy then discovered that he'd been subject to this act of - deception, I suppose, is the only word I can use - and the whole thing blew up. That's when the city started threatening to take Ackerman to court, to seek a Supreme Court interdict preventing him to sign this document. That's when things really started going sour. The then Town Clerk and a couple of other officials then went off, at NOCSA's request, to Lausanne; met with senior officials to discover exactly what the bidding regulations were, because they had been denied access up to then. This made Ackerman absolutely livid because he saw Ramsamy working in alliance and collusion with the city to undermine his - Ackerman's - position by going off to see the IOC without his knowledge. That made things even worse. From then on things started declining; Ackerman was eventually eased out of the whole thing".

Comment

NOCSA wrote a letter to all three bidding cities on 14 September 1993 in which the terms of the bidding process were spelt out.[79] The relevant sentence is in the second paragraph: "We have already informed the cities seeking our nomination for the Games of 2004 that we will present our candidature to the IOC after consultation with the new government. However it is important to note that the candidature of the city chosen by NOCSA is presented to the IOC by the official authorities of the city and NOCSA approximately one and a half years prior to the attribution of the Olympic Games. IT IS UPON THIS OCCASION THAT THE CANDIDATURE BECOMES OFFICIAL".

The IOC Charter emphasises that any organising committee must be able to prove the support of the municipality or council of the city it represents. As it happened, the cities had until 1 October 1996 to submit their official candidature to the IOC.

The Ackerman/Ramsamy clash surfaced in February 1995 even before the first local democratic elections in the Western Cape, which took place in May 1996. NOCSA was quite adamant that on a national level a South African bid would not be official before a new National Government was in place. <u>Why the urgency to bring matters to a head before the first democratically elected Local Government was due?</u>

Clive Keegan on Ackerman's management style:
"Although he (Ackerman) ran a successful family business along certain management lines for years and that management style worked, he doesn't understand things like political accountability. He did not understand the need to get involved in some kind of political process with the local authority. He couldn't understand the political dimensions of things and he thought if he could make a success of Pick-'n-Pay by applying a certain management style, he could do the same with the Olympic bid. The two are similar, but they don't work the same way at all, and that I think, was the root cause of his downfall; that he never really began to understand that running a very successful large retail business is quite different to running a highly politically sensitive process such as the bid. That was psychologically the difficulty behind the whole Raymond Ackerman period".

Clive Keegan's problem with the Ball Committee:
"I had no problems with the new committee at all. I had problems with Ball. At the time I was deputy chairman of the company. The chairman was Steve Tshwete who in fact never attended any meetings at all, understandably. The Senior Vice Chairman was Danie Malan who is based in Johannesburg and although he formally chaired the meetings once or twice a month, I was the Cape Town based deputy and I was the de facto Chairman. I regarded my responsibility as a director of a properly legally constituted company. I regard myself as having certain fiduciary responsibilities ... I also felt that I have a <u>responsibility to the ratepayers</u> of Cape Town and to the City Council which I represented on the board. I also believe that as Chairman I had a certain responsibility to keep track of what was going on. Chris Ball was telling me and the board absolutely nothing! He was keeping information from the City Council. He was acting with almost complete autonomy from instructions of his Board of Directors. And I just decided I could no longer carry on like this; if I wasn't going to be able to exercise my legal duties as a director, I was not going to carry on exposing myself to the risk of being charged with irresponsible incautious behaviour. This of course all happened not long after the whole Boesak thing blew up and a whole number of other scandals whereby fairly senior trustees and directors of NGO's like Desmond Tutu all found themselves embarrassed because they did not behave with the decorum that was expected. If I found that I could not do that job properly, I was not going to carry on. I was also concerned that the whole <u>developmental nature of the bid</u> had been lost sight of. I remain convinced that Chris Ball is really not particularly

interested in the developmental side of the thing and to me that was really the core of the whole bid effort. It wasn't just an attempt to bring 15 days of sporting glory to Cape Town; it was about sporting opportunities, recreational facilities, poverty alleviating programmes and I don't think Ball ever believed in the developmental dimension. Sam Ramsamy certainly did not, and Ramsamy was on occasions actively hostile towards those who said: 'This bid is about development'. He said this bid is about sport, don't ask us to get involved in political upliftment pro- grammes. Those were among the reasons that prompted me to go. The board was just not being consulted in the way I believed Ball was obliged to".

Is it true that Mayor Bantam walked out of a meeting chaired by President Mandela?

Keegan: "That was absolute nonsense. It was a meeting at Genadendal when the President was asked to try and sort out the conflict between the city and NOCSA and Ackerman's company. And the Mayor was asked to come to this meeting at very short notice and he in fact had a prior engagement. He apologised to the President and said he had to leave early".

Is it true that Ramsamy wasn't invited to that meeting?

Keegan: "What happened was that Ackerman asked for the meeting with the President to discuss his problems. Wendy and Raymond arrived at Genadendal thinking it was just them and the President for dinner to find a large delegation from the City Council, a huge delegation from Ackerman's own committee and a huge delegation from NOCSA. So in many ways 'hijacked' is the word, that Ramsamy and the city did manipulate their way into that meeting in a way that Ackerman had not expected".

Is it true that Cape Town 2004 is experiencing cash flow problems?

Keegan: "I don't think it is a crisis. Certainly they have not done spectacularly bet- ter than Ackerman. I don't think its all to do with Ackerman and Ball. There is a scepticism among large business about the eventual ability of Cape Town to secure the Games and while they are prepared to put in advertising revenue to gain some commercial mileage, it's different when it's time to put down hard cash which doesn't pay in equivalent advertising".

Interesting Events and Controversial Comments Concerning the Management of Cape Town's Bid

"Cape Town's Olympic bid Chief, Chris Ball, learned a harsh lesson about Olympic politics this week when he was forced to apologise for critical comments about the tactics of Rome." Ball apparently accused Rome of "skulduggery" and "disinformation" when he was quoted as saying: "Rome is trying to knock us off". Italian Olympic President Mario Pescanti reacted by lodging an official complaint.[80]

More of the same?

Bidco's Spokesman on sports matters, Ronnie Kingwell, could not refrain from a dig at Cape Town's Latin opponents at a Pretoria Afrikaanse Sakekamer meeting on 28 June 1997, when he said: "We see pronouncements coming from the IOC as late as yesterday to say quite categorically there will not be another commercialisation of the Olympic Movement again. Now Cape Town offers really that first opportunity because you can be guaranteed the Greeks and the Italians are going to put their best foot forward in producing another commercial fantasy as such". An unnecessary remark, really; one would expect the Greeks and Italians of all people to emphasise the cultural aspects more than the Americans, South Africans or Australians would do. For example the Citizen of 4 July 1997 described the Greek plans for a "cultural" Olympics which was announced at an open-air concert in Athens. Apparently the intention is to hold special events at Greece's ancient sites for the four years up to the Games.

"To Bid or Not to Bid?"

The Fair Lady elucidated the pros and cons of Cape Town's bid in an excellent article by Diana Streak and Karena du Plessis with the latter expressing her opposition quite cogently; "But no matter whether we win the bid or not, serious questions have been raised about the way Bidco have been operating. Arrogant, dismissive and downright dishonest are some of the adjectives used to describe their campaign. Clearly more community involvement, more transparency, more dialogue and more open debates are sorely needed".[81]

A Joint Failure

"A joint project between Athletics South Africa and Cape Town's 2004 Olympic Bid Committee to bring US and European track and field teams against South Africa's best was canned because of a failure to secure sufficient funding".[82]

Transparency

"Why two large venues, planned for construction if the bid is successful, have been earmarked for private use after the Games".[83] The two developments in question are the Metro Entertainment Centre which is planned on a site owned by the Central Substructure and the Cape Town Exhibition Centre, which will be constructed on land belonging to the South African Rail Commuter Corporation. Both of these very costly developments would be in private ownership after the Games. Vol. 2 of the Bid Books states the costs of the Metro Entertainment Centre as $29 million and the Cape Town Exhibition Centre as $53 million. But the Cape Town Convention Centre ($8 million) planned on land also belonging to the Central Substructure and the Indoor Arena ($14 million) due to be built on a site belonging to the Department of Public Works, are in the same category; they are also due for private ownership afterwards. How transparent have the City Council and Bidco been on these transactions?

Comments by Political Parties

The Democratic Party decided to review its support for the bid because of the risks of bad planning, the Cape Times reported. Western Cape DP leader Hennie Bester specified these risks as "large municipal debts due to capital developments necessary for the Games and environmental degradation in the rush to complete developments and scoop maximum profits".[84]

"One supporter of the bid who is a little miffed at present is Western Cape Premier, Hernus Kriel. It seems that he had offered to lay on some sort of reception or function for the IOC delegation while it was in Cape Town. Apparently, he did not receive any reply from the Bid Committee. As a result, Kriel has been notable by his absence at any of the events during the IOC delegation's visit."[85]

A special cabinet committee was set up to lobby international support for Cape Town's bid. The fact that this committee consisted of ANC members only was heavily criticised by National Party and DP spokesmen. The NP's Nic Koornhof said that the government was creating the impression that the bid belongs to the ANC. The DP's Mike Ellis was of the opinion that the formation of the committee was an insult to other political parties and to the country as such. "There is no room for a party political monopoly of an issue as big as the Olympics," Ellis said.[86]

Andrew Young, the former us Ambassador, declared himself "just a preacher" before an audience in November 1996 when he proclaimed at a special presentation in Cape Town that "Everything I do is about feeding the hungry, clothing the naked and healing the sick". Young was also co-chairman of the Atlanta Organising Committee and an ex-mayor of Atlanta. He however, did not reveal to the audience his involvement as Vice President in a firm of consulting engineers which was to have had a share in the construction of Cape Town's proposed Olympic facilities.[87]

Which brings us to political parties and the only games they know - power games. My first theory for the reason behind Cape Town's somewhat surprising selection as host city was that the government reasoned that parliament would have to move to Gauteng eventually and that the Olympic Games was seen as a conciliatory gesture to Cape Town and as a bonus to advance its tourism base. Remember Cape Town was chosen as bid city before the first general election. After the election, and the NP victory in the Western Cape, the ANC probably saw the added bonus: an Olympic Games with its resultant regional growth prospects that could draw extra thousands of their supporters from the impoverished Eastern Cape to settle and look for work in the Cape Town environs and in doing so, probably strengthening the ANC's already considerable power base in the Western Cape. It is, after all, one of only two regions in the whole of South Africa that is not under ANC control and politicians as a breed are not inclined to share power readily.

Interview with Andrew Jennings, author of the controversial Lords of the Rings which received international acclaim and sold very well in Britain and the Scandinavian countries:

Cape Town wants to host the Olympic Games - how would you advise them to go about it?

Andrew Jennings: "As the Olympics are now, I would say don't, just don't do it. I read enough, and I have friends in the Cape to know that like all of South Africa you have a huge financial task in the years to come, rebuilding, no, building and creating the infrastructure that most of the people in your society are entitled to. What those people, all the people of South Africa don't need, are elite swimming pools, specially designed for top international events and nothing like the pool you take your kids to, or you learned to swim in, or do your club swimming. You simply don't need all these elite facilities, because they don't work for communities."

Jennings on Barcelona: "If you go to Barcelona you will see a whole range of sports facilities that are never used, because Catalonians don't practise these sports. Catalonians are crazy about soccer and bicycles and good luck to them. They are very good at it. But not track and field. It's not part of their culture. You don't get many track meets in that stadium. They are not huge in swimming. It's not a great swimming culture; they've got a sea however. They have now got all these expensive pools that are not used; they are closed down most of the year."

Are they paying more taxes as a result of the Olympics?

Jennings: "Vast tax bills! Because you see Spain went through this nonsense and look at the price they paid; I mean Government has spent so much money they've lost the subsequent elections - the National Government - because they put on that ridiculous expo in Sevilla and the Barcelona Games."

Would you say that is what they will try to do with Cape Town?

Jennings: "It's a mess! Supposing Cape Town wins. I hope for the sake of the people of the Cape they don't win these kind of Games. Then you would be building a bigger airport than you would need in the next twenty years. You would be building roads, all kinds of infrastructure. Then there is cleaning up of the area so that the visitors are not offended by the squalor the local people had to live with forever. It's clear that South Africa must work out its own development plan with the resources it has and at a rate your tax system can accommodate. You don't bring a great hungry cuckoo in the nest, that would grow and grow, squawking and demanding, not just the financial assets, but also your human assets, the intelligent creative people who could be looking at what is needed to improve the quality of life for everybody. Instead the Olympics become a priority for everybody and you end up with facilities you don't need and remember it's bull that the eyes of the world are on it. The eyes of the world are on what they see on TV namely the track and the pool."

Comment

There is no doubt, in my mind at least, that despite all the differing opinions (and Jennings seemed determined to give Barcelona no credit at all), Barcelona will go down as an overall success in Olympic history. It is possible that Barcelona might be seen in future as the epitome of a successful Developmental Games.

Cape Town 2004 - The Bottom Line

There were simply too many shortcomings, inherent weaknesses and uncertainties which could have translated into serious financial losses as well as national humiliation. In the end Cape Town is too far from the core of the South African population to justify R2 billion worth of sports infrastructure. Its accommodation and transport infrastructure were too underdeveloped to warrant a huge construction programme in the hope that future demand will justify the massive capital outlay. Furthermore the general range of services and standards of management were simply not capable of handling 29 sports world championships simultaneously. So, for Cape Town, first prize was not to get the Olympic Games!

If Not Cape Town, What Then?

It is clear that hosting the Olympic Games will not automatically accord wealth and prosperity to any region, because this event by itself will not transform any region's economic base or fundamentals, since it is not an ongoing primary source of demand. Certainly a successful Olympics can enhance the appeal of a Los Angeles, Seoul or Barcelona enormously, but there is the minimum requirement of overall competence and the "fundamentals of appeal" that characterises a city which can already offer its inhabitants a reasonable overall quality of life.

It is clear that the IOC is keen to see a successful African Olympic Games take place, to put it mildly. The strategic side of the solution is simply to draw up the ideal bid situation which would suit South Africa and then to present it to the IOC and negotiate concessions and compromises in advance. The IOC management would be most helpful in this regard and they can save any bidding committee a great deal of trouble and hassle if allowed early inputs. The IOC's operational staff are very competent and experienced. A bid as close as possible to the ideal for South Africa's needs can surely be drawn up with their input. Obviously it would then be entered into the normal bidding process against all other comers. But then the expensive and time consuming local inter-city competition can be disposed of.

There can be little doubt that Gauteng would have to be the centre of such a bid and the timing would have to be right, in other words not before the government's GEAR macro-economic strategy gains momentum. The core of the South African population lives in or near Gauteng; it's where the infrastructure is concentrated, it has been the traditional generator of wealth for the whole of Southern Africa and it is much closer to our African neighbours, especially now that the new highways to Maputo, Windhoek via Botswana and Harare are becoming a reality.

Many events would go to Durban because it is within striking distance of a large section of the population, and it is equipped to host certain events (like yachting and rowing) which might prove expensive or unsuitable for Gauteng. Cape Town has become so sought after in tourism terms that hardly anybody who visits South Africa for whatever reason will want to miss it. Cape Town would, amongst others, play host to the equestrian events because it is free from African horse sickness.

Cape Town would be eminently suitable as a convention/congress centre a la Barcelona, and this would be an extension of its present exclusive tourism niche as it would attract even more high-spending tourists. One can imagine the international prestige a congress in the Parliament Buildings would command.

A South African bid as such would be a more sensible way of hosting the first African Games. But first the violent crime and the culture of non- payment of services, etc must be brought under control. The country as a whole must be reasonably safe and stable before we can attempt the most prestigious event of all. We as South Africans must be able to manage our own future reasonably well before we can move on to these mega-events. Anything less would smack of blatant short-term opportunism.

Footnotes

1. The World in 1997, 1996, pp 83-89
2. CT 2004 Bid books Vol 2, 1996, p 22
3. The Economist 4 May 1996, p 48
4. IOC September 1995, pp 81, 82
5. Rojas 23 February 1996, p 3
6. Financial Mail 12 April 1996, p 49
7. Rossouw 22 July 1996, p 2
8. Woodgate 11 June 1995, p 5
9. Gillingham 25 September 1994, p 9
10. Project Pro September 1994, p 27
11. Ball 3 March 1996, p 22
12. Sharpe 12 April 1996, p 1
13. Weiss 18 April 1996, p 1
14. Dickson August 1996, p 15
15. Vernon 20 October 1996, p 5
16. Beeld 28 Julie 1996, p 3
17. Mc Gibbon 3 August 1996, p 9
18. Proctor Sims June 1996, p 9
19. Dickson August 1996, pp 15-21
20. The Star 22 May 1997, p 3
21. KPMG SA NN Gobodo and Co CA (SA) , p 1
22. Central Economic Advisory Service March 1996, p 1
23. KPMG Consulting February 1993, pp 3, 6, 10
24. Roulac 28 May 1993, pp 7, 8
25. Ball 3 March 1996, p 22
26. Weiss 11 April 1996, p 1
27. Sharpe 12 April 1996, pp 1, 2
28. Weiss 18 April 1996, p 1
29. Hawthorne 16 September 1996, p 63
30. Bryden 19 May 1996, p 26
31. Bulger 6 June 1996, p 1
32. De Villiers 27 October 1996, p 2
33. CT 2004 Bid books Vol 3, 1996, p 112
34. Strategic Environmental Assessment Executive Summary 1997
35. Merrifield 12 June 1997, p 19
36. CT 2004 Bid books Vol 3, 1996, p 72
37. Vernon and Bezuidenhout 16 June 1996, p 3
38. CT 2004 Basic Information Package Vol 1, March 1993, p 12-2
39. CT 2004 Bid books Vol 2, 1996, p 24
40. Makhanya 15 March 1996, p 6
41. Sharpe 16 June 1996, p 3
42. The Star 30 December 1996, p 3
43. The Star 25 July 1996, p 15

44. Vernon 20 October 1996, p 5
45. Deacon February 1997, p 3
46. The Citizen 24 June 1997, p 11
47. The Star 3 April 1996, p 16
48. Beeld 9 Desember 1996, p 2
49. Olivier Mei 1997, p 24
50. Korporaal 28 March 1997 (In CIO N61), p 3
51. Johnson 2 July 1992, p 1
52. Van Wyk 20 November 1994, p 25
53. Gillingham 20 November 1994, p 27
54. The Sunday Times 11 December 1994, p 26
55. Beeld 20 Februarie 1995, p 2
56. The Star 22 February 1995, p 10
57. Gillingham 26 February 1995, p 29
58. Beeld 27 Februarie 1995, p 1
59. Pretoria News 7 March 1995, p 3
60. The Star 10 March 1995, p 5
61. Gillingham and Robertson 12 March 1995, p 3
62. The Star 15 March 1995, p 3
63. The Weekend Star 25/26 March 1995, p 4
64. The Star 31 March 1996, p 5
65. The Star 6 April 1995, p 8
66. Streak 30 April 1995, p 12
67. Bryden 7 May 1995, p 29
68. The Pretoria News 18 May 1995, p 2
69. De Villiers 25 June 1995, p 2
70. The Star 12 September 1995, p 9
71. Beeld 4 Oktober 1995, p 1
72. Ward 24 December 1995, p 29
73. Bryden and Drew 31 March 1996, p 32
74. Beeld 10 April 1996, p 2
75. Bulger 6 June 1996, p 1
76. Thom 12 June 1996, p 1
77. Gillingham 9 December 1996, p 123
78. Weekend Argus 25 February 1995
79. NOCSA 14 September 1993, p 1
80. Bryden 2 March 1997, p 5
81. Du Plessis 7 August 1996, p 77
82. Beer 30 January 1997, p 23
83. Houston 6 - 12 December 1996, p 10
84. The Cape Times 19 April 1996, p 2
85. The Argus 7/8 December 1996, p 28
86. The Citizen 16 May 1997, p 5
87. Gillingham 31 August 1997, p22

CHAPTER 13

THE FIVE FINALISTS FOR 2004

(This chapter is based largely on the "Report of the IOC Evaluation Commission for the Games of the XXVIII Olympiad in 2004").

On 5 September, the 2004 host was announced after the five finalists had made their last presentations.

If the experience of the Australians can serve as a yardstick, the race is usually won before the final week, but it can still be lost during those hectic last few days.[1] The Australians certainly waged a successful campaign because they managed to squeeze out the political favourite Beijing. But just to make sure they did not lose out during the crucial final week, they took 39 tons of presentation material with them to Monte Carlo![2]

Initially there were a record eleven cities in the running for 2004 and they were all visited by the evaluation commission which submitted a written report. Obviously this commission studied the candidature files in detail before visiting the cities. Quite a task, one can imagine, but it is obviously vital to scrutinise the technical requirements of all the finalists before the IOC members vote on them.

So the initial eleven cities were whittled down to five and Sevilla, St Petersburg, Lille, Rio de Janeiro, San Juan and Istanbul fell by the wayside. But to what extent did technical excellence influence the final decision? IOC president Antonio Samaranch made it clear that the 14 member panel struck a geographical balance by including one candidate from South America and one from Africa besides the three European ones. Dick Pound, the IOC Vice President confirmed this when he added "You could pick five European candidates and not be embarrassed other than in a geopolitical sense".[3] So, now we had experienced European finalists which had staged the Games before: Athens in 1896, Stockholm in 1912 and Rome in 1960 and two finalists from regions that had never hosted the Olympics, and in the case of Africa had never even made a bid before.

The losers were understandably extremely disappointed, especially the Turks who slammed the selection as a political one. Togay Bayatli, the Secretary General of the Turkish Olympic Committee, was quoted by Associated Press as saying: "The evaluation was clearly not made on a technical basis. This is the result of a prejudice against our nation, which is stuck between East and West." Istanbul Mayor Tayyip Erdogan called it a "political game". Pound responded by saying that "They knew the system when they got into this ... What's more embarrassing? Do you want to be one of the five or six cities which aren't ready yet or the one that gets only a single vote from your own IOC member in the final round?"[4]

One can only sympathise with the Turks; Istanbul had been through the bidding process before, the necessary funds had been raised already by means of a lottery, the parliament had already passed more than the required Olympic Laws, and in terms of infrastructure Istanbul definitely seemed to be on a par with the rest. For example Istanbul's 36 571 hotel rooms certainly put it far ahead of Cape Town's 9 049 rooms in the accommodation stakes.[5] So it was not a case of not being ready; Istanbul was simply on the wrong continent this time around.

At this stage the Olympic rumour mongers told me that Rome peaked too early and that Athens was in the ascendancy. Apparently Rome had considerable support right at the top; amongst them obviously Primo Nebiolo, the head of the International Amateur Athletics Federation as well as soccer supremo Joao Havelange. But the rest of the IOC staff further down were very solidly behind Athens. Let us compare the five candidate cities on a few crucial issues:

Public Support

Stockholm was trailing badly in this section, because its support had consistently been lukewarm and one just could not see the IOC taking the Games to a city where the majority of the inhabitants, 52 % in this case, did not want it. Athens seemed to enjoy massive support with 96,4 % of the population behind the bid. Buenos Aires was certainly not faring badly with 70,8 % of the public behind it. As far as Cape Town was concerned, the IOC seemed quite uncertain as to what the level of support was. Rome seemed to float a wave of strong positive popular sentiment with 81 % in favour of a Games.

Economic Strength

The Countries Involved in the 2004 Bid

In gross terms there is no doubt that Italy was the giant with a GDP of over $1 310 billion or $1,31 trillion in American terms. In GDP per head terms, the $29 209 Swedish figure was the most impressive.

Country	GDP	GDP per head
Greece (Athens)	$124 billion	$11 900
Argentina (Buenos Aires)	$296,6 billion	$8 470
South Africa (Cape Town)	$136 billion	$3 130
Italy (Rome)	$1 310 billion	$22 900
Sweden (Stockholm)	$260,3 billion	$29 209

(The above figures are from The World in 1997).[6]

South Africa had the lowest per capita income, indicating the lowest productivity coupled with the widest distribution in income and leaving it the most vulnerable. The only other two African countries listed in The Economist Intelligence Unit's Third World in Figures were Nigeria and Zimbabwe with per capita incomes of $310 and $690 respectively.[7] Cape Town is relatively isolated, being 700 km from its nearest urban neighbour. In poor countries distances do matter greatly!

The exact opposite is Rome which is in the middle of the densely populated Italy with 300 people per square km and within striking distance of 200 million affluent Europeans.

Stockholm is central to the four Scandinavian countries with an average GDP of over $31 000 per head. Germany, the Netherlands, the United Kingdom, Poland and the immense Russia are not far away, so attracting spectators would not have been a problem. People could afford to fly or travel by ferry and the transport routes were well developed.

Athens would find it more of a problem to attract millions of spectators since the Greek population was not very large - about 10 million - and its immediate neighbours, Albania, Yugoslavia and Bulgaria were not particularly prosperous. Turkey is close by but it is doubtful whether a Greek Games would have elicited much support from Turkish spectators. Athens was of course a very established tourism destination and strong support from Greek communities from all over the world could be expected, as well as from fellow European Union states. There was also, of course, the strong sentimental appeal of an Athens Games, which would have made it a special event.

Buenos Aires was clearly at a disadvantage when compared with the European cities. It is in a poorer continent and again large distances, as well as less developed transport routes would make it more difficult to sell as many tickets. The six most affluent countries in South and Central America had an average GDP of $4 705 per capita. Argentina, Chile, Paraguay and Uruguay had an average population density of fewer than 20 inhabitants per square km.

It is amazing to find that these five cities from disparate regions expected to sell about the same number of tickets:

City	Number of Tickets	Average Price
Athens	5 million	$40 (R180)
Buenos Aires	5,3 million	$31 (R140)
Cape Town	4,6 million	$40 (R180)
Rome	5,9 million	$40 (R180)
Stockholm	4,1 million	$27 (R122) (IOC report)[8]

One can only deduce that these expected sales figures were not scientific calculations, but were merely arrived at by looking at Barcelona's sales and adding some 30 %. As far as I can ascertain there is only one Olympic Games where ticket sales to foreigners outstripped those to locals and that was in Montreal in 1978 where most entrance tickets went to US citizens. It is also interesting that the richest region in per capita terms, Scandinavia, was prepared to sell their tickets at the lowest average price. How and where the Cape Town Bidco expected to sell over four and a half million tickets at an average price of $40 each, was a complete mystery! It is no wonder that the IOC report assessed the expected $183 million from ticket sales "to be on the high side".

Distribution of Competition Sites

Buenos Aires offered the most compact set-up, with only one site over 31 km but less than 40 km from the Olympic Village.

Athens was planning five competition venues which would be between 31 and 40 km from the Olympic Village. Three football venues were at a distance of over 100 km.

Cape Town intended to have one competition site between 31 and 40 km away; three sites between 41 and 50 km; and two sports, slalom canoeing and yachting just over 50 km from the Olympic Village. The football venues would be spread over the country with Johannesburg, Durban, East London and Port Elizabeth staging preliminary matches. Port Elizabeth, the closest city is over 700 km away.

Rome offered four venues between 31 and 40 km, and six (including baseball and yachting) between 51 and 100 km away. Rome also intended to stage football preliminaries in four other centres more than 100 km from the Olympic Village.

Stockholm had one competition venue (yachting) between 51 and 100 km and six others 100 km away from the Olympic Village. The sports involved were football, volleyball and canoeing.[9]

Transportation

Atlanta required all the capacity of its 51 million passenger a year airport to ferry enough spectators to buy 8,5 million entrance tickets to the various events. That is apart from its extensive road and rail network, of course.

Barcelona had to make do with a 13 million passenger a year airport. Its ticket sales were over three million and spectators could also use buses and trains as Barcelona forms part of Europe's vast road and rail network.

City	Airport Capacity in Passengers Per Year.
Sydney	17 million (1994) plus 2nd International Airport
Athens	10 million plus 16 million from 2nd International Airport
Buenos Aires	10 million approx. 1 International plus 1 Local Airport
Cape Town	3,4 million (1994) plus 2 Military Airports
Rome	30 million Da Vinci plus 2nd International Airport
Stockholm	14 million
Johannesburg	8 million passengers handled (1994).[10]

On the face of it, Stockholm's airport was barely adequate, but Stockholm had extensive seafaring links with the rest of Europe, including Britain and Ireland and its port was geared to cope with 7 million passengers per year. It is universally recognised that 14 million passengers per year is the minimum capacity for an airport that acts as a gateway to a Barcelona size Olympics (three million entrance tickets). It is also imperative that there be a rail or metro connection from the airport to the host city and/or Olympic Village.

Barcelona had an excellent rail connection. Atlanta's Marta was indispensable in terms of transporting masses of visitors to and from the airport. Sydney, realising that highways alone won't suffice, was building a 10 km rail to Kingsford Smith Airport. It is interesting to note that Sydney Olympic Park and Sydney Harbour Zone are connected by road, rail and water transport links.

Buenos Aires did not provide the yearly capacity of its airport. Its capacity was very likely in the eight to ten million passenger a year category, which was inadequate - it was backed by a local airport and extensive metro rail system which transported 800 000 passengers per day.

Rome did not supply the capacity for Leonardo da Vinci airport in the IOC report, but this was a huge airport that handled over 21 million passengers in 1995 with extensive rail links to the city.

Cape Town's airport was hopelessly inadequate in terms of size and capacity and its only link with the city was a highway. Cape Town was the only city amongst the five finalists without underground transport or a tram system.

Accommodation

Visitors need transport facilities on entering the country, and then there should be adequate, affordable, comfortable and safe accommodation.

City	Rooms in City	Rooms in Region
Athens	15 277	24 153
Buenos Aires	12 735	12 653
Cape Town	6 520	2 520
Rome	38 914	18 354
Stockholm	19 675	27 515.[11]

Four cities had ambitious plans to extend accommodation capacity if appointed Host City for 2004, except for Athens, which stated quite categorically that it would utilise its present infrastructure. Buenos Aires intended adding between 6 300 and 9 000 new rooms. Cape Town hoped to construct almost 6 000 rooms. Rome listed 2 520 new rooms in the four and five-star category, but did not mention other grades. Stockholm would enlarge its accommodation capacity by 3 800 rooms in the city and 4 800 rooms in the region, if awarded the Games.

It is clear from what we have seen in terms of transport and accommodation capabilities that there was a significant difference among the cities. It is actually astonishing that these five cities intended to host the same sized Olympic event. In terms of infrastructure Rome was the giant, Athens not far behind, Stockholm, while a smallish city, well equipped in terms of infrastructure and probably the best in what the IOC report describes as "very high technological standards and capabilities". Buenos Aires was a likely candidate to host a 30 % smaller Games than the European hosts.

Cape Town, the first African candidate, was seriously hampered by its lack of infrastructure and relative isolation. In spite of an "impressive depth of analysis and planning" it would definitely not have been able to cope with an Olympic Games larger than 1,5 million ticket size. That was 50 % of a Barcelona size Games and would have stretched Cape Town's resources to the limit. That would still have been a bigger event than the 1960 Games held in Rome when 1,4 million tickets were sold and packed Rome to capacity in spite of having 22 000 hotel and guest house rooms available.

Nowadays the number of athletes, officials and sponsors is much higher, so the total accreditations are about four times higher and that also requires an enormous increase in resources.

To illustrate the sheer growth in the number of accreditations host cities are expected to cope with, in the case of Rome in 1960 it is pretty certain that the total number of accreditations did not exceed 35 000, whilst Sydney is presently preparing for 150 000 accreditations in 2000.

The Flexible Budget

The huge variation in certain aspects of the budget clearly indicates how difficult it is to predict accurately the costs of staging such a large once-in-a-lifetime event.

Just to compare the costs of staging the sports events:
Sydney 2000 is preparing for expenditure to the tune of $564 million, Cape Town expected the lowest with $97 million, Athens was preparing for $250 million, Buenos Aires for $115,5 million, Rome for $163,8 million and Stockholm for $233 million.[12] Perhaps lower labour costs were expected to favour the two Southern hemisphere countries, because the other aspects of the operating side of sports events are quite standardised, according to stringent IOC regulations.

It is in the "visitor accommodation" section of the Capital Investment Budget of the IOC report where one can pick up the extra costs incurred by the fact that the two Southern hemisphere countries are less developed. The expected expenditure in this section was nil for Athens, $600 million for Buenos Aires, $453 million for Cape Town, nil for Rome and nil for Stockholm.[13] So either Buenos Aires and Cape Town elicited these huge figures to get government guarantees for a larger amount or else they obviously expected large scale expenditure in order to produce sufficient accommodation.

Security is an interesting aspect of the modern Olympic Games. In terms of cost it is not easy to compare different cities, because the security situations might be completely different and the size and composition of the security forces can vary considerably. The other aspect of security is a more philosophical one, as security did not really seem to feature seriously in earlier Games like Paris 1924, Los Angeles 1932, London 1948, Helsinki 1952 or even Rome 1960. Why has it changed for the worse? Is it because of a shift in human expectations or a transformation in the aspirations of groups or nations, or simply excess individual freedom that is not linked to social responsibility?

Without a doubt Atlanta has been the biggest spender on security of all Olympic hosts so far. The Atlanta Journal-Constitution of 10 July 1997 reported an expected total expenditure of $303 million on this controversial aspect of the 1996 Games. Atlanta tried to cope with fewer security personnel (30 000) and much more technology. Seoul with 80 000 and Barcelona with 45 000, utilised more personnel. For the five finalists the security figures seemed low with Stockholm at $27 million, Buenos Aires with $40 million, and Rome expecting to spend $50,4 million. Cape Town, the most dangerous contender, hoped to make do with $52 million and Athens was the highest at $75 million. Sydney initially budgeted to spend $41 million on security in 2 000 which seems a bargain when compared to Atlanta, but then one has to take into account Sydney's relative remoteness and the reduced threat of terrorism.[14]

Local sponsorship or relative lack of it is the one large part of Sydney's current financial dilemma. The rest is quite predictably unexpected cost increases (Michael Knight, NSW Olympics minister admitted this in May 1995). Nothing new really: London already had this problem in 1908, and this won't be the last time either that the huge pressure to "sell a host" to the public and the IOC results in over optimistic budgets. But let's return to 2004's expected revenues from local sponsorships, which was of course a separate issue from the TOP or international sponsorships. The expected figures, according to the IOC report were:

Athens	$200 million
Buenos Aires	$80 million
Cape Town	$114 million
Rome	$125 million
Stockholm	$178 million
Sydney	$321 million.[15]

When these figures were reflected as a fraction of the GDP of the various countries, it became even more interesting; Athens, 1,6 placed the heaviest load on its private sector in terms of expected sponsorships. Perhaps Greece was relying on a hidden strength. Hundreds of thousands of successful Greek individuals and firms abroad might contribute as they did for the 1896 Games in Athens.

Cape Town at 0,84 was much lower than Athens but still above the over-optimistic presently suffering Sydney with 0,79. Then followed Stockholm at 0,68, Buenos Aires with a very conservative 0,27 and Rome with an extremely low 0,09. It was the relatively wide range of these figures which was worrying. Was Athens that much more creative with figures, more adept at securing sponsorships, or just plain optimistic? As far as the television revenue and TOP are concerned, figures were about the same and predictably reliable because of the IOC's central role in negotiations.

Sports Venues

Cape Town topped the list with 16 new installations required, including a 75 000 seat Olympic Stadium, which on its own would cost $78 million. The new competition sites on average would cost $21,25 million each. (The IOC report listed 16 but only 14 were in the Bid Book).

Rome needed to have only eight new sports sites constructed; no new Olympic Stadium was required, since the Football Stadium used for the 1990 World Cup would suffice. Nevertheless construction costs worked out at a staggering $71,75 million per site.

Athens had an existing stadium which would host the 1997 World Athletics Championships and could be used as an 80 000-seat Olympic Stadium. Athens would require 10 <u>new installations</u> in terms of competition facilities and these would cost a total of $297,5 million - <u>$29,5 million each.</u>

Buenos Aires could boast the lowest total expenditure on sports infrastructure with eight <u>new competition sites</u> required at an expected $148,8 million, which worked out at <u>$18,6 million per site</u>. The 60 000-seat River Plate Stadium, built for the 1978 Football World Cup would be modified to serve as a 65 000-seat Olympic Stadium.

Stockholm would construct an expensive new Olympic Stadium at $269,2 million; this would be a 70 000-seater. The 6 <u>new competition sites</u> would cost an average of <u>$48,16 each</u> with a total of $289 million.[16]

Sydney is presently constructing a 110 000-seat <u>Olympic Stadium</u> at a cost of $515 million; that is about <u>$4,7 million per thousand spectators</u>. Stockholm's would be <u>$3,84 million per 1000 spectators</u>, whilst Cape Town's Olympic Stadium expenditure would come to <u>$1,04 million per thousand spectators.</u> That would surely indicate that construction costs in South Africa were very low indeed.

It is interesting to note that while admitting that the South African Broadcasting Corporation was willing to act as host broadcaster, Cape Town was the only instance in which the IOC Report expressly stated that the Organising Committee of the Olympic Games reserved the right to establish a separate Olympic broadcast organisation.[17] Cape Town's would have been the first Olympic Village within striking distance of a nuclear reactor - Koeberg Nuclear Power Station is about 20 km away.

In the end it is skill, organisation and resources that really count. For sheer natural beauty, Cape Town with the majestic Table Mountain, and scenic Stockholm, spread over 14 islands, would take some beating. Either of these would be the city one would choose to get away from it all. Somehow these two cities did not evoke the bustling big city images of traffic jams and pollution that Rome and Athens tend to conjure up. Buenos Aires, on the other hand, was probably suffering from an identity crisis, as it is a relatively unknown new-world city without a specific image.

However to make this mega event a reality has much more to do with skill, organisational capabilities and massive resources than majestic settings or spectacular scenery.

The relentless struggle between these five formidable candidates certainly reflects the realities of the world we live in today, as well as some of the fears and aspirations for the future.

Footnotes
1. McGeoch 1994, pp 35, 272
2. McGeoch 1994, p 283
3. Associated Press 12 March 1997, pp 1-2
4. Associated Press 12 March 1997, p 2
5. IOC Report 1997, p 300
6. The World in 1997, 1996, pp 83-89
7. The World in 1997, 1996, p 89
8. IOC Report 1997, pp 344, 345
9. IOC Report 1997, pp 132, 133
10. IOC Report 1997, pp 308, 309
    Italian Embassy (Rome)
    Argentinian Embassy (Buenos Aires)
    SATOUR (Johannesburg)
11. IOC Report 1997, pp 300, 301
    CT Bid books Vol 3, 1996, p 46
12. IOC Report 1997, p 334
13. IOC Report 1997, pp 338, 339
14. IOC Report 1997, pp 336, 337
15. IOC Report 1997, pp 334, 335
16. IOC Report 1997, pp 134, 135
17. IOC Report 1997, p 326

CHAPTER 14

ATHENS 2004 -
CLASSIC GAMES OR GREEK TRAGEDY?

And you shall know the truth, and the truth shall make you free

John 8:32

How the IOC members voted on the fifth of September 1997

First round:	Athens	32	Rome	23	Stockholm	20
	Buenos Aires	16	Cape Town	16		

Second round:	Cape Town	62	Buenos Aires	44

Third round:	Athens	38	Rome	28	Cape Town	22
	Stockholm	19				

Fourth round:	Athens	52	Rome	35	Cape Town	20

Fifth round:	Athens	66	Rome	41	Athens won by 25 votes.

Cape Town's Hangover

All the signs are that, by eliminating Cape Town, the IOC redeemed the South African government and Olympic authorities from an Exxon Valdez in terms of wasteful and misdirected expenditure.

As if to confirm Cape Town's unsuitability, the violent battle between the drug lords and Pagad on the Cape Flats intensified to such an extent during October, that it was deemed "a direct challenge and threat to both the Constitution and the State" by police chief George Fivaz after a meeting attended by the security big guns which included the Safety and Security Minister, the Defence Minister and the South African National Defence Force chief.[1] At the same time, the Financial Mail warned that "hospitality sector expansion creates overcapacity which could send many (hotels) to the wall". The required boost in foreign tourism was not materialising, because of South Africa's crime problem.[2]

It seems that Cape Town's Olympic Bid Company is not even destined to fade away gracefully. The financial director Michael Fuller, according to the Cape Times, predicted a shortfall of R1,5 million, after a meeting of bid company auditors, council officials and Fuller. Only a few days later, chief executive Chris Ball contradicted Fuller and said the company had R5 million in its bank account. This prompted Arthur Wienburg, former Cape Town City Councillor to urge the Bid Company to open its books: "This bid was heavily funded with public money and there is only one way to show true transparency......They are morally duty-bound to show us the books".[3]

Cape Town 2004 would have been an African Montreal, an expensive and enduring international embarrassment to the Olympic Movement. But the IOC management surely realised this and there are signs that they actually were worried that this "encouragement to the first African bid" might get IOC members carried away. First there was the discreet search for relevant critical information, mentioned in 'personal recollections', then the 'air tickets for the wives of African IOC members' scandal on the Tuesday, three days before the selection when Reuters carried the message " Late bets are on Cape Town".[4] According to this report Cape Town surged to second favourite with London bookmakers William Hill, whose spokesman Graham Sharpe was quoted as saying: "If money talks, Cape Town will win, despite the majority of Olympic-watching pundits writing it off as a realistic contender". Maybe these gamblers were backing on the effect of a powerful, emotional speech expected from President Mandela: an oratory masterpiece along the lines of the Jacques Chirac piece de resistance for Paris in 1985 which so nearly gained the winning trophy for the French city.

An interesting Reuters survey of Olympic sports federations, sponsors and journalists who frequently write about the Games, revealed that these respondents expected Rome to be favoured by the IOC because of its apparent ability to guarantee stability after the turmoil of Atlanta. One opinion was that "Rome has the best, most proficient National Olympic Committee in the world. It also has a great history and tradition in terms of sport". It was also clear that the sports professionals on the whole preferred Stockholm. Two thirds of them said they would go for "clean cool Stockholm" after the "sweaty chaos of Atlanta". Athens was seen as a sentimental favourite, which has contributed much to the Olympic Movement, but the traffic and pollution counted against it, the participants felt. Buenos Aires and Cape Town were not taken seriously as contenders for 2004 in this survey. In Cape Town's case there was a concern about "safety issues" and that it might not be a prudent move financially. "Panellists were concerned that Cape Town would be better spending money on other community facilities".[5]

Anyway the revelation about Cape Town's offer of first class return air tickets to Lausanne definitely impeded the city's campaign. (By Thursday, the day before voting, Cape Town odds had weakened to joint second favourite with Athens).[6] But this was in no way decisive as Cape Town was never a threat to the two front runners and only managed to outlast Stockholm as a result of the votes gained from the elimination of Buenos Aires. The whole episode demonstrated that the African symbolism affair was taken more seriously by the betting public than the

IOC which has the responsibility of seeing that events actually can be staged successfully. How NOCSA could have made such an elementary mistake, clearly violating the $200-maximum-for-gifts rule is a mystery. Ramsamy is an experienced Olympic role player and it is almost inconceivable that he was not cognisant of the offers. It is more likely that Ramsamy was not as enthusiastic about Cape Town's ability to stage the Games as his position compelled him to be, that the tickets-to-wives issue might very well have been used by him and the IOC at a critical stage just to make sure the IOC members got the message that Cape Town and Stockholm were not to be taken too seriously. (Stockholm was accused of offering to transport furniture back home for visiting IOC members - but was later cleared). After all, Ramsamy had warned the South African public in 1995 that a Cape Town Games could cost R21 billion, which at the time was nearly four times the expected capital outlay of R5,6 billion.[7] This shock coincided with his battle to oust Ackerman and ever since then, there have been numerous allegations that Sam Ramsamy was not really supportive of Cape Town's bid.

Caustic Comments

Ian Chadband in the London Sunday Times on the Sunday before the crucial vote: "There are many imponderables. Could President Mandela's planned dramatic intervention in Lausanne - not so much a plea as a demand for the completion of the five rings by giving Africa the Games-transform Cape Town's internally divided, problem-ridden pipe dream into a winner? Has the recent series of small fires and minor explosions in the 1912 Stadium, supposedly the work of anti-Olympic saboteurs, fatally wounded Stockholm's bid? How much did the empty seats at the world championships affect the image of Athens? The bidding has become extremely sophisticated, with PR consultants drafted in to convince IOC members that black is white; in other words, that Cape Town is not riddled by violent crime, that Athens and Buenos Aires have no pollution or environmental problems, that Rome will not be milked by incompetence or corrupt officialdom, that everyone in Stockholm is mad keen for the Games".[8]

Martin Gillingham in the Sunday Independent came to the inevitable conclusion that "The likely explanation is that Cape Town never had a chance of winning, and its inclusion in the final five was more a gesture of encouragement by the IOC that the time may soon be right for an African Games".[9]

Darryl Accone, The Culture Desk, in analysing the response to Cape Town's defeat on the following Sunday: "Nothing disclosed our callow naivete and petulant immaturity as nakedly as the reaction to Cape Town's failed bid to host the 2004 Olympics. In the unseemly riot of recriminations, guilt trips and conspiracy theories that followed Athens' victory, everyone blamed someone else ... Just how many more miracles, or placebos, does our infant international nation demand?

Exactly when will we realise that we cannot emotionally blackmail the world on the basis of our transformation, no matter how laudable that will always be?

"Most of all, when will we have the maturity to carry the can? It's always someone else's fault, never our own. A sober look at the Cape Town Olympic bid should long ago have revealed that it was a masterpiece of manipulation".[10]

Lessons from Lausanne

The simple lesson is that as Olympic participation has always been only for the very best amongst athletes, the sheer scale of the modern Olympic Games has made the staging of it such a daunting prospect, that only the economically vibrant, well managed, infrastructurally sound regions should attempt to host it. Unlike a Soccer World Cup, the cost and complexity of a modern Olympic Games have made it an almost unattainable ideal for the cities of the Third World. But where is the IOC heading with the Olympic Movement? What lies ahead in the 21st century?

The Olympic Road to Ruin?

Any movement or corporation or organisation has an inherent culture, a system of values that is central to the very being of the institution. The problem is that in this organisation a definite dichotomy in core values was inherited. The sentiments of de Coubertin's exclusive amateur club of well-to-do gentlemen for whom taking part was paramount, differed drastically from the culture of the ancient Games where the festival had a religious undertone and the intense competition was an all-or-nothing affair. As we have explored from chapter 1, there is a unique aura attached to the Olympic Games, a mysterious magic almost, that is unequalled in the world of competition. Richie tried to encapsulate this fascination: "The Olympic Games are revered by some as the pinnacle of hallmark events. They are steeped in tradition, held relatively infrequently and are dedicated to excellence. They represent a sports event of unequalled stature".[11] But the Olympic Movement has always had to contend with the real and harsh world. It has survived the blatant political manipulation of the cold war era successfully. The Olympic Movement has managed to adapt well to the stringent managerial demands of the modern knowledge society. But will it survive the onslaught of commercial excess?

To what extent will commercial pressures dictate the future of the Olympic Movement? At what stage does commercial interests start to interfere with core values? Maybe it would be useful to try and first ascertain what those core values are? Georges Du Brie sketched the dilemma "After the somewhat unfortunate Olympics in Atlanta last summer, the IOC found itself forced to consider the raison d'etre of the Games. For years they had talked about the Olympic 'ideals' without too much thought about what they were. Then suddenly last summer Atlanta showed them what they weren't".[12]

While the Olympic Charter [13] refers to respect for universal fundamental ethical principles, the preservation of human dignity and the encouragement of a peaceful society, the important ideals and values tend to be confusing and even contradictory. In terms of sports competition as well as the contest to host the Games, the rivalry is intense and the tendency is to try almost desperately to find ways to gain an advantage over the opposition. Athletes resort to illegal substances, competing cities tend to favour inducements that range from free air tickets to scholarships. So while the Olympic ideals are tinged in rosy descriptions of fraternity, friendship and fair play, the reality is more often than not the opposite. De Coubertin's well known principle that it is not the winning that counts, but the competing, is also contradicted by the high standards set for both competitors and host cities, which guarantee absolute exclusivity. With the increasing commercial pressures on winning and records, the public's association with the Olympics as an event that has been linked with only the best, is reinforced. But the problem is that television dictates what is good for viewing and ratings and we end up with beach volley ball as an Olympic sport. Surely the Olympics should be about sports where the gold medal is the ultimate accomplishment. You can lose every contest but, in any track or field event, or in weight lifting or in gymnastics, wrestling or swimming, the gold medal is the supreme achievement. The same goes for a World Cup victory in soccer or a Wimbledon trophy in tennis. Certain sports are simply Olympic sports according to popular perception and others will never be, and the Olympic Movement is risking a precious heritage by not being able to recognise or define those that are bound to remain iffy recreational or entertainment affairs.

John Bryant, the Deputy Editor of The Times wrote in June 1996: "Those who have already spent too many hours watching wall to wall television coverage from Atlanta will sigh with weary relief as the real Olympics eventually begin today. Enough of beach volleyball, enough of women's soccer, enough of team dressage. At last they will bring on the real athletes. What we need is a definition of what constitutes an Olympic sport and a drastic pruning of the events that do not qualify. The Games need cutting down to size".[14]

Samaranch has been tremendously successful in moulding the IOC into a more honest, open organisation in tune with society's requirements, where athletes don't have to rely on dirty notes in brown paper bags any more (American Dwight Stones who used to be a top high jumper in the seventies, recently revealed how he had to haggle for bonus money before attempting to break world records)[15] and where the previous excesses committed by competing cities are regulated quite effectively. But the weakness of the present IOC President is his tendency to want to bring and keep all powerful role players on board in order to preserve unity at all costs. One example is the preference for the almost unknown tae kwon do martial arts sport which has Olympic status in preference to the vastly more popular karate just to accommodate Korea's influential IOC member Mickey Kim.

So we have an Olympic bus that is dangerously overloaded because the number of sports, competitors and participating countries just keep on increasing. At the recent athletic World Championships held in Athens, 200 nations took part, that is already three more than at Atlanta just a year earlier. And this over extended bus is driven by a complex propellant, namely commercialism. These inherent dangers were recognised by Samaranch himself when he was quoted in 1992 by Hill as saying: "We shall be discussing the size of the Olympic Games as there is a number of competitors which we cannot exceed without causing great harm to the Games".[16] and also by Simson and Jennings when Samaranch stated : "Olympic sport must not become unequivocally the agent of world capitalism".[17]

Whilst the great number of competing nations is in tune with the IOC's all important universality ideals, it is the variety and complexity of all the different sports that make the hosting of an Olympic Games such an expensive and complex affair. When the sponsors' demands are added, the 5 000 luxury hotel rooms for instance, it becomes an almost impossible task. It is no wonder Time Magazine's Kate Noble wrote as follows about the choice for a 2004 host: "Perhaps there should be a gold medal for masochism. City authorities must know that hosting the Olympic Games is likely to bring them as much grief as glory." ... "But with the cost of hosting the Games rising, the winner of this race could end up the loser".[18] Which brings us to the victor of the 2004 tug-of-war.

Will Athens be Able to Cope?

The ancient Greek capital is a city that is associated in modern terms with traffic jams, air pollution and internal dissent. The Greek economy, which is going along steadily with a 3,1 percent growth forecasted for 1998 and inflation at a 25 year low is not as large, productive or vibrant as the Spanish one was before the 1992 Games. The Olympic spectacle has certainly added substantially to its girth since 1992. Barcelona had about 113 000 accreditations (Olympic family and organising staff) whilst Sydney is expecting this figure to rise to 150 000. As we have seen in the previous chapter, Athens is much smaller than Rome and not nearly as accessible as Barcelona or Rome.

There is no doubt that the Greeks will be able to produce spectacular opening and closing ceremonies and the atmosphere should be something to savour, given the special status Athens has in terms of Olympic heritage. But to cope with a Sydney-sized Olympic Games might prove an almost impossible task for the Athenians and 2004 might well see the real Olympic shambles that's been predicted for some time. Whilst the Australians are extremely competitive by nature and as a result keen to show the world they can 'hack it', the Greeks are encumbered by a feeling of historical supremacy which often manifests in an attitude of passive arrogance (which cost them the 1996 Games). If Atlanta with its massive hi-tech airport and highly integrated transport systems struggled to cope with Olympic traffic, it is difficult to imagine how Athens, which is unduly stressed by its normal traffic, is going to manage the Olympic influx. Severe traffic jams and pollution forced the Greek authorities to implement a system linked to the registration numbers whereby cars were only allowed on the road on alternate days.

Of course the commercial basis of the Olympic Movement may overheat like a stock market before then and these commercial values may start to decline. A recent survey has shown that 40 % of Australians recognise Quantas as an Olympic sponsor (it was part of Atlanta's promotion), but only 15 % see Ansett (the rival Australian airline) which has paid over $25 million to be part of Sydney's effort, as an Olympic sponsor. There is serious doubt whether Ansett, a much smaller company than Quantas, will be able to find the required $90 million over the four years to ensure maximum benefit of its Olympic status.[19] There is a real danger that the value of sports advertising is already overrated, that public interest might become saturated by too much top class competition or that the focus in terms of sport interest might even shift to the grey area between pure sports and pure entertainment. The Stadium Australia shares issue is one large commercial Olympic venture that has flopped and the IOC has taken an important step to try to stabilise the commercial foundations by negotiating a $1,3 billion long term deal with General Motors, amongst others, to secure sponsorship for the next six Olympic Games.

General Motors would certainly require a well-planned and executed long-term Olympic association to secure major benefits, because the signs are that the motoring behemoth did not make major marketing strides from its $40 m Atlanta association. The Harris poll, which involved six surveys taken from February to August 1996, showed that 51% of respondents recognised General Motors Corporation as a sponsor at Atlanta, but when asked the same question of Ford Motor Company, 43% named this major GM competitor a sponsor as well. Is it worthwhile to spend all those millions just for an 8% advantage? The Harris Poll, which was published in The Wall Street Journal also indicated real benefits for PepsiCo Inc from the Coca Cola Olympics. Incredibly, Pepsi was the fourth most cited sponsor in the Harris surveys - while informed observers agreed that the '96 Games were certainly not drug free, they were unanimous about the total absence of Pepsi.[20]

Perhaps there was this deep urge amongst IOC members, to return to the classical simplicity of earlier Olympic celebration as symbolised by the beautiful, all marble Panathenaic Stadium, when they voted for the 2004 host. Unfortunately the excess Olympic baggage that will be brought to the Greek capital is heavy and complex. Whilst the demands of hosting is definitely growing, the claimed bene-fits are being questioned increasingly. In Australia John Morse, the Managing Director of the Australian Tourism Commission has warned that "The Sydney 2000 Olympic Games would not be an economic panacea for South Australia or the nations as a whole".[21]

If the IOC is serious about the long term future of the Olympic Movement, it should discard all the superfluous sporting baggage. At The Centennial Olympic Congress held in Paris in 1994, several speakers alluded to the need for serious change to this aspect of the Games. Richard Palmer, the Secretary General of the British Olympic Association: "As far as Programme changes are concerned, and these must inevitably come, these should be guided by a reflection of the sports that are played worldwide, and by the tradition of the Games and NOT by the demands of the entertainment industry". Etienne Glichitch, the President of the International Hockey Federation: 'These problems are becoming more and more numerous and more complex as the number of National Olympic Committees increases, and as the sports themselves, their disciplines, their variations and their combinations grow in number, not forgetting the proliferation of associated professions, the members of which earn their living from sport. Solving these problems requires this process of runaway expansion to be brought under control". And Debra Jevans, Secretary General of the International Tennis Federation: "The more practical and pressing problem now, however, is the growth of the Olympic Games themselves. The origi-nal great amateur festival of sport is now an enormous global spectacle, a victim of commercial success. Over the past four Olympiads, the number of medal sports has increased from 21 to 26 and the number of athletes from 5 900 to 11 500, not to men-tion additional number of coaches, captains and officials. This level of growth is sim-ply not feasible........The Olympic Games is now accepted as having reached its max-imum size. The number of cities with the capability of hosting the Games is limited. The infrastructure requirements and the costs associated are becoming beyond the potential of any but the major cities of the world".[22]

After all Samaranch said in 1992: "The Olympic bus is full. Take one more passen-ger, someone else has to get off".[23] But the problem of gigantism requires more drastic action. In the Ancient Games, a hero was welcomed through a special hole knocked in the city's wall. In the modern context, the formidable wall of commer-cial greed and political opportunism has to be knocked down by courage and fore-sight in order to preserve precious core values. In practice a lighter and leaner Games will be more manageable, the advantages and risks more predictable and the staging of it accessible to more regions and cities. Such a return to a purer Olympics would make the real Olympic sports more identifiable and secure long term commercial as well as emotional values.

The Olympic focus has simply become too blurred and indistinct and the IOC might well be forced to make the stark choice between the political expediency of power play (to keep important sports federations or individuals on board) or to safeguard the core of the Olympic Movement itself.

This decision will determine whether Athens 2004 will be a chaotic Games or the beginning of a new, pure and classic Olympic era.

Footnotes
1. Pretoria News 20 October 1997, p 3
2. Pincus 17 October 1997, p 50
3. Pretoria News 13 October 1997, p 3
4   Reuters Information Service 2 September 1997
5. Iley 4 July 1997, p 39
6. The Star (BR) 4 September 1997, p 1
7. Gillingham and Robertson 12 March 1995, p 3
8. Chadband 31 August 1997, Internet
9. Gillingham 7 September 1997, p 2
10. Accone 14 September 1997, p 3
11. Richie (In Cummings and Mihalik) 1984. p2
12. Du Brie 1997, p 47
13. IOC 1995, pp 10,11
14 Bryant 26 June 1996, p 16
15 Reuters 1997
16. Hill 1992, p 242
17. Simson and Jennings 1992, p 22
18. Noble 18 August 1997, p 59
19. Charles 21 July 1997, p 3
20. John Helyar 24 February 1997
21. Innes 15 July 1997, p 9
22. IOC 1994, pp 42, 43, 48
23. Miller 1992, p 187

BIBLIOGRAPHY

BOOKS

Allison, L 1993. **The Changing Politics of Sport.** Manchester: Manchester University Press.

Brough, S 1989. **Economist Atlas.** London: Hutchinson Business Books.

Callahan, R E, Fleenor, C P and Knudson, H R 1986. **Understanding Organizational Behaviour: A Managerial Viewpoint.** Columbus, Ohio: Charles E Merrill.

Coote, J, Trevor, B, Leitch, S, Lahmy, E, David, R and Bressy, R 1980. **The ITV Book of the Olympics.** London: Independent Television Books.

De Moregas Spa, S M, Rivenburgh, N K and Larson, J F 1995. **Television in the Olympics.** London: John Libbey and Company Ltd.

Drucker, P F 1989. **The New Realities.** London: Octopus Publishing Group.

Epsy, R 1979. **The Politics of the Olympic Games.** London: University of California Press.

Hill, C R 1992. **Olympic Politics.** Manchester: University Press.

Hill, C R 1996. **Olympic Politics.** Athens to Atlanta 1896 - 1996. New York: St Martin's Press, Inc.

International Olympic Committee 1995. **Olympic Charter.** Switzerland: International Olympic Committee.

Jennings, Andrew 1996. **The New Lords of the Rings.** London: Pocket Books, Simon and Schuster.

Johnson, P 1983. **A History of the Modern World.** London: Weidenfeld and Nicolson.

Lovelock, C 1991. **Services Marketing.** London: Prentice - Hall International Editions.

Mc Geoch, R, with Korporaal, G 1994. **The Bid.** Melbourne: Reed Books.

Miller, D 1992. **Olympic Revolution.** London: Pavillion Books.

Nafziger, J A R 1988. **International Sports Law.** New York: Transnational Publishers.

Simson, V and Jennings A 1992. **The Lords of the Rings.** London: Simon and Schuster.

Tosi, H L, Rizzo, J R and Carroll, S J 1990. **Managing Organizational Behaviour. A Managerial Viewpoint.** New York: Harper Collins.

Wallechinsky, D 1992. **The Complete Book of the Olympics.** London: Aurum Press.

Wilson, N 1988. **The Sports Business. The Men and the Money.** London: Piatkus.

PERIODICALS AND NEWSPAPERS

Accone, D 1997. Our response to losing the Olympics shows we have a lot of growing up to do. **Sunday Independent**, 14 September 1997.

A city engulfed by a human tide. 1996. **The Star**, 5 August 1996.

Ackerman opts out.1995. **The Pretoria News**, 7 March 1995.

An African success story. 1997. **The Economist**, 14 June 1997.

A night of celebration and terror. 1996. **Newsweek**, 5 August 1996.

Asking R14-m, but Olympic Company misses key talks. 1996. **The Star**, 25 July 1996.

Atlanta '96 in danger of becoming the 'Coke Games'. 1996. **The Star**, 8 March 1996.

Atlanta briefs. 1996. **The Star**, 31 July 1996.

Atlanta Games denounced as cheap and tasteless. 1996. **The Star**. 14 November 1996.

Back on track after Olympic compromise. 1995. **The Star**, 6 April 1995.

Ball, C 1996. Going for gold in the Olympics. **Sunday Times**, 3 March 1996.

Battersby, K 1996. Why I hate Atlanta. **The Evening Standard**, 25 July 1996.

Beer, M 1997. Lack of cash halts bid to bring US track stars for Cape Town meet. **The Star**, 30 January 1997.

Bernstein, A 1997. Atlanta, model lesson for SA's embattled cities. **The Star**, 26 February 1997.

Bid to end attacks on 'Cape hell run'. 1997. **The Star**, 22 May 1997.

Blacks' tent embassy plan for Olympics. 1997. **The Sun-Herald (Sydney)**, 26 January 1997.

Bryant, J 1996. Time to prune Olympics of events that do not qualify. **The Star**, 26 June 1996.

Bryden, C 1995. Cape Town bid goes ahead but Ackerman is slammed. **The Sunday Times**, 7 May 1995.

Bryden, C and Drew, J 1996. Government support vital for Cape Town bid. **The Sunday Times**, 31 March 1996.

Bryden, C 1996. Games bid has flickers of doubt. **The Sunday Times**, 19 May 1996.

Bryden, C 1996. Tell tale signs as frustrations go on. **Sunday Times**, 21 July 1996.

Bryden, C 1997. Olympic gaffe raises hackles. **The Sunday Times**, 2 March 1997.

Bulger, P 1996. Cabinet supports CT's bid for 2004 Olympic Games. **The Star**, 6 June 1996.

But Hernus isn't. 1996. **The Argus**, 7/8 December 1996.

Cape Town loses international scouts' conference. 1996. **The Star**, 30 December 1996.

Cape violence 'threatens State'. 1997. **Pretoria News**, 20 October 1997.

Carlin, C 1996. And you thought Britain had a bad Games. **The Independent**, 5 August 1996.

Cash crisis looms for Games. 1995. **The Star**, 22 February 1995.

Chadband, I 1997. Late scramble for Olympics. **Sunday Times UK (African Sport Zone)**, 31 August 1997.

Charles, E 1997. Olympic Gamesmanship. **Sun-Herald (Sydney)**, 21 July 1997.

Charlton, P 1997. Doubts about the Minister for the Olympics. **Courier Mail (Brisbane)**, 29 March 1997.

China bid suffers a body blow. 1994. **The Sunday Times**, 11 December 1994.

Chua-Eoan, H 1992. A spirit in Barcelona. **Time International (Special Edition) 139 (27)**, July 1992.

Chulov, M 1997. But with a sting for NSW. **The Sun-Herald (Sydney)**, 30 March 1997.

Conditions met, Ackerman back. 1995. **The Weekend Star**, 25/26 March 1995.

Cause for alarm. 1996. **Financial Mail**, 12 April 1996.

Dark forces lurk beneath the surface of Atlanta's Olympic razzmatazz. 1996. **The Sunday Independent**, 14 July 1996.

Dasey, D 1997. $200 m Games profit. **The Sun-Herald Sydney (CIO N17)**, 30 March 1997.

D-day dawns for council's Olympic bid. 1995. **The Star**, 15 March 1995.

Deacon, T 1997. Cape Town 2004. Communication is the Achilles' heel. **Project Pro**, February 1997.

Deford, F 1996. Let the Games begin. **National Geographic**, July 1996.

Deford, F 1996. **The secret to the universal popularity of the Olympics. Newsweek**, 22 July 1996.

Deford, F 1996. With the whole world watching, the Centennial Olympic Games lit up Atlanta. **Newsweek Magazine**, 29 July 1996.

De Villiers, C 1995. Pay row mars Olympic bid. **The Sunday Times**, 25 June 1995.

De Villiers, C 1996. State underwrites Olympic bid. **The Sunday Times**, 27 October 1996.

Dickson, R 1996. Learning from Atlanta. **South African Transport**, August 1996.

'Die Spele was beslis nie beste' - IOK. 1996. **Beeld**, 5 Augustus 1996.

Doust, D 1996. How Atlanta got the gold. **Millenium Magazine**, April 1996.

DP ' will review its support for Olympic bid'. 1996. **The Cape Times**, 19 April 1996.

Du Brie, G 1997. 2004 Olympics: More Coca-Cola? Or Cafe-ouzo? Maybe grappa? **Sportsworld Japan, (CIO Press Review N74)** 18 April 1997.

Du Plessis, K 1996. To bid or not to bid. **Fair Lady**, 7 August 1996.

Fabricius, P 1996. Despite poor accommodation and organisation, SA police 'made a plan' and learnt a lot. **The Saturday Star,** 10 August 1996.

Fishburn, D 1996. The World in 1997. London. **The Economist Newspaper Limited.** 1996.

Galvin, R 1995. Cost of Olympics 2000 out of control. **The Star (BR),** 26 May 1995.

Galvin, R 1997. Olympics - new chief for Sydney 2000 Games. **Reuters CIO N61,** 27 March 1997.

Games bid team members at odds over finances. 1997. **Pretoria News,** 13 October 1997.

Games new rules. 1997. **The Sydney Morning Herald,** 28 March 1997.

Gillingham, M 1994. Cape Town's billion rand baby. **The Sunday Times,** 25 September 1994.

Gillingham, M 1994. George slams 'unilateral' IOC. **The Sunday Times,** 20 November 1994.

Gillingham, M 1995. Massive clash of two egos threats to Cape Olympic bid. **Sunday Times,** 26 February 1995.

Gillingham, M and Robertson, C 1995. Hosting the Olympics could cost SA as much as R21 bn. **Sunday Times,** 12 March 1996.

Gillingham, M 1996. Power plays with fire. **SA Sports Illustrated,** 9 December 1996.

Gillingham, M 1997. Madiba's magic may not be strong enough to enchant the IOC. **Sunday Independent,** 31 August 1997.

Gillingham, M 1997. SA must learn from its mistakes before the next Olympic bid. **Sunday Independent,** 7 September 1997.

Going for Gold in bid for Olympics. 1996. **The Sunday Times,** 3 March 1996.

Government aid for Olympics backed. 1997. **The Citizen,** 24 June 1997.

Green light for 2004 bid. 1996. **The Star,** 31 March 1996.

Harder than a garden party. 1996. **The Economist,** 3 August 1996.

Hawthorne, P 1996. From Pariah to power house. **Time Magazine**, 16 September 1996.

Helyar, J 1997. Does playing name game at Games work? **The Wall Street Journal.** 24 February 1997.

Homeless in Olympic host city worried about their fate during Games. 1996. **The Star**, 3 April 1996.

Houston, C 1996. Questions need to be answered. **Mail & Guardian**, 6 - 12 December 1996.

How wrong is it going. 1996. **The Economist**, 12 October 1996.

Innes, S 1997. Fingered - Syd and Millie mutants. **The Daily Telegraph Sydney (CIO N17)**, 28 January 1997.

Innes, S 1997. Games 2000 - 'bad year' for a tourism cure-all. **The Advertiser (CIO N133)**, 15 July 1997.

Iley, K 1997. Olympics poll - Rome odds-on 2004. **Reuters (CIO N126)**, 4 July 1997.

IOC check on budget. 1997. **The Daily Telegraph (Sydney) (CIO N74)**, 18 April 1997.

Jeffery, N 1997. UCI to set strict guidelines on bikes. **The Australian**, 16 April 1997.

Johnson, S 1992. Olympic hurdle cleared. **The Star**, 2 July 1992.

Kaapse Spele - stryery op 'n hoogtepunt. 1995. **Beeld**, 27 Februarie 1995.

Kaapstad sal in 2004 gereed wees vir Spele. 1996 **Beeld**, 28 Julie 1996.

Kabinet twyfel oor SA Olimpiese bod. 1995. **Beeld**, 4 Oktober 1995.

Korporaal, G 1997. IOC to watch for further departures. **Sydney Morning Herald (CIO N61)**, 28 March 1997.

Lange, A 1996. With IOC propensity to award Olympics as prize for reform, SA still has a chance. **The Star**, 9 May 1996.

Letter to bidding cities Cape Town, Durban and Johannesburg. **NOCSA**, 14 September 1993.

Lexington, 1996. Victor ludorum. **The Economist**, 20 July 1996.

Makhanya, M 1996. Community wants Olympic Village site. **The Star**, 15 March 1996.

Martz, R 1996. An arena for terrorism. **The Atlanta Journal - Constitution,** 10 July 1996.

Mc Gibbon, C 1996. Main movers behind bid believe Mother City has what it takes to host the big one. **Saturday Star,** 3 August 1996.

Mc Kenzie, S 1997. Olympic tourists join the fast lane. **The Daily Telegraph (CIO N17),** 28 January 1997.

Mc Mahon, L 1997. The broadcast of the Games of the XXVI Olympiad in Atlanta. **Olympic Review,** April/May 1997.

Miller, D 1995. Atlanta Olympics in top gear. **The Star (BR),** 5 May 1995.

Mitchell, A 1997. The Minister and money. **The Sun Herald (Sydney) (CIO N61),** 30 March 1997.

Moore, M 1997. It's a tease to please in the Olympic mascot money game. **The Sydney Morning Herald CIO N13,** 22 January 1997.

Moore, M 1997. Olympic media may be housed in hospital. **Sydney Morning Herald,** 28 January 1997.

Moore, M 1997. Knight of the long knives. **The Sydney Morning Herald,** 29 March 1997.

Moore, M and Korporaal, G 1997. Marathon grinds on for Sydney brokers. **The Sydney Morning Herald,** 29 March 1997.

Myburgh, J 1993. The two sides of the Olympic coin. **The Star,** 22 November 1993.

Noble, K 1997. Olympic beauty contest. **Time Magazine,** 18 August 1997.

Onmin bedreig Kaap se kans op Spele. 1995. **Beeld,** 20 Februarie 1995.

NOCSA 'still open to negotiation'. 1995. **The Pretoria News,** 18 May 1995.

Nog een los Olimpiese bod maatskappy. 1996. **Beeld,** 10 April 1996.

NP, DP slam political Olympic Games bid. 1997. **The Citizen,** 16 May 1997.

Ogden, C 1996. The Post-Miracle phase. **Time Magazine,** 16 September 1996.

Olivier, J 1997. 2004 Dalk net 'n jaar van beloftes. **Insig,** Mei 1997.

Olympic bid: No financial audit done. 1995. **The Star**, 10 March 1995.

Olympic bid. Millions repaid to Ackerman. 1995. **The Star**, 12 September 1995.

Olympic tax bed row is growing. 1997. **The Citizen**, 17 June 1997.

Parsons, T 1996. World blasts Atlanta for commercialism and glitches. **The Star**, 6 August 1996.

Pavlovic, V 1997. Private sector asked to build Olympic water reclamation works. **Sydney Business. (CIO N 72)**, 14 April 1997.

Pincus, D 1997. More than enough room to swing an elephant. **Financial Mail**, 17 October 1997.

Porter, J and McDougall, B 1997. Play as a team. **The Daily Telegraph (Sydney) CIO N61**, 27 March 1997.

Proctor Sims, R 1996. Transport and the Olympics. **SA Transport**, July 1996.

Project Pro. The 2004 Olympic Games. 1994. September 1994.

Reuters Information Service 1997. **(CIO Press Review N130.)** Athletics - money for athletes in 'shamateur days'. 9 July 1997.

Reuters Information Service. 2 September 1997.

Rossouw, Arrie 1994. SA moet net nodige geriewe bou vir vir Spele, sê IOK man. **Beeld**, 22 Julie 1994.

Sachs, J 1996. Growth in Africa. **The Economist**, 29 June 1996.

Sharpe, S 1996. Olympic Games bid costs escalate. **Business Day**, 12 April 1996.

Sharpe, S 1996. Govt to meet claimants for Olympic site. **Business Day**, 16 June 1996.

Smith, P 1996. Africa turns Asian. **The World in 1997**, 1996.

Smith, V E and Springen, K 1996. Psychic scars. **Newsweek**, 5 August 1996.

SOCOG (Sydney Organising Committee of the Olympic Games). **Fact sheet**, 1995.

SOCOG Chief quits. Holway takes over. 1997. **The Canberra Times**, 28 March 1997.

Soundbites. 1993. **The Observer,** 24 September 1993.

Spele in Kaapstad 'kan op ramp uitloop'. 1996. **Beeld,** 9 Desember 1996.

Spencer, G 1997. Sydney finds kangaroos and koalas too cliched to be Olympic mascots. **Associated Press (CIO N15),** 24 January 1997.

Stovin-Bradford, R 1997. Odds on Cape Town winning Olympic bid weaken to 9-4. **The Star (BR),** 4 September 1997.

Streak, D 1995. Ackerman in row over Olympic bid. **The Sunday Times,** 30 April 1995.

Stuart, I 1997. Games 2000 'bad year' for tourism cure-all. **The Advertiser. CIO N133, 1997.**

Sydney 2000 - Costs soar. 1996. **The Star (Sydney),** 24 May 1996.

Sydney 2000, 1993. Special media/telecommunications supplement. **Sydney Olympics 2000 Bid Limited,** April 1993.

Sydney Olympic Committee for the Olympic Games, 1993. **News of the Sydney Olympics 2000 bid.** April 1993.

Sydney's Olympics not Green enough. 1997. **The Citizen,** 29 May 1997.

Symbols of contention. 1997. **The West Australian,** 22 January 1997.

The bleak Continent. 1989. **The Economist,** 9 - 15 December 1989, 313 (7653).

The stadium game. 1996. **The Economist,** 4 May 1996.

The white man's burden. 1993. **The Economist,** 25 September 1993.

Thom, A 1996. 'Culture of crime' serious danger to SA, warns study. **The Star,** 12 June 1996.

Usher, R 1992. Carnival in Catalonia. **Time Magazine (Special Edition),** July 1992.

Van Wyk, J 1994. Gevaarligte flikker vir Kaapse droom. **Rapport,** 20 November 1994.

Vernon, K and Bezuidenhout, J 1996. Olympic bid tripped up by land prices. **Sunday Times,** 16 June 1996.

Vernon, K 1996. Olympic bid suffers a major setback. **Sunday Times,** 20 October 1996.

Ward, A 1995. 'Cape Town in the loop' for 2004 - bid chief. **The Star**, 24 December 1995.

Weiss, A 1996. Massive bill for 2004 Olympics. **The Argus**, 11 April 1996.

Weiss, A 1996. R5,6 billion bill for transport looms. **The Argus**, 18 April 1996.

Wheel comes off the Olympics. 1996. **The Daily Telegraph**, 23 July 1996.

Who's misleading whom? 1995. **Weekend Argus**, 25 February 1995.

Woodgate, S 1995. **The Star**, 11 June 1995.

World slams Olympics shambles. 1996. **The Star**, 24 July 1996.

Wulf, S 1996. Duet Song. **Time Magazine**, 29 July 1996.

STUDIES

Botella, M 1993. **Impact of the Olympic Games on Barcelona tourist attractiveness.**

Central Economic Advisory Service, March 1996. **Impact study of the 2004 Olympic Games.**

Central Statistical Services (CSS). 1994. **Statistics in brief.**

COOB '92 SA Barcelona.

CT 2004. 1996. Cape Town Bid Books, vol 1.
CT 2004. 1996. Cape Town Bid Books, vol 2.
CT 2004. 1996. Cape Town Bid Books, vol 3.

CT 2004. March 1993. **Basic information package of CT 2004 feasibility study.**

City of Barcelona Press Communique 1992: JG 0103 A
City of Barcelona Press Communique 1992: 0608 A MDF
City of Barcelona Press Communique 1992: 0103 A JG
City of Barcelona Press Communique 1992: 0201 A JM
City of Barcelona Press Communique 1992: 0405 A AB
City of Barcelona Press Communique 1992: 0309 A JMC
City of Barcelona Press Communique 1992: 0202 A JH

Cummings, P R and Mihalik, B J 1994. **The impact of the Atlanta Summer 1996 Olympics; assessing resident perceptions.** Georgia.

Dong-Wook, L 1988. (5WIH of Olympics). **How to prepare Olympics and its task.**

International Olympic Committee (IOC) 1992. **Olympic Charter.** Lausanne.

International Olympic Committee 1995. **Manual for Candidate cities for The Games of the XXVIII Olympiad.** Lausanne.

International Olympic Committee 1997. **Report of the Evaluation Commission for the Games of the XXVIII Olympiad in 2004.**

KPMG Consulting. 1993. **Manchester 2000. Economic benefits and opportunities of the Olympic Games.** Manchester.

KPMG South Africa. NN Gobodo and Co Chartered Accoutants (SA). **The Olympic Games 2004. Preliminary study. Economic benefits and opportunities.** Department of Sport and Recreation.

Merrifield, A 1997. **The Impacts of the Olympics on the Construction Industry.** CSIR Pretoria.

Nel, P C 1996. **The 1996 Atlanta Centennial Olympic Games. Security Operations Review.** SAPS. Pretoria.

Newsletter of the City of Barcelona 1992: 7.

Olympic Assessment Team 1997. **Strategic Environmental Assessment of the Cape Town 2004 Olympic Bid.** Cape Town.

Organising Committee of the XIX Olympiad 1969. **Official Report.** Mexico City.

Pro Sport München 1973. **Official Report.** München.

Rojas, J 1996. **Turisme de Barcelona.** Barcelona.

Roulac, S 1993. **Lessons for Atlanta from the 1984 Los Angeles Olympic Experience.** California.

Swaffield, J (Sir) 1979. **A feasibility study for a 1988 London Games.** London.

Xth Olimpiade Committee. **The Games of the Xth Olympiad Los Angeles 1932 Official Report.** Lausanne.

A list of interviews:

Gert Potgieter, University Pretoria (Pretoria). February 1993.
John Limna, BOA (London). February 1993.
Alfred Bosch, COOB92 (Pretoria). March 1993.
Miquel Botella, COOB92 (Barcelona) July 1993.
Josep Rojas, Bureau de Turisme (Barcelona). July 1993.
Dan Moyo, NOCSA (Johannesburg). July 1993.
Bill Enevoldson, Manchester 2000 (Manchester). July 1993.
Pere Miro, IOC (Lausanne). July 1993 and June 1996.
Wendy Ackerman, Original CT 2004 (Cape Town). April 1996 and March 1997.
Paul Johnson, CT 2004 (Cape Town). April 1996 and March 1997.
Mike Fuller, CT 2004 (Cape Town). April 1996 and March 1997 (telephonic discussion).
Clive Keegan, CT 2004 and City Council (Cape Town). March 1997.
Ben Groenewald, SAPS. March 1997.
Andrew Jennings, author (London). June 1996.
Fekrou Kidane, IOC (Lausanne). July 1996 (brief discussions).
Clive Grinaker, Grinaker Sport Management (SAA - 10 000 m above sea level) March 1997 (brief discussions).

Early Warning!

Sunday Times 02-06-1996

THE South African public is constantly being exposed to pronouncements about how good the Olympics will be for Cape Town. If it is not Chris Ball's "If Cape Town wins, we all win", it is Edward Griffiths lecturing us on how glorious the benefits of the games would be (Sunday Times, April 28).

But is it really that simple?

A serious analysis demonstrates that Cape Town's shortcomings as an Olympic host in size, location and required infrastructure are obvious and fundamental.

The population estimate for the Western Cape was 3,6-million for the April 1994 election, with the nearest urban area, Port Elizabeth, more than 700km away. Compare that with the population of Barcelona, the 1992 host. Situated in densely populated Catalonia, it has a population of more than six million. It is less than 90 minutes' drive from the French border and 50 minutes by aircraft from Madrid (population: four million).

Atlanta, the host this year, is less than two hours' flight away for 210-million Americans. Sydney, the host in 2000, has a population of 3,7-million and is situated in New South Wales, where more than six million people reside.

In countries more developed than South Africa, more people can afford to fly relatively long distances to attend sports events. The gross domestic product of Australia is US$20 200 (R88 274) a head, the US equivalent is $28 440, while the Spanish figure is $14 000, compared with South Africa's $3 370.

Cape Town's relative isolation counts against it in terms of its potential to sell tickets, its ability to provide informal accommodation and adequately utilise sports infrastructure.

More than three million tickets were sold for the Barcelona games, contributing eight percent to the city's revenue. Of these, 80 percent were sold in Spain. The 5,6-million tickets that will be on sale in Sydney are expected to add 14 percent to the city's revenue.

The first African games are expected to sell only 750 000 tickets.

A number of people in Cape Town are likely to open their homes as bed-and-breakfast establishments for the games but, with at least 150 000 visitors a day expected, Cape Town is bound to have an accommodation problem.

Another mark against the city is the level of utilisation of stadiums and sports facilities.

The International Olympic Committee is critical in its analysis of the long-term need for expensive sports infrastructure. With its relatively small population, there has to be a serious question mark over a capital outlay of nearly R2-billion on sports facilities in

Cape Town's shortcomings as an Olympic host are apparent to anyone doing his homework, writes PIETER DE LANGE

Cape bid far below Olympic standard

Cape Town.

A glance at any map will confirm that Cape Town is not favourably situated for would-be spectators from the rest of Africa. The distance figures confirm this. The aggregate distance to Cape Town from Zimbabwe, Swaziland, Mozambique, Lesotho, Botswana and Namibia is just under 10 000km.

With an average per capita income of less than $500 a year in these countries, it would be almost impossible for hundreds of thousands of sports enthusiasts to attend the Olympics in Cape Town in significant numbers.

Even if they could afford the travel costs, the average projected ticket price is R640. In Barcelona, 85 percent of the tickets sold for less than R100 each. The average ticket price for Atlanta is R280.

Accommodation requirements for the Olympic Games are formidable. Apart from the Olympic village needed to house athletes and team officials, about 16 500 hotel rooms are needed. The International Olympic Committee stipulates that at least 5 000 of these should be in a "superior category".

Barcelona, with 40 000 hotel rooms within striking distance of the Olympic action, struggled to provide enough accommodation. Sydney, with more than 30 000 hotel rooms, is building many more. *The Economist* (May 4 1996) reports that many people in Atlanta are letting their flats for the Olympics because the city offers "within it's 55-mile (88km) radius only 55 000 hotel rooms".

A mere 5 622 hotel rooms are available on the Cape Peninsula.

Barcelona's airport could handle 12 million passengers a year. Atlanta's airport handles more than 51 million, with direct service to 25 international cities. Sydney's airport was used in 1994 by 17 million passengers, and a second airport was approved before the games were awarded to the city.

Johannesburg international airport's capacity has been enlarged to 11 million passengers a year. Cape Town's airport can handle only four million, with a scarcity of back-up airports in close proximity.

Barcelona's operating budget totalled $1 737-million, Atlanta's estimate is $1 573-million and Sydney hopes to contain its expenditure to less than $1 200-million.

Cape Town's figure is in the order of $850-million (R3 615-million). This is optimistic indeed when taking into account that the city has an underdeveloped transport system and inferior sports facilities, and can expect much higher security costs, the highest telecommunication expenditure ($270-million to Barcelona's $175-million) and less revenue from ticket sales. Then there is the huge capital outlay required for improved infrastructure.

There are also strategic disincentives. The city experienced its first setback when the National Olympic Committee of South Africa ousted the bid committee it appointed.

Public confidence diminished and the bidding process had to start anew. The vexing question of who is accountable for the R8-million reportedly owed to the Ackermans still remains.

With a boom in tourism and economic growth of more than five percent, one cannot help but wonder if Cape Town needs the Olympics.

The Cape's charm is based on a delicate blend of factors including natural beauty, a sense of history and an easygoing atmosphere. By committing Cape Town to a huge construction programme such as would be required for the games, the city would inevitably find itself on the highway to mass tourism. This could change its character forever.

Is it worth the risk?

● *Pieter de Lange is a dentist who did a research project on the Olympics in his final year of a Unisa MBL course*